Fashion FOR DUMMIES®

by Jill Martin and Pierre A. Lehu, with Dana Ravich

WILEY

Wiley Publishing, Inc.

Fashion For Dummies®

Published by
Wiley Publishing, Inc.
111 River St.
Hoboken, NJ 07030-5774
www.wiley.com

WILEY

About the Authors

Jill Martin: Jill Martin is a fashion expert and three-time Emmy-Nominated television personality. Jill appears regularly on NBC's *Today* discussing everything from the latest trends to how to shop on a budget. She is well-known for the wildly-popular "Ambush Makeovers." Jill has done in-depth coverage from the Golden Globes and Oscars, conducting celebrity interviews and discussing red-carpet fashions. A contributor to *US Weekly* magazine, the Long Island native can also be seen frequently on *Access Hollywood, Extra, Entertainment Tonight,* and *The Insider.* A diehard sports fan, Jill is also a broadcaster for the New York Knicks, reporting during pregame and postgame shows and doing celebrity interviews at halftime. She is a graduate of the University of Michigan and is currently living in New York City developing her own clothing line. To learn more about Jill, check out her Web site (www.jillmartin.com).

Pierre A. Lehu: Pierre Lehu began as a publicist, working with a wide variety of celebrities, and over time broadened his working repertoire to include the roles of lecture agent, literary agent, manager, and writer. Having been instrumental in launching the meteoric rise of Dr. Ruth Westheimer as a celebrated sex therapist, he soon became her "Minister of Communications" and in that capacity was co-author on many of her books, including two *For Dummies* titles, *Sex For Dummies* and *Rekindling Romance For Dummies* as well as more than ten others. He also acted as co-author for Rocky Aoki, the founder of the Benihana chain of restaurants, on *Sake: Water From Heaven.* A double graduate of NYU (BA and MBA), he resides in Brooklyn with his wife and is the father of two.

Dana Ravich: Dana is a fashion stylist and works in the fashion and entertainment industry styling models and celebrities for editorial shoots, catalog, advertising, and television. She got her start at *Mademoiselle* magazine in New York and then moved on to E! Entertainment TV and the Style Network in Los Angeles, styling the networks' hosts for everything from *E! News Daily* to red-carpet Oscar coverage. During her time in Los Angeles and then Miami, Dana styled shoots for *Glamour; O, The Oprah Magazine; In Touch; Us Weekly; People; Fitness; Shape; GQ;* and *Vanity Fair.* Her advertising clients have included Coppertone, L'Oreal, Olay, Perry Ellis, and MTV. She has also worked closely with and advised designers and buyers. A graduate of Columbia University, she is now back in New York and continues to work in fashion.

Dedication

We would like to dedicate this book to all the women out there who want to *look* as good as they *feel*.

Authors' Acknowledgments

From Jill: I would like to thank Pierre Lehu for asking me to be his partner-in-crime on this amazing project. It has been quite a journey, and I cannot thank you enough for your expertise and kindness . . . you are the consummate professional.

I would also like to thank Dana Ravich, my collaborator and friend, for your invaluable contribution and support. You made this process fun and exciting, and your expertise was a perfect fit to sculpting this book.

To my fabulous mother, father, and brother Jonathan, who always put up with my craziness. Thank you for all of your support and for always believing in me. I have the best family in the world. I am so, so lucky. And now, I will make every family function, I promise! And to Dan Le Batard for teaching me the importance of perfect punctuation.

There are so many other people who contributed to the book who we all cannot thank enough: Designer Betsey Johnson and Agatha Szczepaniak for letting us shoot our cover at the fabulous Bestey Johnson boutique; Photographer George Kalinsky for his expertise and dedication; Rebecca Taylor, Angela Cranford, and Avi Gerver for all of their hard work on the shoot; Stylist (and co-author) Dana Ravich along with Makeup artist Bella Sirugo; Jennifer and Mark Miller for letting us use their amazing jewelry; The celebrities and designers who shared their fashion wisdom: Kathie Lee Gifford, Hoda Kotb, Tory Burch, Nancy O'Dell, Sara Blakely, Tracy Reese, Liz Lange, Cynthia Rowley, Lisa Rinna, Tori Spelling, Tommy Hilfiger, Shoshanna Gruss, Selita Ebanks, Beth Stern, Tyson Beckford, and Michelle Smith; Allison Ross Levitan, Andrew Waranch, Jill Fritzo, Alison Brod, Steve Herz, and Jeff Feldman for their help; Lindsay Sobel for the great introduction to Pierre; Maury Rogoff for her support; and Amy Rosenblum for always being my biggest fan.

From Pierre: This book was born as a result of holding our class reunion at Vera Wang's, so thanks to my Friends Seminary classmates one and all. And if it weren't for Dr. Ruth Westheimer, I wouldn't have gone to the *Today* set where I saw Jill Martin reporting on fashion, so thank you Dr. Ruth for that connection and for everything else we've shared during our 28-year long adventure. And without Jill's expertise, dedication, and persistence, this book would never have blossomed the way it did, so Jill, thank you, thank you, thank you. And one more thanks to Jill for bringing Dana Ravich along for the ride as her contributions have been invaluable . . . and, of course, thanks to Dana for her hard work.

To my wife, Joanne Seminara, it's been thirty plus years of counting our blessings, and I can't thank you enough. And our two most important blessings are our children, Peter and Gabrielle — thanks for all the joy you've brought us. And Pete, an extra thanks for bringing Melissa on board. And to our family members, mine who are gone and whom I miss so much, and to all the Seminaras, an extended thanks.

Others who also deserve my thanks for their help and support include Merle Frimark, Teresa Jusino, Lindsay Sobel, and Lindsay Weiner.

And all three of us want to thank everyone at Wiley who've made this project possible and who've been so helpful in pulling the many, many details together to make this fabulous book, including Lindsay Lefevere, Tracy Barr (we put you through a lot, but it was worth it!), Diane Steele, Alicia South, Lauren Bishop (you're such a talented artist!), PJ Campbell, Melisa Duffy, Kathy Nebenhaus, and Stephen Kippur.

From Dana: Thank you to my most inspirational friend and biggest supporter, Jill Martin. I am so glad you asked me to be a part of this most incredible experience. And, of course, to Pierre Lehu, thank you for letting me join you. It has been truly a joy working with you. I would also like to thank my family for their love and unwavering support — Robert, Lucy, Rachel, Lyle, Helen, Lou Lou, and Leo. And to Sarah Hamilton-Bailey, Michelle Jonas, Amy Hall Browne, Renannah Weinstein, Jennifer Smith, and Adam Glassman: Thank you for all of your support and everything that you have taught me.

Publisher's Acknowledgments

We're proud of this book; please send us your comments at http://dummies.custhelp.com. For other comments, please contact our Customer Care Department within the U.S. at 877-762-2974, outside the U.S. at 317-572-3993, or fax 317-572-4002.

Some of the people who helped bring this book to market include the following:

Acquisitions, Editorial, and Media Development

Project Editor: Tracy Barr

Acquisitions Editor: Lindsay Sandman Lefevere

Assistant Editor: Erin Calligan Mooney

Editorial Program Coordinator: Joe Niesen

Technical Editor: Danielle L. Smith

Illustrator: Lauren Bishop

Senior Editorial Manager: Jennifer Ehrlich

Editorial Supervisor and Reprint Editor: Carmen Krikorian

Editorial Assistants: Jennette ElNaggar, David Lutton

Art Coordinator: Alicia B. South

Cover Photos: © George Kalinsky

Cartoons: Rich Tennant (www.the5thwave.com)

Composition Services

Project Coordinator: Patrick Redmond

Layout and Graphics: Laura Campbell, Carrie A. Cesavice, Joyce Haughey, Brent Savage, Erin Zeltner

Proofreaders: Laura Albert, Linda Seifert

Indexer: Potomac Indexing, LLC

Special Help: Elizabeth Staton

Publishing and Editorial for Consumer Dummies

Diane Graves Steele, Vice President and Publisher, Consumer Dummies

Kristin Ferguson-Wagstaffe, Product Development Director, Consumer Dummies

Ensley Eikenburg, Associate Publisher, Travel

Kelly Regan, Editorial Director, Travel

Publishing for Technology Dummies

Andy Cummings, Vice President and Publisher, Dummies Technology/General User

Composition Services

Debbie Stailey, Director of Composition Services

Contents at a Glance

Table of Contents

Introduction

"I don't know what to wear!" "Do these pants make my butt look big?" "Is this outfit too boring for my big date?" Chances are you have had one (or all) of these thoughts at some point in your life. (I know I have!)

Fashion is a topic so many women need help with and don't know where to turn. Many women find navigating through the fashion world difficult. Your budget, body type, and personality all play a part in the choices you make every morning when you get dressed. But whatever your style, knowing a few basic rules can help you whenever you bounce back to that annoying question, "What am I going to wear today?"

Now trust me, I am not going to preach that you should be dressed up, looking like you are heading to a black-tie affair everyday. (I am well aware of how hard it is to carry on a full life and try to look good doing it.) So as you read through this book, understand that it is not just about *what* you wear, but *how* you wear it.

Getting dressed in the morning should be fun. You should open your (soon-to-be-if-not-already) organized closet and enjoy putting together different combinations. I know, I know . . . figuring out what to wear can be exhausting. But after reading this book, you'll have the tools you need to look stylish for any occasion. I want you to learn what works for you and your body type and what makes you feel most confident. I truly believe that confidence is your best accessory.

On NBC's *Today* show, Colorist to the Stars Louis Licari and I pluck two lucky ladies out of the crowd and give them a complete makeover. These women come down to the plaza wanting a change (many of them have either looked the same for years or have never developed a style of their own.). In just a few hours, hosts Kathie Lee Gifford and Hoda Kotb bring these women out totally transformed. Now, I am not saying that the second you finish reading this book, you'll become a whole new person. What I can promise is that you'll have a better understanding of what works for you and your body type. My mother read this book and called me saying, "I am donating anything that is not a 10!" You'll soon discover what that means, but trust me: To get my mother to give anything away takes a small army.

We have all been through mini-makeovers in our lifetime. Now it's your turn!

About This Book

When I was approached to write a *For Dummies* book, I said what many of you would probably say: "Oh those yellow and black books — I love them!" But then I thought, "How could there *not* be one on fashion?" They have *Dummies* books for just about everything. I read one on golf and my best friend's husband read one on how to use a BlackBerry. But sure enough, no *Fashion For Dummies* existed then. And I was glad, because I really feel that I can help many of you who are tired of waking up in the morning and thinking, "I have nothing to wear!"

On NBC's *Today,* I appear on fashion segments that cover everything from trends to budget shopping. My main goal in every segment is to teach women how to look and feel their best. I believe there is a formula to looking and feeling good every day when you leave the house, and over the years, I've developed a few tricks to help you get through your busy day while always looking your best. In this book I give you the tools you need to develop your own style. I also show you exactly how to orchestrate some of these ideas, so as you go through the book, take a close look at the illustrations.

I know how overwhelming a book like this can be, but here's the story: You don't have to read this book all in one sitting, and you never have to read it all the way through if you don't need or want to. The great thing about *For Dummies* books is that everything is segmented. Look at the Table of Contents and decide what you want to focus on. The only thing I ask is that, if you're not going to read this cover to cover, go to Chapter 2 before reading anything else and take my style quiz and read about my 10 System to be able to really understand how you should approach building your own style.

Conventions Used in This Book

I am a person who understands everything in numbers. If a friend calls and says she's depressed, I immediately say, "How depressed, 1 to 10?" (10 being the most you can be). This is how I communicate, and I use this system in every aspect of my life, including what makes it into my closet. Every single piece I own, from a sizzling dress to a pair of sweatpants, is a 10. What I mean by that is that particular piece of clothing is the best it can be. My gray sweatpants are cozy, fit me properly, and look cute on me. My black dress hugs me in all the right places, does not look faded in any way, and is a classic style that can take me to almost any occasion. For a piece of clothing to get into my closet, it needs to meet certain requirements, and I want you to adopt this process as well. After reading this book, there should not be anything hanging around that does not make you feel your most fabulous. For that reason, the most important convention in this book is my reference to this system. You'll see that I refer to it often.

As you read this book, you'll see I suggest things you should splurge on and those you can save on. Price doesn't interfere with my 10 System. (I have an

H&M dress that's a 10 and was under $30 — it's fab!) In addition, don't get overwhelmed thinking you need to go buy everything new. Revamping your closet is a process, and the items that are must-haves, most of you already have in your closet.

Other than these things, there are a couple other conventions you need to know about:

- ✔ *Italic* is used for emphasis and to highlight words or terms that I define.
- ✔ The action part of numbered steps appears in **boldfaced** text.
- ✔ Web addresses appear in `monofont`.

What You're Not to Read

Again, *For Dummies* books are great because you don't *have* to read one chapter to understand the next. So if you are very interested in accessories, but not in pajamas, you can skip the PJs chapter and focus only on the accessories chapter. (Use the Table of Contents to find the chapters you want; you may even discover a different topic you want to explore!)

As you read, watch for the Technical Stuff icon. This appears beside extra information for those who like to delve that much further into a topic. You can read these paragraphs if you're interested but skip if you're not. Even without reading these bits, you can still get all the info you need to understand the topic being discussed. Same goes for the sidebars, the shaded boxes. If you see one that doesn't pique your interest, skip it and move on.

Foolish Assumptions

I am laughing as I write this because I do not think *any* of my assumptions are foolish! But I have made some assumptions about you:

- ✔ You want your style to reflect your personality, and you want to look your best each and every day, but you just don't know how to do it.
- ✔ You know what you love about your body and what you dislike about it and you want to find out how to accentuate your best parts and camouflage the ones you would rather downplay.
- ✔ You've got a ton of clothing sitting in the back of your closet that you've never worn. Many of the pieces still have the tags on them and others are in sizes too big or too small, and while you had every intention of wearing them when you bought them, now don't know what to do with them.

If any of these assumptions fit, you've definitely got the right book in your hands.

How This Book Is Organized

This book is *very* organized. Believe me, I've gone through it over a million times! But even more than this book being organized, you have to be. The beginning of your makeover does not start at your favorite boutique with you buying out the entire store. Before you whip out that credit card, you need to develop your personal style, figure out your body type, and decide what styles work for you. After doing this and seeing what you already have in your closet, you can then assess what you need. To help you accomplish all of these tasks, I've arranged this book into parts so that you can easily find the information you need.

Part I: Fashion, Style and You

If you're like most women, you're searching every morning looking for that perfect outfit. In order to confidently decide what you should and shouldn't wear, you need to know the basics. Trends, developing your own style, and figuring out what looks good on you helps you develop the skills you need to make getting dressed easier. Sounds good, right? Before you hit your favorite store though, read (and reread) this part.

Part II: Mastering the Basics of Garment Construction, Fabrics, and Color

Even after you read Part I, it's not time to go shopping. You still have to learn about the clothing you are about to buy. Before you start filling up your closet, you need to know what goes into making a quality item. This part explains how to recognize a well-made garment, how to pair patterns and colors, and how a particular piece of clothing goes from being a designer's vision to a must-have in a store near you.

Part III: Stocking Your Closet without Going Crazy or Broke

This book may not come with a winning lottery ticket, but in this part, I explain how you can manage your clothing budget so that you'll come out a winner after every shopping expedition.

In addition to managing your budget, I also offer various ways to help you begin to build your new, fabulous wardrobe. Should you hire someone to help you or would you rather do the research all on your own? This section is filled with information that will help you make the best decision for you.

Part IV: Dressing for Any Occasion

"What am I going to wear to *that?*" How many times have you gotten an invitation and asked yourself that question? Without the right information, getting ready for a big night out (or big night in) can be stressful. Speaking of stress, are you in the camp of never knowing what to wear on those in-between days when the seasons change? In this part, I go over how to get ready for anything and everything from a day at the office, to a formal event, to a cozy night in.

Part V: Finishing Touches

Getting dressed in the morning isn't just about the clothing you choose. A perfectly wrapped present is nothing without the bow . . . and that is how I feel about accessories. One necklace can take your outfit from frumpy to fabulous. In this section, we go through all the different options you can use to spice up an otherwise simple look and what works best for your body type.

Speaking of what works best, what you wear underneath your clothing is just as important as what you are actually wearing. Underwear, bra straps, or pantyhose gone wrong is never a good look. In this section, I give you the tricks and tips you need before you even put on a stitch of clothing.

Here's another essential for all women: fabulous shoes. The heel or flat you choose to put on with your favorite outfit can make or break a look, so choose wisely!

Part VI: The Part of Tens

We've all been fashion victims at one point or another, but there is a way to avoid fashion faux pas. In this part, I go over the most common mistakes and how to avoid them. I also show you how you can go from day to night in a flash. Most days of the week, I leave the house at 7 a.m. and don't return until after dinnertime. I've perfected a number of ways to make your day outfit turn into something that works come evening and share ten of them so that you're ready when a spontaneous plan comes your way. This part ends with a list of my favorite Web sites where you can get many of your must-haves and find helpful fashion information without ever leaving the house.

Icons Used in This Book

As you read through this book, you'll see icons popping up. Obviously, different ones mean different things. I wanted to familiarize you with them so you can know what to stop for. Here are the icons you'll be seeing throughout:

When you see this pop up, check out the accompanying paragraph. You'll find shortcuts, bits of advice, and answers to many questions you may have asked yourself while reading that particular topic.

Some of what I have to tell you really needs to be absorbed because I refer to it many times throughout the book. If you see this icon, you'll know to pay extra attention.

The text accompanying the Fashion Fix icons helps you get out of any fashion emergency. These are great tips that you will (and should) remember every time you leave the house. Fashion Fixes can save you a lot of headaches and help you make it through common fashion disasters.

I use this icon to highlight inexpensive alternatives to pricier items. Even if you don't love *exactly* what I am suggesting, you can still find helpful suggestions for saving money while building a fabulous wardrobe.

Pantyhose with open-toe shoes! Need I say more? Everyone should read the text that appears next to the Fashion Faux Pas icons because I saved these for those fashion no-nos I feel *very* strongly about. These are mistakes that you should avoid no matter your age, body type, or personality.

Not everybody cares about the technical stuff, but others find it fascinating. For those of you who eat up details like how dresses were made in the 19th century and why a woman's shirt-buttons are opposite a man's, keep a look out for this icon.

Where to Go from Here

So where do you start? If you're not planning to read this book cover to cover (no offense taken), then start with Chapter 2. That chapter gives you information you cannot be without when moving on to other chapters. Also, if you feel you need a little guidance, the Table of Contents and Index point you in the direction you are looking to go.

Finding your personal style and building a great wardrobe isn't brain surgery. So have fun! I promise: The new you is only a few pages away!

Part I
Fashion, Style, and You

The 5th Wave — By Rich Tennant

"I'll just wait for the knock-off."

In this part . . .

Y ou learned to dress yourself by the time you were, say, 5 years old, right? Eventually, you became a teen, and shopping for the trends was a must. Now you're all grown up and, as an adult, you're an expert on what does and doesn't look good, right?

Not necessarily. Before you can confidently judge what you should and shouldn't wear, you need to know the basics about fashion, about developing your own style, and about your body. You'll find that information in this section. Don't buy one more stitch of clothing until you finish reading this key information.

1

Fashion 101

In This Chapter

▶ Who's who in the fashion industry

▶ Taking important steps toward developing your own style

▶ Fitting your wardrobe needs into your budget

▶ Making the impression you want

True elegance and style comes from being confident and feeling comfortable in your own skin.

Tory Burch, Fashion Designer

You may have been born naked, but minutes later a nurse wrapped you in swaddling (how chic an outfit is that!), and you've been wearing clothes ever since. While some women have mastered the art of fashion and look fabulous all the time, many still struggle to figure it all out. If you are one of the women still searching for what exactly to wear every day, you've come to the right place. Whether you're going to the grocery store or heading to a gala, I want you to feel your best at all times, no exceptions.

As children, most of us were dressed by our parents. As teenagers, you likely just followed the trend du jour. But as adults, the options are endless. Because the choices are so vast, how can you possibly arrive at your very own style? After all, while you may find your one true love after dating less than a dozen people, you can fall in love with a dozen pairs of shoes in one store alone. Now, the ideal solution for many people would be to hire a personal shopper and leave the decision-making to expert hands. Unfortunately, few people can afford that route. So the next best plan is to gain a better understanding of how to develop your personal style. This chapter gives you all the info you need to begin that journey.

The Real Trendsetters

Literally thousands of fashion designers around the world are busily turning out mountains of clothing, and as the media continues to focus more and more attention on the fashion industry, hundreds of new designers are trying to make their way into the field every year. With so many working fashion designers, it's not surprising that you, the fashion consumer, have a flood of new clothing to choose from. If you feel like you're swimming upstream in this tide of satin, leather, and beading, try to take comfort in knowing you're not alone.

While each new fashion season brings out a variety of new styles that make you feel like everything in your closet is dated, not every designer has an impact on the latest trends. There's a filtering process between the designers' creations and the hottest trends that land in your closet. Figure 1-1 shows a designer outfit and a mass market outfit based on that design.

You may wonder how all those who make the cut seem to know that it's time to raise hemlines or douse the world in plum. You may also wonder what role, if any, the buying public has in this process. Getting the answers to these questions helps you figure out what you need to wear day and night.

Although fashion may seem like a one-way street, with all the clothes streaming out of Seventh Avenue and into the malls and boutiques nearest you, the truth is far different. Quite a number of people actually set the trends: designers, buyers, fashion houses, the fashion media, and, believe it or not, *you*. You have a much greater influence on what designs actually end up in the stores than you may think. The following sections outline the key players.

Designers

Designers are people with creative vision. They have an idea about the way clothing should look, and they take this idea all the way from an initial sketch to an actual sample to, hopefully, a store near you. Top designers display their latest creations at shows held in New York, Paris, and Milan (see Figure 1-2).

Figure 1-1: From the runway to real life.

Naturally the big name designers have more clout than those that are lesser known, but even they aren't operating in a vacuum. Everyone in the fashion industry has his or her finger in the wind, trying to decipher what the next trend may be. And the fashion designers aren't the only ones navigating public taste. The buyers (who pick and choose from the designers' collections, determining what makes it from the runway to you) also have a huge impact.

Figure 1-2: A design on a runway.

Buyers

Buyers are the people who decide, for every upcoming season, what will be hanging on the clothing racks in a store near you. Every store — from large department stores to small boutiques — has a buyer (or buyers). The buyers for the major retail outlets are one of the most important filters of the fashion trade. They have to be sure about what they're buying, because if the general consumer has different tastes, the stores end up with a ton of extra merchandise that will just end up on the sale rack.

Back in 1919, an attempt was made to artificially change the course of fashion. Pressure was put on the fashion industry to stop raising hemlines because showing so much leg was thought to be damaging America's morals. Designers responded and agreed to send hemlines back downward. The only problem was that women weren't fans of the new fad, and so the longer skirts and dresses bombed, and American women roared into the 1920s wearing flapper dresses.

Fashion houses and their ads

Fashion houses are the companies behind the bigger name designers. They're considered *houses* because the company bears the designer's name, even after the designer has retired and someone else has taken over designing the label. The fashion houses influence trends and, consequently, sales through the use of advertising. If you look through a fashion magazine, you see that most of the pages are ads. These ads, which are just as visually interesting and informative as the editorial pages, can have quite an impact. For example, department stores didn't want to stock designer jeans back in the 1980s, but the ads placed by the jeans companies created the public demand, and it wasn't long before those jeans were in every store.

Fashion media

Another important set of players is the fashion media, which is led by the major fashion magazines such as *Vogue, Elle,* and *Harper's Bazaar.* The fashion media decode what's happening on the runways and download all the information to you. Anyone interested in fashion looks to these trend-setting publications (or their Web sites) to see what's in style and what is the next "must have."

Long before the designs hit the stores, the magazines' editors choose what to feature in their magazines from the hundreds of looks on the runway. Because the fashion shows are about six months ahead of the next fashion season, and the fashion magazines are sent to the printer two to three months ahead of when they hit the newsstand, the editors, who consult closely with the fashion designers, try to look ahead and anticipate what will be popular. Because of their position as a fashion authority, their decisions exert a considerable amount of influence.

The other players

Other prognosticators also have a role to play. One example is the *Color Marketing Group,* a non-profit organization made up of design profession-als from all sorts of fields, from fashion to interior design, who get together every year and decide that, say, powder blue will be "the" color for the next year. That sets off the fabric and yarn manufacturers to stock up on material for the fashion designers in this color.

Trend forecasters also play a role. Most of the big design houses have either in-house staff whose job it is to know what trends are coming around the corner, or they hire firms (yes, there are firms that do this) that special-ize in predicting trends. These people are well versed in what's cool in the celebrity world, with teenagers, and pretty much everything going on in pop culture. They also have to keep abreast of what all the other designers are doing. Not only do they know what's going on now, but they are also steps ahead. Remember, the designers are designing their collections way ahead of when the trends will be "in." They show their lines six months ahead of when they will be in stores and are designing even further ahead than that.

And stylists like Dana Ravich, who along with Pierre co-authored this book, dress stars for big red carpet events and for appearances on television shows or in print. If a celebrity is wearing a dress from an up-and-coming designer, that could be his or her ticket to fame, too.

You

The designers, buyers, and magazines can tell you what's in style and guide you toward what to buy, but at the end of the day, it's up to you. What makes the most sense for you, your lifestyle, and your body type determines what you purchase. After you develop your personal style, you can take cues from all these outside influences in order to navigate through all this information and make the choices that are right for you.

Getting Your Personal Style Started

Some of the factors that go into deciding what to wear include where you live, what your interests are, where you work, what you like to do when socializing, and what colors and styles suit your body type. By weaving all these factors together (as Chapter 2 does), you can create your own personal style. To find out what belongs in your personal wardrobe, see Chapter 7.

Decide which trends can work for you

If you pick up a fashion magazine and look at the outfits the beautiful models are wearing, you may think, "What does this have to do with how I dress?" But even though you may not buy one of those designer outfits, it can give you clues on how to dress fashionably.

To begin with, when flipping the pages of a fashion magazine, stop and take a good look at those outfits that attract you. Decide what you find appealing about that particular look. You should even take notes. If you see a dress with an off-the-shoulder style showing off the model's collarbones and that's a body part you like, take note. If, while flipping the pages, you see that several other designers are also making off-the-shoulder styles, you've spotted a trend that you'll want to make yours.

Because magazines usually show photos of clothes for coming seasons, these designs may not yet be in stores. So tear out the pictures that you like. They can help when you're shopping because you'll know exactly what to look for. And if you're tempted to buy a random dress at the end of the current season just because it's on sale, the pictures you're carrying around will inspire you to wait for the style you're seeking. This is especially important if your budget only allows you to buy a few pieces.

Know your body

Of course clothing comes in all different sizes, but just because an outfit comes in your size doesn't mean that it suits you. Some designers know how to make creations that can be adapted to women who don't fit the runway mold. Other designers have a great eye for color and fabric, but when it comes to cut, they're more the one-size-better-fit-all types. Your job is to learn what your body shape is and find out what types of clothes flatter your figure. If you find a designer whose fit works for your body, check out the rest of his or her line. Chances are good that all the pieces will fit you well. (Go to Chapter 3 for help in identifying your body shape and developing a better understanding of what clothes can make you look your best. Go to Part IV for advice on how to dress fashionably for any occasion.)

Many women buy clothes that don't fit, using the excuse that this gives them the incentive to get into shape or lose ten pounds. Some brides are able to meet such goals because they're aiming for one particular and very important day in their lives, but most women don't end up ever wearing those clothes. Of course, if you are aiming to lose weight (great!); I'm not trying to discourage you. But a more practical (and successful) strategy is to invest in pieces you can wear as the beautiful you that you are right now.

Make educated purchases

To make educated purchases, you have to understand a few fashion basics, like what styles look best on you, what fabrics are appropriate for certain seasons, and what colors are *you.* If you are not equipped with all the information you need, shopping efficiently can be challenging.

When you shop, look at the short term ("I just love the way this looks on me") and the long term ("Is this something I must have in my closet?"). If you see a pair of trendy gladiator sandals, ask yourself, "Is this something I need, or should I use this money toward a great black cashmere cardigan?" Buying trendier, less expensive items is fine, but buying quality pieces that can last you many seasons is essential. The decision-making process isn't just about the way an article of clothing looks, but also how it was made. Head to Chapters 4 and 5 to pick up the required basics.

Determine where you want to fit in

A key to building your wardrobe is to decide what you want your overall personal style to be. If you're a mother of three and spend most of your days playing with your children and carpooling, a good portion of your wardrobe will be geared to that. But you are also a woman with a personality of your own, and your wardrobe should have pieces of clothing that work off the playground as well.

So what should determine your style? Would you prefer to look like you'd fit right in walking down the streets of a fashion capital like New York, Milan, or Paris? Or are you more comfortable adopting the style more popular to the area where you live? (Figure 1-3 shows two outfits, one that would look good in a fashion center and another that is more mainstream.) Or do you want to identify with a particular group? If you work in an office, you need to understand the dress code of that environment, and when socializing among your friends, you want to dress appropriately for the occasion, all the while being true to your personal sense of style.

Figure 1-3: Your personal style is defined by many different aspects of your life.

During the course of a week, or maybe even a very hectic day, you could change your outfit over and over again, depending on where you are and where you're going. But rather than consider playing clothes chameleon a chore, look at it as an endless series of opportunities to look gorgeous and express your personal style. To do that, you need to build up confidence in your ability to dress in the right attire no matter what the setting.

Figure out how you want the world to see you

What you choose to put on your body when you wake up in the morning says a lot about how you feel on any particular day. Even the most basic outfit can say so much. Take jeans and a T-shirt, for example — an ensemble most women can relate to. The number of combinations you can put together with these two items is endless, but each look sends out a very different message. If you're going for cute, you can pair a T-shirt with *boyfriend jeans* (a baggy jean that's often cuffed and distressed) and flip-flops (see Figure 1-4). If you're going for "hot and sexy," add jewelry and stilettos to your basic look, and you've gone from simple to sexy in a flash (see Figure 1-5). For a more sophisticated look, try a blazer over your T-shirt with a trouser jean and black pump (see Figure 1-6). And a cute sweatshirt with a pair of ripped jeans that you've had forever can show that even on a casual Sunday, you put effort into looking cozy yet adorable (see Figure 1-7).

Figure 1-4: A casual, cute look.

Figure 1-5: A great pair of jeans and high heels is a sexy look.

Now I understand that after a long work week, the last thing you want to do is try to look hot while running to get the newspapers. What I am saying is that, in the split-second of choosing what to wear for the day, make an effort to go the more flattering, put-together route. Doing so not only gives you more confidence to start the day, but it also prepares you for anything (or anyone) that comes your way! You may think of jeans and a T-shirt as only one kind of look, but even the most basic outfit can represent many different aspects of your personality, as Figures 1-4 through 1-7 show.

Most of the time, you pay attention to what you're wearing because you're going out of the house. When you're home relaxing, you're likely to throw on any old thing or your favorite sweats. (And, of course, that's okay.) However, sexiness and personal style develop only with confidence. My point? You should feel your best at all times. If you're sitting at home, do it in your favorite sweats and your coziest T-shirt. If you're heading to the market in sweats, make them look casual but sexy (yes, there is a way to make sweats look cute!).

To motivate yourself to abandon the "it doesn't matter how I look" mentality, try this: Remind yourself that you *may* run into someone you haven't seen in years. Nine times out of ten you won't, but you may. I want you to look great and feel fabulous at all times because then you'll impress the person who is most important to you: *you*.

Figure 1-6: Jeans can be very sophisticated.

Figure 1-7: Even cozy can be stylish.

Go for diversity

A spice rack with 25 herbs lets you express yourself so much better than a spice rack with only salt and pepper. The same is true of your wardrobe. The more variety you have to choose from, the more you can express your personal style, which is only possible when your wardrobe has the depth to match all sorts of moods.

When shopping, look at each purchase to see whether it expands your repertoire or is just another item like most of the others in your closet. Sure, you may love wearing gray, but if you already have numerous tops in your favorite color, try grabbing a top that highlights a different part of your personality. But always remember to buy only items that you'll wear. Don't buy a green top just because you don't have one, if green isn't a good color for you. The goal is to expand your wardrobe and express your style, all while staying in your color palette and wearing clothes that suit your body type.

If you're not sure of the vibes you want to give off when you're getting dressed in the morning, pick an outfit that allows you to add some variations. If you choose a monochromatic blouse, for example, stick a scarf (or a pair of fabulous chandelier earrings) in your purse, so that you can jazz it up if you end up going out for a drink after work. Try to think ahead. If your outfit is one that can be livened up, you'll be able to say, "Let's go" when someone suggests doing something fun.

Build your wardrobe to include both basics and trendy stuff

For most photo shoots, the person being photographed hires a stylist who brings various outfits to choose from to achieve the perfect look. When Dana and I were choosing what to wear for the front and back covers of this book, we just went shopping in my closet. We were laughing, saying, "We really do practice what we preach!" I had every basic item we needed to convey to you exactly what we wanted to. My point? Having basics in your wardrobe is a must. (The black dress on the back of the book is one I've had for eight years.) Now, I am not saying I don't have trendy items in my closet — I do. But I'm careful when buying something that I know will be out next season, and I don't spend as much money on it as I do on something I know will be around for a while. Your closet, too, should include the basics and a few trendy things.

Fitting Your Style to Your Budget

In creating a style, you're going to run into a reality check, otherwise known as your clothing budget. If you happen to have an unlimited amount of money to spend on clothes, then you can skip this section. But because most people do have to watch what they spend, learning to shop within your budget is an important skill to develop.

Spend more on the basics, less on the trendier things

Some people approach clothes shopping as they do their grocery shopping. They make a list of what they need and go out searching for the cheapest price. While stretching your food dollars this way can be quite effective, it doesn't always work with clothing. I encourage you to spend more on certain staples, items that will take you from season to season and look rich with any outfit. Trendier items are the pieces to save on because they may only last you the season. (In Part III, I explain what to look for so that even your "save" items will look like splurges.)

Sales are great times to buy staples, seasonless items, and classic pieces. Although the store just needs to clear space for new shipments, that classic pair of black Calvin Klein pants marked down and down again may fit perfectly in your wardrobe. Sale racks often take time (and patience, for that matter) to look through, but don't walk by because you feel like sales mean something is of poor quality. Quite often, it's just the opposite. (To find out more about this topic, check out Chapter 7.)

Take stock of your wardrobe

The temptation for many women to go out and buy clothing is a strong one. If you think your wardrobe has a hole that needs filling, you could just take the first opportunity to hit your local stores or surf the Web. But at some point you'll likely run into the ceiling of your clothing budget, and you don't want that to happen at a time when you need the perfect dress for a special occasion.

So don't always be so quick to look for an opportunity to shop outside your closet. Shopping can give you a psychological boost, but if you're using it as a way to lift your spirits rather than as a way to create a look for yourself, then you're almost certain to miss both goals. Rather than reach for your credit card every time you feel like it, do what every clothing store does several times a year: Take inventory.

If you don't take stock of what you already have in your closet, you're likely to buy the same thing over and over again because that's what you're drawn to. Being organized and allowing yourself to really see what you have gives you the freedom to buy new pieces you may have otherwise overlooked.

I'm not suggesting you enter every item you own into an Excel spreadsheet. Still, you should take some time as a new season is about to arrive to go through all your clothes and give away whatever isn't perfect for you. (For more on how to pare the ordinary or unexceptional from your closet, see the next section for a brief introduction on my 10 System and Chapter 2 for additional details.) At the same time, make a list of what you need and put down as many details as possible. For example, "a white button-down shirt to wear under blazers" may top your list. That way the next time you're looking through the racks in your favorite store, you'll able to fill in the gaps in your closet.

Some people give away items as soon as they buy a new one. While that method preserves closet space, it places unnecessary limits on you — especially if you're a good shopper. There's no reason to get rid of one pair of navy slacks just because you buy another pair, especially if you can wear the new pair in a different way. Maybe you wear one pair to work with ballet flats because they're too short to wear with heels. Another pair of navy slacks that you *can* wear with heels wouldn't be considered a repetitive item in your wardrobe. Although both slacks look similar, they serve different purposes.

Invest only in 10s

My main goal in this book is to help you concentrate on quality instead of quantity. I would rather you own one black blazer that fits you perfectly and is of the best quality than four that are "eh" — which leads me to my 10 System: Every item you have should be evaluated on a scale of 1 to 10, and only 10s should remain in your closet. Every blazer, sweater, or pair of jeans (shall I go on?) must fit this requirement to keep a place in your fabulous closet. As you go through the next chapters, keep this scale in mind. (To find out more about the 10 System, see Chapter 2.)

Throughout this book, you'll find tips on how to shop for key items, especially in the chapters in Part IV. Because these important garments have to be close to perfect, they may require the extra expense of being altered by a professional tailor. Although I try to help you save money throughout this book, in some instances, I encourage you to spend a little extra because it'll pay off in the long run.

Prolong that new clothes feel

Putting on a new article of clothing is a great feeling. Even if no one notices, you know that your mood has been elevated. But after a while, that blouse (or pants or scarf) joins the ranks of all the other items in your closet. Even though it's no worse for wear, it loses the punch it once had on your emotions. It's no different than if you ate your favorite dish over and over. After a while, you'll yawn instead of salivate when you see it on the menu.

While you can't stop this process, you can slow it down. Learning how to reinvent pieces you have is key. For example, a white button-down shirt can take you many different places. It can be worn under a sweater, as in Figure 1-8. When you are on vacation in a tropical place, it can be tied over a bathing suit and paired with a long skirt (see Figure 1-9). If you're heading to work, it can be worn with a sweater-vest (see Figure 1-10). And finally, if you're off to a fancy event, you can dress it up by pairing it with a sequin skirt, as in Figure 1-11.

Figure 1-8: Look casual yet sophisticated with a white button-down under a sweater.

Figure 1-9: Your white button-down will have you looking beach-chic.

Excessive buying is not the best way to establish personal style. Being smart and having key, versatile pieces in your closet will make you the fashion queen you want to be!

A Last Important Point

Throughout this book I talk a lot about personal style. My hope is that you'll use all the information here to figure out the overall image you want to project to the world. When all is said and done, no matter what you're wearing, you have to be yourself. If that means certain styles are not for you, so be it. But with so much to choose from, you can be sure to find pieces that are perfect for you. And by the time you've finished reading this book, you'll know just how to be the stylish woman you've always dreamed of being!

Figure 1-10: A vest can be a perfect complement to a white button-down shirt.

Figure 1-11: You can dress up your white button down if heading to a fancy affair.

2

Impression Management: Developing Your Personal Style

In This Chapter

» Knowing what your clothing says about you

» Finding your fashion identity and defining your style

» Streamlining your closet

» Shopping for your new style

Be confident in your clothes and wear what you feel best in. If you're not comfortable in what you're wearing, it will show.

Tracy Reese, Fashion Designer

What you wear reveals so much about you. That's why choosing what to put on every day can be so hard. If the clothes you put on reflect your personality, then every day you're making choices that show the world a little something about yourself. These choices can actually affect how you go about the rest of the day. So when you get dressed every morning, you're revealing how you feel, showing an aspect of your personality, and preparing yourself for what type of day it's going to be. (Amazing, right? Did you realize that old sweater you put on last week may have been the cause for your chaotic day?)

In this chapter, you discover how to create and manage your own personal style so that you always leave the house feeling fabulous! And please don't look at this as some massive project. This aspect of your life is in your control and is very easy to manage. You are steps away from walking out the door every day with a new, confident look — so get ready!

What You Wear: The Key to Confidence and a Window to Your Personality

You can find many definitions of what it means to "be fashionable." When I talk about a personal style, I don't mean that your clothes need to reflect what the latest issue of *Vogue* shows, What I mean is that your clothing should reflect you and your personality. Here's why:

✔ **How you look on the outside reflects how you feel on the inside.** Are you full of confidence or more the shy type, raring to go or in need of a nap, ready to meet any challenge or looking for any excuse to dive under your desk?

✔ **How you look affects your attitude, your decisions, and often what plans you choose to make (or, more importantly, not make).** You never know what the day is going to bring, so you should be prepared for all situations (within reason). If you leave the house in the morning looking so-so, you're less inclined to accept that spontaneous invitation for drinks or dinner after work. You don't always have to be dressed up in cocktail attire, but if you look great and are confident in your outfit (even if it isn't as dressy as you'd like), you'll be more inclined to accept the invitation.

✔ **The way you look and feel about yourself influences your confidence.** One of the sexiest things a woman can own is her confidence. You want to look fabulous at all times because, let's face it, you should always look like the fabulous person you are! Confidence is your best accessory

Figure 2-1: Looking and feeling your best boosts your confidence.

(see Figure 2-1). When you walk into a place thinking, "I look smashing!" others will think the same thing. Trust me.

This chapter (and this book, for that matter) is all about empowering you. And the first step in grabbing some of that power is recognizing that your appearance is very much in your hands to mold; you have complete control over it. If you believe you're not good at selecting your clothing and the process isn't any fun, you probably haven't yet figured out the right way to do it for *you.*

What to Aim for When Creating Your Own Personal Style

Personal style is about finding a look that best expresses your personality. It's also about coordinating looks and really accentuating your physical attributes while camouflaging the areas that need a little help. In fact, your personal style is something that is going to carry you through your adult life. Yes, it may change a bit over time. And yes, it will and *should* incorporate some of the latest trends, but it's *not* about blindly following what appears in the pages of the latest fashion magazines.

A key to creating your own style is knowing the difference between fashion and style. *Fashion* is what is current and in the moment according to magazines and top designers. *Style* is something you develop according to your personality and body type. So while miniskirts and knee-high boots may be the latest fashion, they may not be appropriate for you because of your body type, personality, or both. That doesn't mean you have to abandon them entirely. You can incorporate parts of a particular look into your own style. If a miniskirt is the wrong length for you, try a pencil skirt that comes to your knee. If skirts aren't in your repertoire at all, try a pair of boots under some great-fitting slacks. If the current boot has a pointy toe, wear one in that style and you'll be incorporating the latest trend in a way that works with your style.

Accentuating your personality

You can shape your personal style in many ways. The choice of what distinguishes your personal style from somebody else's, such as a specific color or chunky jewelry or stiletto heels, should be one that suits your personality. If you love to be the topic of conversation at a cocktail party, investing in statement jewelry may be the way to go. Many women feel sexier in heels, so maybe topping off each outfit you wear with an unbelievable pair of pumps or sandals is your style. (You get the drift, right?)

Feeling comfortable whenever you head out the door gives you added confidence. And this part of the puzzle is a lot of fun. It really allows you to play with accessories, shoes, scarves, and bags. Plus, it gives you the freedom to buy and wear things that are unique to you!

Using clothing to complement your personality

It's great to experiment to see how you can bring out other facets of your personality. You'll be surprised how a different look can make you feel. Consider these examples:

- ✔ If you aren't used to being the center of attention and tend to dress in darker or more subdued colors, try something a bit bolder. If putting on a red dress is too much at first, start with a big accessory to brighten up your outfit or try a red top with jeans to ease into dressing in brighter colors. Play around with different combinations to discover which ones you feel comfortable in. Maybe you'll decide to dress up an otherwise plain outfit with a pink scarf. That scarf will show the world that you were careful about what you chose to wear, but it won't do it in such an obvious way.

- ✔ If you love being the center of attention and are always wearing showy or ornate pieces, you may want to try toning your look down from time to time.

- ✔ If you have a fabulous figure (good for you!) and love to show it off, try a more subtle approach occasionally, which is also very sexy. (It may sound cliché, but less really is more.) Having a little mystery in the mix is always good.

 You have to feel comfortable in the clothing that you wear. Your style is a reflection of your personality. While experimenting is great, especially when you're developing your style, being confident and expressing your true self is the most important thing. Find out what works for you and your body type and develop your wardrobe around that.

Using clothing to project the image you want

In creating your style, you not only want to reflect who you are, but you also have to be focused on the image you want to project. While you should always stay within your comfort zone, it's okay to push the envelope a bit. For example, if you're very conservative and are looking to dress a tad sexier but you're not sure how to do it, take baby steps. Instead of wearing your little black dress with pumps and pearls, try a stiletto heel and a great pair of chandelier earrings. This takes your look from simple to sizzling with just a couple of changes, while staying within what's comfortable for you.

Showing you're in control

One of the great cries of women everywhere is, "I don't know what to wear!" Now it's one thing to say that in the privacy of your own home, but when you walk out the door, you don't want anyone else wondering, "What was she thinking!?" You want to have control over your wardrobe and, more importantly, give the impression you have that control (even if you were in total panic five minutes before leaving the house). It's all about looking put together as opposed to looking thrown together!

Keep in mind that looking put together doesn't mean that everything you have on matches perfectly. To be honest, women who wear everything matchy-matchy look more like fashion victims than mavens. The idea is to create an overall image that makes those looking at you think you were in complete control when you selected your outfit.

Only one item you're wearing should pop. If you choose a patterned blouse, keep the rest of the outfit simple (see Figure 2-2). If you have an intricate necklace with a lot of beading, make that necklace the center of attention and go with one color when choosing the rest of the outfit (see Figure 2-3). This rule definitely has exceptions, but it serves as a great jumping-off point.

Yes, you can break these rules, *if* you know what you're doing. Mixing and matching patterns is definitely possible, but the key is that one or both are

Figure 2-2: Pick one item to pop in your outfit.

very subtle and the color scheme must match. For example, you can wear a pinstripe pantsuit with a floral blouse. If the pinstripe is subtle, the blouse can take more of center stage (for more on matching patterns and colors, see Chapters 4 and 5). As long as the colors in the suit and the blouse are in the same family, or one is totally neutral, you're good to go. Before you mix patterns, be confident you know what you're doing. If you're not sure, keep it simple and pair either pattern with a solid.

Reflecting different moods

To reflect every possible mood, you need the clothes to do that. When you go shopping, think about how a particular item of clothing or accessory can help you expand your ability to express yourself. If everything you own is very loud, how are you going to dress when you're in a quieter mood? Or if everything you own is very subdued, you don't have the option of really dressing up if you're invited to a great party.

I'm not saying that if you love wearing all black, you need to ditch your entire wardrobe. What I *am* saying is that if black is your choice of color, make sure you have accessories, shoes, or bags that make your outfit pop when an event calls for it. Different colors make you feel different ways, so keep your options open!

Figure 2-3: Let your accessory be the focal point.

 I love to wear all white. I think it's extremely fresh and clean-looking. But white isn't appropriate for all occasions. I wouldn't wear all white in the dead of winter to a dinner party. My point? The color you wear (and the part of your personality you want to project) depends on the time and place.

Fitting perfectly — literally and figuratively

Every woman should develop her own personal style and create a wardrobe to express it. Building a style is a gradual process that happens as you find and collect pieces that fit into the big picture. Does that mean you have to look the same all the time? No. It's okay to have subsets of style. The image you want to project at the office is going to be different than on the tennis court. But you have to remember that you're projecting an image in both places. If you're going to have a personal style, those images generally need to be compatible.

With that said, I know how overwhelming and confusing building a wardrobe can be. It may take some time before you have the confidence to walk into a mall or department store and instantly say, "Oh, that fits perfectly in my closet." Finding items that are a perfect fit (and I mean that in both senses of the word) can be difficult. But look at it this way: Because you have so much to choose from, differentiating yourself from everyone else becomes a little easier, and after all, that's really your goal.

Defining Your Personal Style

There's no end to the type and amount of items you can purchase to jazz up your wardrobe. What you choose defines your personal style. So if the items you select are all of the latest fashion, then your style is going to be high fashion. If you choose to wear T-shirts and jeans every day, that too is a style statement. By carefully choosing what you wear every day, you're projecting an image. The following sections help you get started in developing your own personal style.

Getting familiar with fabrics and styles

To have the confidence you need when buying clothing, you must become familiar with the different fabrics and styles. That way, when you grab an item from the clothing rack, you can be absolutely sure of what you're buying. (For more information about what to look for, see Chapter 4.)

Keeping up with what's "in" is also important. Picking up a fashion magazine every month is a great way to stay in the loop. And remember, the ads are just as important as the editorial pieces. Chapter 8 has the details on what to look for, but for now you just need to know that the magazines, as well as what you see celebs wearing on talk shows or the red carpet, can give you a glimpse into what's hot. Even if you examine only one of these outlets, you'll be able to pick up the basic trends like the latest hemlines, colors, cuts, and fabrics.

Considering your characteristics

What about you can be part of your personal style? Lots! Your lifestyle, age, profession, attitude, and hobbies all play a part in defining your personal style. Here are some guidelines:

✔ **Lifestyle:** Are you a single woman living in the big city or the mother of three running an entire household? When you're on vacation, do you head for Broadway or the beach? The answers describe your lifestyle and, in turn, help define your personal style.

✔ **Age:** Everyone wants to look younger, right? The desire to knock off a few years is natural, and your wardrobe is one of the ways to do that. There's nothing wrong with wanting to dress in the latest trends, but do it in an age-appropriate way. Some trends transcend generations. Asymmetrical necklines (see Figure 2-4), for example, were big at the Oscars and Golden Globes in 2009. Celebrities of all ages were wearing one-shoulder dresses as they graced the red carpets. It was just *how* they were wearing them that was different. Don't be afraid to get in on the latest trend if it's something you love. Just make sure you do it in a way that fits your age, personality, and body type.

If you like a current trend but feel it may be too youthful-looking for you, it probably is. This is true of fashions that reveal the most skin and are the most adorned. Use your judgment when trends veer in this direction, and err on the more conservative side.

✔ **Profession:** If you work in an office, the dress code is likely different than if you work in a store or at a school. Although you have to work within the constraints of your particular industry, you should be able to express your style no matter what the dress code.

Figure 2-4: One-shoulder dresses, a trend that can work at any age.

✔ **Attitude:** Whether you're a free spirit or someone who's more conservative, your clothing can reflect your attitude. Use your wardrobe to express yourself.

✔ **Hobbies:** What you do in your free time determines your look as well. Whether you're running errands or running on the beach, your outfit reflects your personality and what you like to do.

Figuring out your current style

In order to start building your closet properly, take this easy quiz. (Sorry to take you back to the 8th grade, but it's a necessary first step!)

Pretend you're a personal stylist who's been hired to give *you* advice. Try to look at yourself as an outsider would when answering the following questions. Nobody knows you better than you do, but if you've never done a self-examination like this (and you probably haven't), what you find out may surprise you. Have fun with this, be honest with yourself, and let your true personality answer every question.

Taking a style quiz

What's your style? Take this quiz and find out! Circle the answers that best describe you:

1) You are most comfortable in

    A)   long, flowing dresses

    B)   cable-knit sweaters

    C)   a bikini

    D)   the latest trend

    E)   a white button-down shirt and jeans

    F)   a fitted sweat suit

2) When not working, you feel most like yourself

    A)   in a romantic vacation spot

    B)   on the tennis court in a country club

    C)   on a beach

    D)   in a big city

    E)   at home hosting an intimate dinner party

    F)   in your SUV with the kids

3) Your accessory of choice is

   A) an armful of gold bangles

   B) a strand or two of pearls

   C) a rash guard

   D) the new "it" bag

   E) big, round, black "Jackie O" sunglasses

   F) a diaper bag

4) The perfect everyday shoe for you is

   A) flip-flops

   B) loafers

   C) barefoot

   D) stilettos

   E) flats

   F) sneakers

5) You tend to wear

   A) mostly white

   B) lots of navy blue

   C) bright colors

   D) head-to-toe black

   E) anything neutral

   F) dark colors

Evaluating your answers

Now that you've taken our style quiz, find out who you are and how to define your look. If your answers fall mostly in the A's, B's, C's, or so on, you fall pretty neatly into one of six groups, outlined in the following sections.

Mostly A's: Group 1 — The bohemian

You are a true bohemian (see Figure 2-5). You love wearing loose-flowing, romantic tops, skirts, and dresses. You tend toward looking casual, yet pretty. Most of your clothes can go from day to night. You look like you just walked off the beach, no matter what time it is, because you have a relaxed, easy vibe about you. Your color palette includes white, off-white, white, and more white, earth tones, brown, and some beachy colors like turquoise and coral.

Figure 2-5: The true bohemian.

Figure 2-6: The prep.

Mostly B's: Group 2 — The prep

You love to wear your polo shirts. You pair them with crisp pants or shorts, depending on the weather and the activity. You are likely to be seen in shorts at the country club during the day and pants at the evening barbeque. The cable knit sweater is the cornerstone of your wardrobe. Your color palette is navy blue, kelly green, and pink — all paired with crisp white, if not one another. Your wardrobe is also filled with bold prints, such as plaid, madras, and argyle, for when you're in the mood to be noticed. The prep look (see Figure 2-6) is totally "old school" yet multigenerational and current as well.

Mostly C's: Group 3 — The surfer chic

If you answered "C" to all or almost all the questions, you are the quintessential surfer chic (see Figure 2-7). Your number one priority is how big the waves are. You don't care what's going on in the real world. Your world is the beach. You spend your mornings and evenings, and all day if possible, at the beach and out on the waves. Your outfit of choice is a bikini and rash guard, with sheepskin boots (of course). Your color palette is red, yellow, and blue — all paired with sand or off-white. The bright colors are reminiscent of all the beautiful foliage in Hawaii. Plus, they let other surfers know you're coming when you catch the big wave!

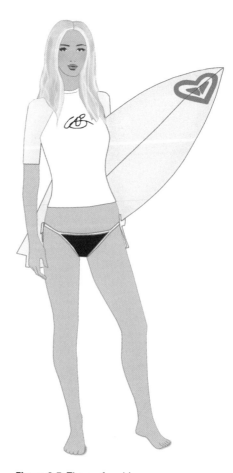

Figure 2-7: The surfer chic.

Figure 2-8: The fashionista.

Mostly D's: Group 4 — The fashionista

If you answered "D" to all or almost all the questions, welcome to group 4. You're the ultimate fashionista (see Figure 2-8)! You love the big city. You adore your uniform of all black with stiletto boots, stiletto pumps, or stiletto sandals. You love to dress up, be in all the latest trends, and wear all designer names. You're *never* a fashion victim, and even if you can't afford the high-end designer labels, you look like you do. You know which pieces to spend your money on and how to make the whole look appear expensive. You never miss an issue of *Vogue, Elle,* or *Harper's Bazaar.* Your color palette is black and more black, paired with the color of the moment, which is, of course, "the new black."

Mostly E's: Group 5 — The classic

You're in group 5 if the letter E came up the most, which makes you a total classic (see Figure 2-9). You have an easy way about dressing and are always put together and chic. You stick very close to the basics. You can buy your clothes at Gap or on Madison Avenue, or a combination — after all, a classic is a classic. Your wardrobe consists of white button-down shirts, jeans and slacks, the perfect black blazer, the perfect little black dress, and a fabulous trench coat or two. You also have a drawer full of beautiful scarves and a closet full of gorgeous purses. Your color palette is denim, white, and black, with splashes of color here and there in the form of an accessory such as a scarf or purse. Clothing is basically neutral in color. The ultimate example of a classic is, of course, Jackie O.

Figure 2-9: The timeless classic.

Mostly F's: Group 6 — The suburbanite

If you answered mostly F's, you fit comfortably into group 6, the realm of the suburbanite (see Figure 2-10). You have a casual lifestyle outside the big city. You spend most of your time taking care of everyone else, but you manage to squeeze in an exercise class, a trip to the gym, or a run outside when you can. Errands and shuttling the kids take up a huge portion of your time, so you need to be comfortable, yet still feel stylish. A cute, well-fitting sweat suit is your go-to outfit first thing in the morning, and it generally carries you through all the day's activities. If an evening activity is on the agenda, a quick change to slacks or jeans and a sweater or nice T-shirt does the trick. Your color palette consists of darker colors like navy, gray, and black. These colors are flattering and slimming and don't show stains or wear and tear from all your daily activity.

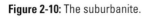

Figure 2-10: The suburbanite.

Help! I didn't have "mostly" anything

If your answers didn't indicate a definite tendency toward one look or another, it means that you don't currently dress in any particular style but throw on something generic to fit the activity. If that's the case, this is an area you can work on. The easiest way to do so is to answer the questions according to how you picture yourself and see your life, rather than what it currently may be.

You don't want to have too many styles going on at the same time. Of course, as your social settings change or your mood shifts, you want to be able to adapt your style to fit your needs at the time. But while there's no doubt that you'll have to massage your style regularly to get it to fit your schedule, you also don't want to abandon it on a regular basis. Rather than attempting to develop different styles for different occasions, work on finding ways to use your personal style as a common thread in any outfit you put together.

Even if you aren't entirely categorized by one group or another, picking a style and going with it can make life a lot easier. I'm not saying you can't delve into other looks when the mood strikes or the occasion arises — but to develop a personal style, you need to narrow it down.

Building Your Stylish Wardrobe

After you have an idea of the direction you want to go in, you can get started searching for the tools — that is, the clothing and accessories — that can help you to meet your goal. Woo-hoo! Time to have some fun. Your closet is about to get a makeover, and so are you! The next section has the details.

Using my 10 System to create the perfect closet

Once you decide on your style direction, it's time to focus on what you have going on behind those closet doors. Quality, fit, and style are the most important factors when creating your wardrobe. This means everything in your closet should be first-rate, whether it's a formal gown or sweat pants. So here's the deal about your closet (and read this sentence over and over again): Everything in it is a 10 — that is, the best — or it's about to be. If it isn't a 10, guess where it's going? Yup! Out the door. Nothing less than a 10 is acceptable. No, not even to just run to the market, walk the dog, or lounge in at home.

In order for your clothing to be considered a 10, it has to pass the following test. And, yes, you must go through your closet piece by piece, trying things on and asking these five questions of every single item. These questions are in no particular order and are all equally important. Be ruthless! This is not a multiple-choice portion of the book. Every criteria in this list needs to be met or the item is out the door like a bad date!

You must be brutally honest with yourself. Sometimes it helps to have a friend with you, someone whose fashion sense you trust (but any *really* honest friend will do). It makes the whole process a lot more fun, and you can do it for each other, so you both benefit.

What condition is it in?

Before you even try anything on, take a look at each garment and survey its condition. Is it permanently stained? Are there holes beyond repair? Is it stretched out to the point that it no longer fits well? Is the material pilly (does it have those little round nubby things that cling to lots of sweaters in particular)? If you answer yes to any or all of these questions, you don't even need to try it on. Toss those pieces straight onto the donation pile.

Does it fit?

If it passed the quality control test, the next step is to try it on. Does it fit? And, more importantly, is it flattering? Is it really a 10? Do you feel like a million bucks when you put it on? If not, it's outta there.

If you have a blouse that goes perfectly with a particular pair of pants but it happens to be a little tight so that it shows off that bulge around your tummy, then it's the wrong choice for you. Ditch it! If you feel uncomfortable about its defects, you won't wear it no matter how well it goes with the pants. Better to get rid of that blouse and avoid feeling conflicted every time you see it than to keep it just because it's the only blouse you have in that color.

Is it in style?

Is the piece in style? If not, is it more of a classic piece that will always be in style? Or is it a high-quality item that may come back into style? (The latter scenario is rare. Even when things come back into style years later, they're always a bit different. Remember the shoulder pads in the 1980s? Well, when they tried to bring them back recently, the pads were on a much smaller scale and the whole trend didn't really take off again, so those pieces weren't worth keeping anyway.) So, if the piece isn't a classic and is truly last year's trend (or even last decade's trend), out it goes.

Is it relevant to your current life?

How does this garment fit into your life? Is it an old college sweat shirt? Are they your spinning shoes, and you haven't seen the inside of a gym in years? Is it a sweater set from your younger, more conservative days? Take stock of your day-to-day life and your activities, and then evaluate what you actually need and actually wear. Do you need office clothes, workout clothes, party clothes? It can be all of the above, but if you don't play tennis anymore or don't work in an office anymore, or if anything in your life has changed that affects your wardrobe, then you need to be okay with letting these pieces go. Don't get sentimental about your old suits. If you don't use them, someone else may be able to. Isn't that a lot better? And just think about how nice your closet will look with less clutter!

Where to take the things you don't want

After you know what you're getting rid of, the next thing is to figure out what to do with the outgoing piles. Here are the options:

- **Charities:** Any number of charities would be more than thrilled to receive the goods you're unloading, such as homeless shelters, women's shelters, and other charitable organizations like *Dress for Success*.

- **Vintage shops:** If it's truly a vintage piece, designer, and really worth something — just not something that still fits you or your life — you can try selling it to a high-end vintage shop.

- **Consignment shops:** If the item isn't really vintage or high-end but is in good condition, relatively current, and is a recognizable brand with possibly some resale value, then by all means take it to a consignment shop. You may be able to get some cash for it. Some shops pay you only if or when they sell the items (hence, the name "consignment.") Other shops pay you upfront for the merchandise.

Nothing feels better than purging all that excess from your closet. You'll be so happy you did. Just think about all the room you'll have for all your fabulous new clothes. Plus, you'll actually be able to see what great pieces you already have and can use to start putting together fashionable outfits.

Do you ever actually wear it?

This is where you really have to be straight with yourself. We all have things in our closet that we're either "saving" or we just think we may wear someday in this other life we're not living. Sometimes, the piece isn't really your style or color, but you think it's a nice top and you may find a reason to wear it one day. Trust me, you won't. If it's something you put on and then change out of every time before you leave the house, you really don't feel comfortable in it, so don't even bother. Just get rid of it.

If there's even a question, a maybe, it's out. Seriously.

Obviously, if your ex-boyfriend gave you a sweat shirt back in high school, you can keep that. Yes, even if it's full of holes. But there better be a really good story behind any item you choose to keep that isn't a 10!

In with the new: A-shopping you will go

Dressing in style doesn't mean that every single item you wear every day has to be brand new. Although some women have the luxury to do that, the vast majority of women don't have the money, the time, or the storage for all the clothes and accessories needed to accomplish that. Nor do you have to throw out every thing you already own to develop a personal style. Your shopping goal at this point is to add classic-looking basics and pieces that truly express the new look you want. That means you want to begin purchasing any fashion essentials that you're missing.

The following basic items are the building blocks for every wardrobe. Incorporate them with other pieces to express your personality and style. When you shop for these items, consider your body type and fit when choosing the cut, length, and style that works for you. I explain how to determine what you need for your body type in Chapter 3:

- Little black dress (LBD)
- Black blazer
- Crisp white button-down shirt
- Black trousers
- Knee-length black skirt
- Classic beige trench coat
- Black leather bag
- Dark denim jeans
- Pair of black pumps
- White cardigan sweater (to layer)
- Black cardigan sweater (to layer)
- Set of pearls
- Diamond studs (can be cubic if need be — just keep them small)

You may already have some of these items, but are they really high quality? If not, replace them with high-quality items. For these staples, it's okay to spend a little more. (You can wait for a sale, but keep in mind that some of these items don't go on sale very often because they're always in demand.) If you don't have the money for a new one now, it's better to wear your old raincoat for another season and buy a really good one next year. Remember, you're not on a schedule. Building a stylish wardrobe is a gradual process.

These staple garments are the basis of your wardrobe; they have their own style — classic — and that speaks volumes. After you establish your basic wardrobe, you'll add additional pieces to create your personal style.

As you shop, keep these tips in mind:

- **Choose clothes that blend in rather than stand out.** Creating a style using accessories is easier and less expensive, but for those accessories to shine, you need clothes that frame them, not overwhelm them. So make sure you have enough solids in your wardrobe. Having solids that you can wear over and over is easier on your budget and makes putting outfits together easier, too. You can do this with neutrals, which can be anything in the white, black, gray, or beige family.

✔ **Shop online or use the Web if you lack the time to go shopping.** If you're completely frazzled when you hit the mall, then your attitude may stop you from seeing how a particular article of clothing can help you to express yourself. Offsetting this lack of time are all the new ways to shop, especially the Internet. If you can't get to a store, set aside some time at night when you can surf the Web. Even if you don't buy anything, you can print out the type of clothes you like. Then when you go to a store, you can follow the decisions you made when you weren't so stressed out.

✔ **Buy things you like.** Even if you buy an item at a time, after a while they'll start to match up. After all, they all suit your taste, and with that common denominator, eventually they'll mesh. So if you see a blouse that you really love but you feel like you have nothing to go with it, buy it! Trust me, you probably already own something it will go with, or you'll buy something soon enough that will be its perfect mate! By the way, 99 percent of all the blouses you own will go with jeans, a black pencil skirt, or classic black pants. (Just an FYI for when you say to yourself "I have nothing to wear with this!")

Getting help from the pros

As you shop for pieces to include in your new stylish wardrobe, asking a salesperson for assistance is often helpful. She'll know the lay of the land and can direct you straight to what you're looking for so you can avoid wandering around aimlessly (to later purchase something you don't need).

When you find a helpful salesperson in one department, let her know which department you're going to next and ask who you should ask to see. Chances are, she'll be able to guide you toward another salesperson who "gets" it.

If you think that you're really clueless and you need more than just a department store salesperson, then you need to find a fashion consultant. A salesperson is limited to the clothes in that store, but an outside professional can steer you toward a variety of stores where you can find what you need. Hiring a fashion consultant can also be a good first step in the process of deciding what your personal style should be. The two of you can create your style, develop a game plan, and go out shopping. Then, if need be, you can continue to shop on your own or engage the consultant on a regular basis to go on shopping trips — either with you or for you.

For more information on how sales associates, personal shoppers, and fashion consultants can help you, go to Chapter 8.

3

Dressing to Flatter Your Body

In This Chapter

- Being realistic about your body type
- Accentuating the parts of your body you love and camouflaging the ones you don't
- Flattering your figure no matter what your size
- Knowing when to have your clothing altered

Not every trend is going to work for everybody, or body type. Determine what works for you and what does not.

Shoshanna Gruss, Fashion Designer

Just because an article of clothing is in style does *not* mean it belongs in your closet. I know, I know, sometimes you walk by the window of your favorite store, you see that perfect dress, and you say to yourself, "I have to have it!" Well, before you whip out your credit card or wallet, *wait!* Just because that dress looks fabulous on the mannequin does not mean it'll look fabulous on you. If you try it on, and it looks nothing like what it looked like on the mannequin, put it down; do not buy it. If it's not a 10 on *you,* it won't be a 10 in your closet (see Chapter 2 for information on my 10 System).

How can you ensure that everything you choose is a 10? You need to pay attention to your size and body type. These are key factors in deciding what you can and can't wear. I don't mean to steer you away from trying to make the latest trends work for you. I just want you to figure out the best way to flatter your figure so you look and feel your best. This chapter tells you how.

Golden Rules and Good Advice for Finding Clothing that Compliments You

Every woman has something to complain about when she looks in the mirror. (If you don't, good for you — you can move to Chapter 4!) But if you're like most women, once you fix the one thing that bothers you, another seems to emerge. You lose weight; now it's time for smoother skin. You get your teeth whitened; now it's time for buffer-looking arms. The journey never ends. Why do so many of us feel the constant dissatisfaction? One theory is that the closer we get to "perfection," the more annoying other imperfections feel! (Exhausting, isn't it?)

With that said, we all have parts of our bodies that are great and parts that, well, just aren't. You need to be honest with yourself, know what your strong features are, and then pick stylish items for your wardrobe that flatter those areas. The key is to find a style that compliments your shape, size, and stature. The following sections show you how.

I'm not saying that *some* items in your closet should highlight what works best on you. I'm saying *all* of them should. You should always be your sexiest self, whether in sweaters, sweats, or sizzling evening wear.

Whatever your shape, you may have noticed that some designers fit you better than others. Why? Because each designer uses a *fit model* as the standard for their sizing, and each fit model is different, which means that each designer's garments fit differently. Because it costs more for manufacturers to provide a variety of fits for every garment, they just stick to the one baseline fit and size up and down from there. So if you find a particular brand that works for your body, see what else is in that designer's line. Chances are good that many of the line's items will also work for you.

Getting key measurements

Most women have a good idea what their measurements are, but rather than assume you know, get an accurate measurement. Going to a tailor will give you more accurate measurements, but you can certainly get a close approximation handling the measuring tape yourself. The measurements that you definitely need are your chest, waist, hips, and inseam. You may also want to add your thigh and upper arm measurements. Figure 3-1 shows where to place the tape to measure each of these areas.

When taking these measurements, use a cloth tape measure,
not a metal one. Make sure that,
when you circle your chest,
waist, or hips, the tape is level
and neither too tight nor too
loose. Also measure yourself on
your bare skin, not over clothes.
And this may sound silly, but
don't trust your memory — be
sure to write the measurements
down!

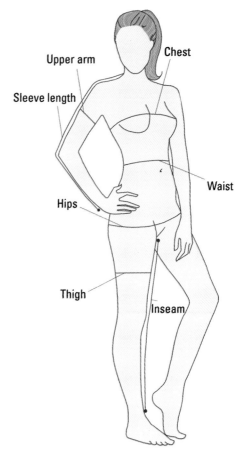

Figure 3-1: Measure yourself properly.

✔ **Chest:** Measure the circumference of your chest. Place
one end of the tape measure
at the fullest part of your
bust, wrap it around (under
your armpits, around your
shoulder blades, and back
to the front) to get the
measurement.

✔ **Waist:** Measure the circumference of your waist. Use
the tape to circle your waist
(sort of like a belt would)
at your natural waistline,
which is located above your
belly button and below your
rib cage. (If you bend to the
side, the crease that forms
is your natural waistline.)
Don't suck in your stomach,
or you'll get a false measurement. If you generally wear your clothes
below your waist, take that measurement as well.

✔ **Hips:** Measure the circumference of your hips. Start at one hip and wrap
the tape measure around your rear, around the other hip, and back to
where you started. Make sure the tape is over the largest part of your
buttocks. Because making sure the tape is level back there can be hard,
try to do it in front of a mirror.

✔ **Inseam:** This is the distance from the uppermost inner part of your thigh
to the bottom of your ankle. You can measure your inseam in two ways.

   • **With help:** While you're wearing a pair of pants, have a friend
   stretch the tape from your crotch to the bottom of your ankle.

- **Without help:** If you have a pair of pants that fit you perfectly (and they shouldn't be too loose around the waist), measure the inseam of the pants, again from the crotch to the hem.

The proper inseam on a pair of pants you're going to purchase will depend on the height of the heel you'll be wearing with them.

✔ **Thigh:** Measure the circumference of the fullest part of your thigh. Wrap the tape measure around your thigh from front to back and then around to the front. You may be tempted to cheat by lowering the tape measure a few inches but then you won't get an accurate measurement.

✔ **Upper arm:** Measure the circumference of your arm. Wrap the tape measure around the widest part of your upper arm from front to back and around to the start point.

✔ **Sleeve length:** Get help for this one because it's hard to do yourself. Place your hand at your waist (your elbow should be bent at a 90-degree angle). Then start at the middle of the back of your neck and measure to your shoulder, down your arm to the elbow, and then on to the wrist.

You may need a family member or friend to assist you with the measurements. If you have a garment that fits perfectly, measuring the garment rather than your body can be a good substitute.

The fruit basket: Determining your shape

What is the ideal shape today? I bet you're saying, "It depends on who you ask." If you look at many fashion magazines, you'll likely see the ideal as tall and thin. If you ask the average male, he may say a woman who is "curvaceous." And if you ask yourself? Hmmm, that may take a little while to answer. But here's the deal: In order to begin to build a wardrobe that expresses your personal style, you must determine what your shape is.

Okay, don't roll your eyes, but yes, I'm asking you to assess your body and then compare yourself to a piece of fruit. You've probably heard these terms before, but perhaps this is the first time you'll actually identify yourself with food that usually works as a centerpiece on your kitchen table.

The shape of many women can be described as bearing a similarity to either a pear or an apple. Now, take a look in the mirror and decide which of these you resemble most. If you're a pear, you tend to carry your weight around your hip and bottom area, and if you're an apple, you tend to carry your weight in your upper body.

Once you know your shape, your next job is to figure out how to use fashion to accentuate the parts you love and help hide the parts you don't. By discovering how to draw attention away from problem areas, you then have the general knowledge you need to dress in the most flattering way for your body type, no matter the occasion.

Whether you're a pear or apple does *not* mean you're overweight. Apples simply carry their weight in their upper bodies, and pears tend to carry their weight around their hips and bottoms. The trick is to use your clothing to make your figure more proportioned on top and bottom. What if you don't fall into either category (some women are cut pretty straight up and down; others are fairly proportional)? Fortunately, you don't have to be either one or the other to make this information work for you. No matter your shape, you can use the advice I give in the following sections to make the most of your clothing! Plus, you have more leeway with what looks good.

The most common fruit: The pear

The most common shape for women is the pear shape (see Figure 3-2). What that means is that the widest part of your body is below your waist, around your hips. Remember, you can be tall, short, heavy, or skinny and still be pear-shaped.

Figure 3-2: A pear-shaped woman.

If you're a pear, your fashion goal is to elongate your figure so that you look less bottom-heavy. The first line of attack to reaching this goal is to balance your hips and your shoulders while showing off your curves. The key here is to accentuate your top half. For example, if the eye is drawn to your cute top or the scarf around your neck, it takes the focus off your bottom half.

Always wear something darker and slimming on the bottom, like dark jeans or slacks, or a dark knee-length pencil skirt or A-line skirt. And, no, that doesn't mean that you always have to wear black on the bottom, but make sure that the bottom is solid in color and darker than whatever you have on top.

As a pear, you want to direct attention to your tops. Fun colors, prints, or details at the neck all serve the purpose of drawing the eye away from the hip area. Just make sure that your tops don't end at your hips because that draws unnecessary attention there. Figure 3-3 shows how combining a tailored, flared pant with an attractive, eye-catching top can play up a pear's best features.

Read on for even more pear-pleasing suggestions:

✔ **Go for clean, tailored lines on the bottom.** Whatever you wear on the bottom should always be more tailored, such as flat front pants. With skirts, the A-line or flared skirt is a great piece to use as a base to accentuate a beautiful selection of tops. Stay away from pleats, side pockets, or anything that is going to add dimension to this area.

If you wear a belt, make sure it's slim and the same color as your pants (a wide belt draws more attention to the area you're trying to deemphasize). If you belt a dress, make sure the belt sits higher up at your waistline rather than your hips. Better yet, wear a top that's gathered around the stomach. Doing so hides your tummy if you need to, while creating dimension someplace other than your hips.

Figure 3-3: The perfect outfit for a pear.

- ✔ **Wear pants or jeans that have a flare on the bottom.** A flared leg draws the eye away from your hips and creates a more flattering line for your whole body. Conversely, stay away from capri or tapered pants. They drive the eye right to the hips.

- ✔ **Check out tunic tops or dresses.** You can wear a tunic top or dress as long as it fits properly. (Don't wear a tunic top or dress if it's in any way clinging to your belly or your hips.) One that fits properly gives a clean, elongating line while camouflaging everything underneath. The great thing about this style is that it accentuates your arms and your whole upper body and makes you appear taller and leaner at the same time.

- ✔ **Make use of jackets.** Jackets are great for pear-shaped people because they usually have interesting details around the neckline and give more structure to the shoulder area, where you're trying to direct the focus. When wearing a jacket, choose one that ends past your hips, not at them. A longer jacket, such as a cute blazer, creates a long, lean line and covers the hip area.

- ✔ **Experiment with different necklines.** A deeper, more plunging neckline elongates your upper body and draws all the attention upward. Try wearing a long necklace to fill in the neckline, which also adds to the lengthening of your upper body.

- ✔ **Show off your shoulders.** The shoulders are a great and sexy part of a woman's body. Especially if you're pear-shaped, you want to show them off by wearing off-the-shoulder tops that expose one or both shoulders. These tops immediately attract attention and steer the eye exactly where you want it. Ruffles or puffy sleeves on your top are also great for pears.

When you keep it simple on the bottom, you have so much room to play with tops and accessories. You can start to stock your wardrobe with great fitting pants, jeans, and skirts, and then play with colors, prints, and less expensive, trendier items on top. Try a fun scarf around your neck, a fabulous necklace, or a great pair of earrings. These items all serve to draw the eye up to your best feature — your face!

Choose materials that hold their form like wool slacks or denim. They flatter and streamline your shape. Avoid any tight knits on the bottom because they cling and accentuate your width.

The next most popular fruit: The apple

Apple-shaped women (see Figure 3-4) are fuller around the middle. If they gain weight, it shows up around their belly and upper body. They're usually larger-breasted and their upper arms and shoulders are broader, too. Their legs tend to be thin and their butts tend to be flat.

Figure 3-4: An apple-shaped woman.

As an apple, you want to emphasize your strong points (your bust and legs) while camouflaging your weaker ones (your midsection), keeping it all in balance. Since the idea is to draw the eye toward those parts of your body that shine and away from those that don't, you want to show off your great legs.

- ✔ **You can wear patterns, just follow these guidelines.** Any large pattern is going to draw attention, so don't wear a large pattern on top. Wear a small, subtle pattern on top, or save the patterns for the bottom. A great print skirt with a solid sweater set is a great way to express yourself while also flattering your figure.

- ✔ **If you have a fuller chest area (and are comfortable accentuating this area), draw attention to it.** Doing so keeps straying eyes from your midsection. Wear a sexy V-neck. (Ooh la la!)

  Wear bras that support your bust. And any straps on your tops should be wide enough to cover your bra straps. (See Chapter 14 to find out more about the different types of bras.)

- ✔ **If, like most apples, you have great legs, short skirts are in order.** If you're in the office, the shortest your skirt should be is just above the knee. If you're going out for a night on the town, go a little higher!

- ✔ **A-line skirts also work with your figure.** Since they flare out from the waist, A-line skirts offer balance and proportion to your upper half.

✔ **If you don't have much of a backside, and you want to give the illusion that you do, wear pants with back pockets.** Your jeans should have a rise lower than your natural, wider waist. Don't wear pants with pleated fronts, as that only makes your middle look larger.

Don't wear pants that are too tight, even if you have good legs, because that makes your top seem extra large. Remember, while you want to emphasize your better attributes, the challenge is to do so while also keeping your overall look in balance.

✔ **Go for longer jackets.** Your jackets should be on the long side, never ending at waist level. Make sure they come down to your hips to create a long, lean line right over your waist and tummy area. And opt for single-breasted jackets that you can keep unbuttoned. A double-breasted blazer that needs to be buttoned to look right only makes you look larger on top.

✔ **Opt for drop waists.** A dress or top with a drop waist (that narrows down at the point of your hips instead of your true waist) bypasses any constricting fabric around the tummy area and makes your torso appear longer and leaner overall.

Figure 3-5 shows an outfit appropriate for an apple-shaped woman. It hides the problem areas and accentuates the positive features.

If you're an apple with great legs, you can get away with anything on the bottom, even knits. As far as your top goes, stay with materials that offer more structure, like a straight cut cotton blouse, or something blousy like silk. Both of these camouflage the midsection. You want to avoid tight knits on top because they cling and accentuate this area.

Where's your waistline?

Another common attribute of women is to be either short-waisted or long-waisted. To determine your own "waistedness," follow these simple steps:

1. **Measure the distance between your armpit and your waist.**

2. **Measure the distance between your waist and the bottom of your bum.**

Figure 3-5: An A-line skirt is a great cut for an apple-shaped woman.

3. **Compare the measurements.**

   If the two aren't equal, you're either short- or long-waisted: If the first measurement is shorter, you're short-waisted. If the second measurement is shorter, you're long-waisted (see Figure 3-6).

Short-waisted women

Maintaining balance is one important key to flattering your figure and dressing for your body type. If you're short-waisted, you're going to look out of balance with a top half that appears smaller than your bottom half. Finding ways to make your top half look proportionate to your bottom half, by making your waist appear longer, helps you achieve balance.

✔ **Try a top with vertical lines.** These lines give the illusion that your top half is longer than it is. The stripes can be as subtle as a pinstripe blouse — anything that keeps the eye moving up and down right over your waist works.

✔ **Wear tops that you can leave untucked.** This is another way of hiding where your waist actually is.

   A deep V-neck draws the focus upwards and away from your waist (this is a little tip that works for everyone — not just short-waisted women).

Figure 3-6: A short-waisted (left) and a long-waisted (right) woman.

✔ **Avoid dresses with a waistband.** If you do need a belt, choose a narrow one that's in the same color as your outfit to minimize the attention to the waist area.

✔ **If you wear prints, limit it to your top and make sure your top ends by your hips.** This hides your true waistline, and the break between the pattern and the solid bottom make your waist seem longer than it really is.

What you don't want to do is draw attention directly to your middle, as the left-hand model in Figure 3-7 does. The wide belt at the waist accentuates the short waist, making the top half look out of proportion with the bottom half. The tunic top, on the other hand (also in Figure 3-7), elongates the waistline and makes the body look balanced.

Figure 3-7: A don't (left) and a do (right) for short-waisted women.

Long-waisted women

The problem that long-waisted women have is that their body type makes their legs seem shorter. If you're a long-waisted woman, you need to use your clothes to add length to your bottom half:

- ✔ **Choose dresses that have an A-line or an empire waist.** These styles make your waist appear higher than it is, thus making your legs appear longer too.

- ✔ **Choose shirts that cover your waist.** The short, stomach-baring shirts are a problem for long-waisted women. When these types of shirts were the trend, it became difficult for long-waisted women to find tops that didn't look like they'd shrunk in the dryer. (By the way, *anyone* over the age of 12 should avoid this trend at all costs. No adult women should ever wear stomach-bearing tops. And, no, it doesn't matter if you spend every day at the gym!)

- ✔ **Choose pants that are at your natural waistline or a bit above.** You definitely want to avoid hip huggers because they make your legs look even shorter.

Never feel as though you're not "in" if you aren't wearing what are supposedly the current trends. Even the fashion industry makes mistakes. You don't have to follow its lead! As I've mentioned before, don't let a trend dictate what you wear. Not all trends work with all body types, and you don't want to be a fashion victim. Better to stick with your own style and wear clothes that flatter you.

- ✔ **Opt for short jackets.** The bolero style, for example, can be very elegant on a long-waisted woman.

- ✔ **Wear heels.** They add length to your legs.

- ✔ **To heighten the effect of longer legs, make sure your shoes match your bottom.** If you're wearing a skirt or dress, matching hosiery also adds to that effect, as does a wide belt that matches the color of your bottom.

Whatever you do, avoid styles and cuts that make your legs look shorter (see Figure 3-8). Low-waisted jeans with a shorter top only accentuate your long waist, cut you in the middle, and make your legs look shorter. High-waisted pants, on the other hand, will elongate your legs, and raise the appearance of your natural waistline (also in Figure 3-8).

Figure 3-8: A don't (left) and a do (right) for long-waisted women.

Tackling other problem areas

The preceding sections concentrate on the waist and hips because those are the most common problem areas, but there are others as well:

- ✔ **Full arms:** If your arms are very full, try wearing tops that extend the shoulder, such as a drop shoulder. Adding a colorful shawl in cooler months can also work well. And, of course, tops with lots of fabric in the sleeve can also disguise what's underneath.

- ✔ **Long necks:** If you don't like your neck because you feel it's too long, use scarves, turtle necks, cowls, or high collars to make it appear less elongated.

✔ **Short necks:** For a short neck, you want to expand the neck area by making it seem that the area just below the neck appears to be a part of it. For that, keep your neckline open by unbuttoning a top button or wearing V-necks.

✔ **Too-large or too-small chest:** If you want to make your chest area seem smaller than it is, a fuller top deemphasizes what's underneath. You can also wear darker, solid tops with a higher neckline. These minimize the look of the bust area and make it appear smaller. If you have small breasts and want them to appear larger, try wearing tops in lighter colors or with prints. These draw attention to your bust and also make it appear bigger, as do V-necks, sweetheart necks, or any neckline that shows off the bust area. And a very colorful scarf tied in a knot at chest level draws the eye there and accentuates the bust as well.

Remember these two general principles: Cover problem areas with some creative fashion sense, and highlight the other parts of your body that you find attractive to draw the eye there.

Getting Your Size Right

Clothing is available for all body types. Whether you're buying pieces from the general misses collections, the petites department, or the plus-size department, make sure your clothing fits you properly.

Clothing sizes are never exact because no two people have the exact same measurements. In many instances, the compromises that you have to make to wear "your" size are not that noticeable. Other times, you really must have your clothing altered to get the right fit. If you can find a manufacturer whose size is really close to yours, buy whatever you need and like from that designer's line.

Petites

Regular misses clothing is designed to fit a woman who is 5 feet 5 inches. If you're significantly shorter than that, even if some measurements like your waist or bust match a particular regular size, many others like sleeve length or inseam won't. So women on the shorter side need to shop in the petite section in order to get the best fit.

As you'd expect, if you're shorter than average, your goal for your wardrobe is to make yourself seem as long as possible. So petites should wear clothes that don't cut them off in the middle but rather offer the eye the longest possible line.

✔ **Clothing that offers vertical lines such as stripes or is monochromatic (or has colors in the same family) are your best bet.** If you wear patterns, make sure that they're smaller (larger patterns can overwhelm you). Stay away from opposites, such as a stark white shirt and black pants. These color combos cut you in the middle. If you want to wear contrasting colors, make sure that the overall look remains *vertical* so you maintain a longer appearance. For example, go ahead and wear a red blouse with a charcoal gray skirt, but make sure that you also have a matching charcoal jacket.

✔ **As a petite, you want to avoid horizontal lines.** Wide belts or sashes shouldn't be a part of your wardrobe, unless they're the identical color of your outfit.

✔ **Detailing can also be useful.** A long skirt with a line of buttons down the side adds length to the eye. A wrap dress with an edge that stands out, for example one made of satin, offers a long diagonal line, which has much the same effect as a vertical line.

✔ **Need I mention heels?** Shoes are most women's favorite accessory, not to mention biggest weak spot when shopping! Women *always* make an excuse to buy more shoes. Well, petite women, as long as you can walk in them, break out the high heels! They'll give you a couple extra inches and, in most cases, give your confidence a boost, too.

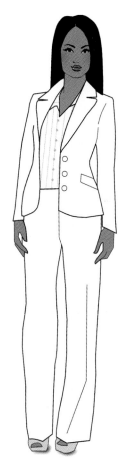

Figure 3-9: A pinstripe top is a good choice for a petite woman.

Figure 3-9 shows an outfit that makes a petite woman look taller because of the pinstripes and because the color scheme is the same from top to bottom.

The taller woman

Many tall women likely didn't love their height growing up. (It's never easy being the tallest girl in the class!) But get older and being tall is likely easier. Now it's just about finding clothing that flatters your long body!

Unless you're over 6 feet tall or have some real figure flaws that you're trying to hide (refer to the earlier section "The fruit basket: Determining your shape"), you'll have an easy time shopping and finding clothing that works and looks great on your body. Most models and *fit models* (models designers use to size their clothing) are on the taller side, and so most designers cut according to those models.

The Baby Phat line of clothing is designed by Kimora Lee Simmons who is 6 feet tall, and tall women report that she has adapted her line to suit taller women, so you may want to check out her clothing line. You can find Baby Phat designs at Macy's as well as online at www.babyphat.com.

If, for some reason, you're uncomfortable with your height and want to draw attention away from it, your goal should be to differentiate your top half from the bottom to keep the eyes from seeing you as one long, lean line. To accomplish this, you can use horizontal stripes or a wide belt. Both keep eyes from looking you up and down. Another way to accomplish this is to wear different colors on your top and bottom halves. Black and white does this well, as do any two contrasting colors. A taller woman can also use larger accessories, like a large bag and chunky jewelry. If your accessories are eye-catching and/or in bright colors, they attract all the attention. Figure 3-10 demonstrates how you can wear a contrasting black belt to cut the body in half and make it appear shorter.

If you're really trying to appear shorter, flat shoes (obviously) help. Tons of cute flats are out there these days, from boots to ballet flats to sandals to flip-flops. The variety is endless and a very welcome addition to most tall women's wardrobes!

Figure 3-10: Tall women look great in contrasting colors and flats.

Plus sizes

If a size 14 in misses clothing is too small for you, you fall into the plus-size category. You'll have a larger variety to choose from and a much easier time finding clothing that fits properly and works on your body type if you shop in the plus-size department.

As a plus-size woman, you're still a fruit (lucky you!) and need to follow the rules that fit your body shape (head to the earlier section "The fruit basket: Determining your shape" to get the appropriate tips).

In addition to the fruit tips, as a plus-size woman, you're going to look better in solids or small patterns because with so much extra material, any larger pattern is going to make too strong an impact. If you wear plus sizes, a monochromatic look will help elongate your appearance, as Figure 3-11 shows. Of course, while muted colors are going to blend in more, don't be afraid of color. If the clothing fits right, is flattering, and accentuates your better attributes, go for it. Bright accessories and statement jewelry are also a great way to make any basic outfit pop.

Since a little added height also makes you look more proportioned, wearing heels is a good idea, especially when you dress up. If you're showing your legs and wearing hosiery, don't wear hose with patterns or bright colors, however, because that makes your legs look larger. Better to stick with dark tights or flesh-colored hose.

Figure 3-11: A monochromatic look.

Depending on your exact shape, low-rise pants may be good for you because they don't squeeze you around the middle (assuming that's your widest part). You want to avoid wide belts because they draw the eye to your waist. When you wear a belt, choose one that matches the color of your top or bottom. Doing so deemphasizes your waistline.

If you haven't done so already, try out Spanx (head to Chapter 14 for these and other undergarments). Spanx are made to hold you in basically wherever you need a little help! They should become your best friend whether you're a size 2 or 20!

If you're plus-size and constantly choose loose dresses because you think they hide what you're insecure about underneath, stop! Loose dresses with an abundance of material make you look even bigger (see Figure 3-12). They also make you look like you don't have any shape at all and do nothing to accentuate the attributes you should be showing off.

Just because you're plus-size doesn't mean you need to be wearing mu-mus. Make an effort to find clothing that flatters your body. Every woman has beautiful parts and those should be accentuated, not hidden under a tent. Along those same lines, be careful that your clothing is not too tight. Avoid materials that cling to your body, like spandex.

Evens and Odds: Understanding Clothes Sizing

In most settings, two is twice as big as one, but not in women's clothing. In the past, most women either made their own clothes or had them custom-made, so there was no need for standardized sizes. But once most women started buying their clothes ready-made, a system of standardization was required. In the early 1950s, the National Bureau of Standards, a government agency, was called in to study the situation. An Acting Secretary of the Subcommittee on Body Measurements for Wearing Apparel Sizes was appointed and various engineers and mathematicians were brought on board. After three years of hard work, the standards were set.

The operative word in the preceding sentence is "were." Even though the federal government spent three years working to figure out standard sizes for clothing, this relatively easy-to-understand system didn't last long because women started to grow larger. In order to please women who didn't want to

Figure 3-12: Don't choose anything that resembles a mu-mu.

have to say they were buying sizes that were at the higher end of the scale, the fashion industry introduced _vanity sizing,_ which effectively moved every size down by four notches, so what was once a size 10 became a size 6. In 1983, the government threw up its hands and got out of the sizing business altogether, and so sizes today are a bit of a free-for-all. Because the government doesn't dictate standard sizes anymore, you can't always be confident that what a label reads on one garment will be at all similar to another. In other words, a size 8 made by one manufacturer does not necessarily fit the same way a size 8 from another manufacturer does.

Today the only vestige of the old standard sizes can be found in patterns, which have steadfastly retained the old sizing formula.

Nowadays clothing manufacturers have developed their _own_ systems and the result can be a bit confusing. Consider these examples:

- **Junior clothing includes only odd numbers, 0–13.** The fit is more youthful, which generally means smaller and younger in style. If you're past your teenage years, you should generally not be buying junior clothing. It most likely won't fit properly and is not really age appropriate.

- **Women's clothing (often called "misses") runs from sizes 0 to 14, even numbers only.** These sizes are for most women, unless you're petite, plus-size, or still young enough to wear junior sizes. These garments are cut with the assumption that women have fuller figures, taking into account the bust and hips.

- **Plus-size clothing in most clothing lines is anything above a size 14.** However, there have been recent changes made with women's or misses clothing. Now you can find some misses clothing up to a size 20. A true plus size will be designated, say, 18W. The difference is that the plus size is cut larger in the bust and middle.

So what does all this mean to you? If you understand that the size indication on a garment is only a rough guideline, you'll be much more careful to try on every item you buy before you make the purchase so that you won't have drawers filled with clothing that doesn't fit properly.

The Beauty of Altering

Just because you're a size 6 and the label on the dress in your hand says "Size 6" doesn't mean that dress is going to fit you. Instead of getting frustrated by this, find yourself an expert tailor. Yes, it's going to force you to spend some of the money you normally would on buying clothes on getting the ones you have fixed, but you'll end up with a wardrobe filled with clothes that fit you like a glove. Believe me, you can do more with a closet full of clothing made up of all 10s than you could with a lot of 5s laying around.

Here's the situation with getting things altered: Do it when it makes sense. If you find the perfect dress in a size 14 but are yourself a size 2, you shouldn't take the dress to the tailor to make it fit. But if you find a perfect dress that just needs to be a little shorter, or the waist needs to be taken in, or the arms are too long, the tailor should be your next stop.

A great fit is nearly priceless. So if the clothing is really worth it — it looks great and makes you feel great — invest the money to have it tailored properly. If it doesn't fit properly, you can bet it's not a 10 (refer to Chapter 2), and it shouldn't be in your closet, let alone on your body!

Finding someone schooled in the art of altering clothes can be difficult. Here are some suggestions:

- ✔ **Department stores** often have tailors on the spot who can measure you and do the necessary work. If this is an option, grab it. The department stores know the tailors' work well and use them time and again. You're pretty much guaranteed quality workmanship.

- ✔ **Dry cleaners** are often a good source, either because they have a tailor in house or know of someone. If you need something like a simple hem, the dry cleaner is a safe bet. If the alteration is more complicated, consider an alteration shop.

- ✔ **Alteration shops** specialize in alterations and should be able to do what you require.

A referral from someone who has used a good tailor is always your best bet. The last thing you want is to experiment with a new tailor if you have a complicated alteration or the garment was very expensive. You may want to have two people, one who is less expensive and you can trust to do little jobs (like the hem on a pair of pants) and another who specializes in dressy dresses and more complicated items.

Not so long ago, most women could sew a simple hem. (I can't, so don't feel badly if you can't either.) That was because pants only came in one long length and so they all had to be hemmed to the proper length. Then manufacturers started selling pants, especially jeans, in a multiple of inseam lengths and the concept of having clothes altered started to fade, especially as sewing machines became less and less common a household appliance. (If you don't own a sewing machine or are laughing at the notion of it, you're not the only one!)

Part II
Mastering the Basics of Garment Construction, Fabrics, and Color

In this part . . .

If you read Part I, you know about your body type and have a general idea of the kinds of cuts and styles that look good on you. So now you're ready to go out and work on that fabulous new wardrobe, right? Sorry, not yet. Before you start filling up your closet, you have to know more about the clothing you're actually buying. This part explains concepts such as how to recognize a quality garment, how to pair colors and patterns, and how a garment goes from being a twinkle in a designer's eye onto a rack in a store near you.

4

Fundamentals on Fabrics and Garment Construction

In This Chapter

▷ Identifying common fabrics

▷ Understanding fabric characteristics like texture and weight

▷ Judging the quality of a garment by how it's made

▷ Finding what works when mixing and matching different fabrics

I'm a big fan of anything made out of T-shirt material. I put it on and immediately feel relaxed.

Kathie Lee Gifford, *Today* Host

When I want to kick back, I grab my cotton sweats and tanks . . . preferably fresh out of the dryer.

Hoda Kotb, *Today* Host

A true fashionista can distinguish between designer clothing and knock-offs in a millisecond. The main way of doing that is by the fabric. It's easy to imitate a style, but since one of the main costs of an item is the fabric, imitations are usually easy to spot if you know what to look for. And vice versa, if you find an affordable outfit by an unknown designer but recognize that it was made with quality fabric, then you've found yourself a true bargain.

In order to build your wardrobe properly, you must have a general knowledge of the fabric you're buying. By discovering how to recognize quality materials and construction, you'll be able to make better decisions on what to purchase. This chapter gives you the lowdown.

Fabric Basics Everyone Should Know

The garment industry uses hundreds of different fabrics in the making of clothes. About 220 different fabrics alone can be used to produce a woman's suit, for example. Some of these are variations of a basic fabric, such as the many types of cottons, ranging from broadcloth to Pima, while others are made from various fibers and have unique characteristics, like brocade, which has raised designs on a flat surface. (See the later section "Fabrics and fabric blends" for a list with descriptions.)

How much do you really need to know about fabrics? Actually it helps to know quite a lot. Here's why:

- **One of the keys to dressing fashionably is having variety in your closet.** If you have ten blouses that are identical in fabric, except for their color, it's difficult to put together an outfit that stands out. But if your collection of blouses features lots of different fabrics as well as a variety of textures, weaves, and shades, you can put together outfits that are more unique.

- **Knowing the different fabric varieties helps when you're shopping.** Asking a sales associate for a black blouse doesn't really give her very much to go on. But if you say you want a black silk blouse, you've narrowed down the choices considerably. And if you say a black silk-satin blouse, you've done even more refining. Knowing one fabric from another can also help you as you scan your favorite store and look for that perfect outfit.

- **The care of your clothing is dependent on what it's made of.** Most synthetic fibers, for example, are prone to heat damage, especially hot water in a washer as well as the heat of a dryer or iron.

Practical matters aside, the more you know about fabrics, the better you can become at selecting clothing of quality (which is the only type you should have in your 10 closet; refer to Chapter 2 for more on my 10 System).

Common fibers

There are five natural fibers (cotton, wool, silk, linen, and hemp) and five manmade fibers (acetate, acrylic, nylon, polyester, and rayon). These fibers are the building blocks of most of the material used in clothing. In some instances they're used alone, but very often they're blended together so that manufacturers can combine the look of one fabric (usually a natural one) with the durability of another (usually a synthetic).

Natural fibers

Natural fibers are just that — those that are found in nature. They come from plants or animals, as opposed to being chemically produced. The following lists a variety of natural fibers and explains how they're used in clothing:

- ✔ **Cotton:** Cotton comes from a plant and is the most popular fabric, in part because it breathes. Among the fabrics made from cotton are flannel, muslin, oxford, poplin, seersucker, and terry cloth. Because cotton cloth wrinkles easily, manufacturers often blend it with polyester to make it wrinkle resistant; unfortunately, this pairing also makes it less breathable. However, today you can buy 100 percent cotton shirts that don't need to be ironed but merely thrown in the dryer for a short time because permanent finishes have been added to them that reduce wrinkling. While such shirts are more costly, in the long run they can save you a bundle in cleaning costs.

- ✔ **Wool:** Wool comes from animals and is woven into a fiber that can be made into clothing. Wool retains heat and absorbs moisture without feeling wet so it's particularly good as an outer layer. When treated, worsted wool holds a crease and is smooth and quite durable, making it popular for suits, skirts, and slacks. Among the types of fabrics made from wool are flannel, gabardine, tartan, and various tweeds.

  Most wool comes from sheep, but the wool of other animals — such as alpaca, angora goat (mohair), angora rabbit, cashmere goat, vicuna (a type of llama), and camel — is also used.

- ✔ **Silk:** Silk is made from the hairs in the cocoon of the silk worm, and man has been using this wonderful fiber since 2,700 BC. Silk is one of the more elegant fabrics because the cloth produced is shiny and gives a dressier appearance. Among the fabrics made from silk are chiffon and *doupioni,* a knobby silk found in some men's lightweight suits.

  Keep your silk away from alcohol. If you're going to put on perfume or hairspray, do so before you don a silk garment and allow the alcohol to evaporate.

- ✔ **Linen:** Linen is made from fibers in the stalk of the flax plant. It's the strongest of any vegetable fabric, as much as three times stronger than cotton. Yes, linen wrinkles easily, but it's also easily pressed. Linen is a good conductor of heat, which makes it perfect to wear in hotter temperatures.

- ✔ **Hemp:** Hemp comes from the stalk of the plant whose flowers and leaves make marijuana (but no, the stalk doesn't contain any of the narcotics that give marijuana its punch). Like linen, it wrinkles easily. Because it's considered a "green" fabric, hemp is growing in popularity, but it's still illegal to grow hemp in the United States and so the fabric is usually imported from China.

Cleaning silk

Though many people think silk has to be dry cleaned, it's a natural fiber that was used for eons before such a thing as dry cleaning existed. That means it can definitely be washed, but you have to know how:

✔ Hand-wash your silk garments. The agitation of a washing machine can damage silk clothing.

✔ Use lukewarm water and a non-alkaline detergent and don't leave silk garments to soak. *Never* expose silk to bleach or detergents with brightening agents. If you notice a soapy residue, add a spoonful of vinegar to the rinse water.

✔ To dry silk, lay the garment down on a towel that will absorb the moisture. Don't dry silk in the dryer or in the sun.

Note: If a silk garment has care instructions that say, "Dry clean only," that may mean the manufacturer hasn't taken the precaution to preshrink the fabric and didn't use color fast dyes — in other words corners were cut. If that's the case, make sure you dry clean that item so that it doesn't shrink or fade and ruin the garment.

Manmade fibers

While natural fibers require just some simple processing, manufactured fibers are a little more involved. They start as various combinations of raw ingredients that you may not associate with clothing at all, like petroleum and wood pulp. These substances are turned into fiber using techniques that have only been around for the last century or less. Manufactured fibers can have advantages over natural fibers. For example, they can be made into hollow tubes that offer loft without the weight (such as those found in winter overcoats) and microfibers that are excellent at repelling water.

✔ **Acetate** is made from wood pulp. It can have the look of silk, dries quickly, and drapes well. If you own clothing made from acetate, keep it away from acetate in its liquid form, such as nail polish and nail polish remover. Liquid acetate will damage the acetate fabric.

✔ **Acrylic** is a *synthetic fiber,* meaning it's manufactured from petroleum products. It has the bulk of wool, draws moisture away from the body, and can be washed. It also dries quickly, but melts if it becomes too hot.

✔ **Nylon,** the first completely synthetic fiber, entered the fashion world in the form of stockings introduced in the 1940s. It's lightweight but strong, and its fibers are smooth and dry quickly. After many washes, nylon tends to "pill"; it also melts at high temperatures.

✔ **Polyester** fibers are strong and wear very well. Because it doesn't absorb water easily, it dries quickly. The downside is that polyester doesn't breathe. Unfortunately, polyester got a bad name for itself when it was used in double-knit fabric that was popular for a while in the 1970s and then became overused. Today, polyester is often used in a blend with cotton or other fibers.

✔ **Rayon** is created from wood pulp, and it shares many of the qualities of cotton. It's strong and absorbent, comes in a variety of qualities and weights, and drapes well. If rayon is washed before being made into a garment, it's a washable fabric.

Fabrics and fabric blends

Given the relatively limited number of fibers — manmade and synthetic — that are used to make clothing, you may wonder how there can be so many fabrics. The answer has to do with how a fiber is woven, whether the fibers are blended, and what finishes are applied. This section gives you a quick rundown of a variety of fabrics and fabric blends.

A glossary of fabrics

Below is a quick look at the different fabrics and the weaves that can be constructed from them. It's a good idea to become familiar with these fabrics (at least on a general level) so you know what you're looking at the next time you're deciding between garments.

✔ **Boucle:** A plain or twill weave made from looped yarns that give it a textured, nubby surface.

✔ **Broadcloth:** A fine, tightly woven fabric, either all cotton or a blend, with a slight horizontal rib.

✔ **Brocade:** A decorative cloth that is characterized by raised designs. It's usually made of silk, sometimes supplemented by actual silver or gold threads.

✔ **Calico:** A plain-weave cotton fabric printed with small motifs.

✔ **Cashmere:** A wool, woven from the fleece of the Cashmere goat, that is both very soft and exceptionally warm. Because of the difficulty of separating the fine fibers from the surrounding coarse hair, cashmere is a luxury product.

✔ **Chantilly lace:** Lace with a net background and floral design patterns created by embroidering with thread and ribbon.

✔ **Chiffon:** A lightweight, extremely sheer and airy fabric with highly twisted fibers. Often used in full pants and loose tops or dresses.

✔ **Corduroy:** A fabric, usually made of cotton or a cotton blend, that uses a cut-pile weave construction. The *wale* is the number of cords in one inch.

✔ **Crepe:** A fabric that has a crinkled, crimped, or grain surface and that can be made from several different materials. *Crepe de chine* is made of silk and comes in various widths, with 4-ply considered the most luxurious.

✔ **Duck:** A closely woven, plain, or ribbed cotton fabric that is very durable. It's similar to canvas but lighter in weight.

- **Dobby:** A decorative weave that has small patterns, often geometric.
- **Faille:** A closely-knit fabric that is somewhat shiny and has flat, crosswise ribs. Faille can be made from cotton, silk, or synthetics.
- **Gabardine:** A twill weave, worsted fabric that can be made from wool, cotton, rayon, or nylon, or blended, with obvious diagonal ribs.
- **Gingham:** A fabric made from various yarns, most often in a checked pattern.
- **Herringbone:** A twill weave with a distinctive zigzag effect.
- **Microfibers:** An extremely fine synthetic fiber that can be woven into textiles with the texture and drape of natural-fiber cloth but with enhanced washability, breathability, and water repellency.
- **Satin:** A lustrous fabric most often used in evening wear.
- **Spandex:** A stretchy fabric that offers comfort, movement, and shape retention. It is also known by its brand name Lycra (created by DuPont).
- **Taffeta:** A crisp, tightly woven fabric with a fine crosswise rib that's easily identifiable by the rustling sound that it makes. Originally all taffeta was made from silk, but today it can be made from a variety of synthetic fabrics, sometimes combined with silk.
- **Velvet:** A luxurious fabric once exclusively made from silk but that today can be composed from a number of different fabrics including cotton. The dense loops, which may or may not be cut, give it a plush feel.

Fabric blends

Blending fibers in a fabric can help prevent wrinkling or lower the cost of a garment. Here are a few examples of blends and their advantages:

- **Polyester and cotton:** Polyester is crease resistant; cotton isn't. A garment that blends the two may not need to be ironed or will require less ironing, while retaining much of the comfort provided by cotton.
- **Linen and silk:** Linen creases easily while silk doesn't. By adding silk to linen, a garment won't crease as readily and will drape better.
- **Spandex and cotton:** Spandex is stretchy and durable, and cotton lets your skin breathe. The two make a perfect combination for sports clothing.
- **Cotton, polyester, and rayon:** Cotton offers breathability, polyester strength, and rayon shininess. A fabric with all three offers durability, ultra-softness, and excellent resilience so that if wrinkled, the fabric bounces back.

How fabrics are made

To get the different types of fabrics used to make clothing, the fibers have to be turned into threads or yarns and then woven or knit together. Which fibers (or combination of fibers) are used and how they're put together determine what type of fabric is made. The higher quality fibers used, the better the quality of the fabric and (provided that the fabrics are designed and sewn together well) the better the overall quality of the final garment.

Step 1: The making of the thread

Since natural fibers are originally "manufactured" by Mother Nature, they don't necessarily come in the appropriate format for making cloth, which is why they have to be fabricated. The natural length of a fiber, say the wool that comes off of a sheep, is called the *staple*. The staples are then twisted together to make the thread or cloth that's needed for turning out actual fabric. Manmade fibers, on the other hand, come out of the manufacturing process as threads, as they are mostly chemicals spun together using various processes.

Step 2: Knitting or weaving the threads together

Fibers are manipulated in several different ways to make clothing. The first is *knitting*, which involves using hooks to loop the yarns together. You may be most familiar with the type of hand knitting that people do at home with a single set of needles, but knitting machines can produce much more sophisticated fabrics. Fabrics in the jersey family, for example, are knitted. Knitted fabrics have more stretch than woven fabrics.

Weaving is the most common form of making fabric. A woven fabric is made by interlacing threads of one or more types of material. Originally weaving was done by hand, but then the loom was invented and simplified the process. Today, computerized looms can produce amazing designs. Following are the most common weave designs, as shown in Figure 4-1:

- ✔ **The plain weave:** Early woven patterns were plain, with one set of threads going over and under the other set. The technical term for the yarn going over is the *warp yarn;* the term for the yarn going under is the *weft yarn*. The plain weave is still used today in the making of chiffon and taffeta.

- ✔ **The twill weave:** In the twill weave, the weft yarn passes over at least two but not more than four warp yarns, moving one step to the left or right with each line. The corded effect produced in twilled fabric greatly adds to the fabric's durability. Some examples of twill weaves include denim and gabardine.

- ✔ **The satin weave:** The satin weave is similar to the twill except the warp yarn passes over four to eight weft yarns, yielding the characteristic sheen of satin cloth.

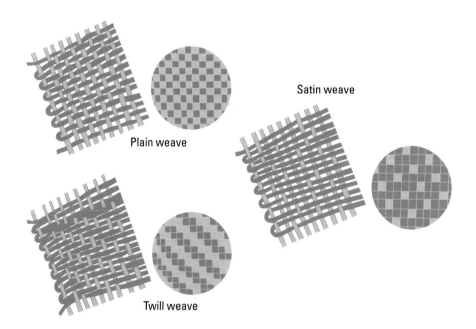

Figure 4-1: Three common weaves: plain, twill, and satin.

Some other common weaves include the rib weave, which has a higher concentration of yarn going in one direction to produce broadcloth and poplin; pile weave, which forms loops used to make terrycloth; and dobby and jacquard weaves, which combine various weaves to make patterns.

Make sure you understand the difference between weaves and fibers. Many different fibers can be woven to make satin, including silk, polyester, acetate, or even a blend. So if you're looking for a satin blouse, don't make the mistake of thinking that all satin is the same, because while the weave is the same, the fibers that are woven together to make satin can be different.

Step 3: Finishing

The last step in making fabric is finishing. A finish can add many types of effects, changing the appearance and texture. For example, *flocking*, which uses adhesives to add material, produces a fuzzy texture. Other finishes add water repellency, moth resistance, flame resistance, or pilling resistance.

Finishing touches from ancient times to today

While finishing may seem like a new technique, and most of the finishes added today are quite new, the Chinese were known to flock cloth in the year 1,000 BC, though for decorative purposes only.

In recent years, a new attribute to clothing has been resistance to the damage the sun's UV rays can have on the skin. By using a high thread count, often with some chemical finishing as well, some fabrics can offer a degree of protection against UV ray penetration. Of course, the garment can only protect the body part it's actually covering.

Understanding how your clothing is made allows you to choose garments that are well-constructed, keep their appearance, and are easy to maintain. If you're buying a trendy item that you don't plan to wear for more than a season, you can use this information to your benefit as well — that is, don't buy a trendy item in one of the more expensive fabrics because it's a garment you don't plan to wear for years to come. But again, if you're purchasing a quality piece for your wardrobe, you want to make sure that you're making an investment in a quality fabric that can stand the test of time.

From smooth to rough: Texture

Texture, the surface appearance of a fabric, is a result of the type of fibers used in the manufacturing process and the weave or knit. Texture is the one element you can both see and feel. Texture is defined by the thickness and appearance of a fabric, and words that describe texture include *furry, soft, shiny, rough, smooth,* and *sheer.*

In general, the more dressed up you're going to be, the more likely the texture of your clothing is going to feel soft to the touch. And because most manmade fabrics can't match Mother Nature when it comes to the combination of softness and durability (think of how strong the light threads of the silkworm are when woven together into cloth), natural fabrics are considered more luxurious than manmade fabrics.

When considering a garment, be aware of the effect the texture has on your overall look:

- **Textures that make you look bigger:** Some textures — shiny textures that reflect light, or thick and bulky textures, for example — make you appear bigger in a garment. Stiff fabrics do the same. In order to avoid looking bigger, try matte fabrics and smoother, less bulky materials.

Also, don't wear fabrics that are too stiff, such as coarse tweed. Figure 4-2 shows the difference between a matte fabric and a shiny one.

If you're petite, you may not want to buy clothing with a very coarse fabric, because while it may add to your size, the coarse look may also overwhelm your small figure.

✓ **Textures that make you look thinner:** Fabrics that have smooth, flat surfaces and a dull or matte surface that absorbs light can make you appear thinner. These fabrics include matte jersey and cashmere.

Soft or clingy fabrics show the shape underneath the garment, which may or may not be something you want. While they don't increase your size as far as width or breadth, they do show every curve, so if you don't want to draw any added attention to your hips or rear, avoid these materials, too. Opt for something with a bit more structure.

Figure 4-2: Matte (left) versus shiny (right) can alter your appearance.

Transparent versus opaque

While most of the material used to make clothes is *opaque,* that is, what lies underneath it cannot be seen, that's not true of all cloth. Transparent cloth is also used in clothing. Transparent fabrics are light and flowing, and they give a very feminine look.

Unless the transparent garment is a piece of lingerie, the wearer usually has some other item of clothing underneath, like a flesh-colored bra under a sheer blouse to maintain whatever degree of modesty is desired. What you wear underneath depends on where you are as well as your level of modesty. If you're going out on the town, you may choose to wear no more than a bra. While in the office, a camisole would be more appropriate (see Figure 4-3).

Figure 4-3: Where you're going dictates how much layering you do.

Key Features of a Garment

Knowing about fibers, fabrics, and weights is only part of the information you need to be a savvy shopper. You also need to know about garment construction. Even if you never buy a hand-sewn designer gown for thousands of dollars, you still need to know what to look for when buying a piece that fits your budget.

Stitching

Most stitching is utilitarian and not something you need to concern your-self with — except when it's not done well and the garment falls apart while you're wearing it (at which point you'll have learned the hard way to appreci-ate good stitching).

The basic stitch is called the *straight stitch*. Other types of stitching include

- **Zigzag:** A stitch used for garments that require some stretch. One stitch goes left and the next right.

- **Baste:** A simple stitch used to just hold pieces of cloth together before final sewing.

- **Buttonhole:** A stitch used to make buttonholes.

- **Back:** A stitch in which the thread is sewn backward as compared to other threads to outline decoration.

In general, stitching (unless it's decorative) isn't supposed to be noticeable because its function is merely to hold the garment together. While stitching often does not add to a garment's appearance, you can often figure out a gar-ment's overall quality — and know whether you're paying a good price for it — by checking the stitching. Some things to look for are

- **How many stitches there are per inch:** The more stitching per inch, the stronger the garment. Sixteen to 20 stitches per inch defines the high-end. Of course, some stitching is merely decorative, such as the type you may see made into a pattern on the back pocket of a pair of jeans.

- **Whether it's machine sewn or hand sewn:** While machine stitching is usually acceptable, in some cases, where attention to detail is demanded, hand sewing is superior. If a garment's label indicates that some hand sewing took place in its creation, you can be sure that it's a quality item, since hand sewing takes a lot more effort and costs more to produce. At the other end of the spectrum, instead of stitching the pieces of fabric together, the pieces may be fused together, a less expensive method of production and one not guaranteed to last very long.

✔ **The type of thread used.** The threads used can be made from various materials. Silk threads are strong yet thin, providing the very best stitching. Cotton threads are next in line, and synthetic threads can perform their job well even though they're not quite as good quality as cotton.

Another way to spot a piece that may not be well-constructed is to look on the inside for seams where the stitching is most apparent. Check to see whether the stitching looks neat and the ends are tied off. If you see a lot of loose threads, then you know this garment is not of the highest quality.

Seams

The *seam* is where two pieces of a garment are stitched together. Major seams are hidden away inside the garment (as opposed to hems, which are seams at the base of edges, such as at the bottom of a skirt, and can't be hidden completely). Note that this isn't true in some articles of clothing, like jeans, where the seams are part of the overall look.

Because most seams are hidden, they're not usually made to look pretty. *French seams* are an exception (see Figure 4-4). These seams are doubled over so that, if visible, they appear a lot neater. (French seams won't work where the material is too bulky, however, because the folded over material makes too much of a bump.)

Figure 4-4: A French seam.

To learn more about the quality of a piece of clothing, do the following when you're looking at seams:

- **Check how tightly knit and strong the thread is.** If the seam appears to be tightly knit together with strong thread, that's the sign of a better quality garment. But if the spacing between the threads is wide and the thread looks weak, you can be sure the manufacturer was cutting corners, and the seam is probably not the only place.

- **Give the seam a good tug.** This gives you some solid evidence of the care that went into its construction.

- **If there's a lose thread, pull on it.** It may just be some extra material, and nothing will happen except that it will pull away. But if the seam starts to unravel when you pull on the thread, put that garment back and start looking for another one.

- **Pay particular attention to curved seams.** Curved seams are used when two curved pieces of cloth must come together, such as when attaching sleeves to the body of a shirt or jacket. While many people learn to sew a simple plain seam in order to make hems, mastering the curved seam is more difficult and a poorly made jacket may not have the proper curved seams where they're required. Figure 4-5 shows a well-sewn curved seam compared to a poorly sewn one.

- **See how much extra material is at the seam.** On a regular pair of pants, you'll notice that there's extra material at the waist seam. This extra material is there so that the seam can be let out. Better quality clothing usually has more material to allow for such alterations. (**Note:** The seams on jeans, called *flat felled seams*, don't provide this extra material. This type of seam was originally used because jeans were considered work pants and the flat felled seam is very strong. The disadvantage is that there is no extra material.)

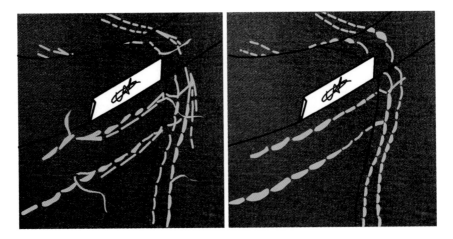

Figure 4-5: Poorly sewn curved seam (left) and a well-sewn curved seam (right).

Making the cut

One of the most important elements in making clothes is the *cut* — how the finished product is put together. The cut not only affects the garment's appearance but also its comfort. In an expensive jacket, for example, the design calls for a curve where the arms get attached to the body of the jacket to accommodate the way your arm moves; you'll notice the difference both in the jacket's appearance and how it feels. In a less expensive jacket, the cut is straight up and down. Not only does it not look as good as the more expensive jacket, but it feels even worse as material hits under your arm instead of flowing around it.

You find such differences in almost every type of garment, from expensive designer gowns to blue jeans. In better quality jeans, for example, the two legs are separate units and the last seam is around the crotch. In less expensive jeans, the legs are part of the front and back and the last seam is up and down the inside of the leg. The first method gives you a much better and more comfortable fit. Figure 4-6 compares a well cut jean with a poorly cut jean.

Figure 4-6: The proper cut (right) makes all the difference in the appearance of a garment.

If you've always wondered how a particular item of clothing can cost so much, it's worth going to a high-end store and trying on some designer pieces (even if you never plan on buying anything). Often, you'll see how different the fit and feel actually are.

Mixing and Matching Fabrics

Here's the thing about mixing and matching fabrics: You can as long as it looks right. The following sections have the details.

Fashion rules aren't just arbitrary edicts sent down from above. Instead, they're based on a common denominator: what looks right and what doesn't. While not everybody agrees on these rules, the vast majority of people do find certain looks pleasing and others unpleasant. Using this as a guide certainly makes it easier for you to choose your outfit each day.

A word about weight

In the fashion world, *weight* refers to the thickness of the thread. The thicker the thread used, the heavier the cloth that is woven from it. In most cases, especially when comparing very similar fabrics, the heavier a fabric is, the more material it contains, the higher the quality, and the more it costs. The difference in weight is sometimes more apparent in the simplest of garments. If you have a choice between two cotton T-shirts and you're wondering why one is a lot more expensive than the other, pick each one up and compare their weights. Odds are that the heavier one, which has more cotton threads per square inch, is the more expensive one.

Three standards for measuring weight are ounces per linear yard, ounces per square yard, and grams per square meter. It's important to know which unit is being used when being given the weight of a cloth because something that would be lightweight in one would be heavyweight in another. In the United States and Asia, fabric weight is more likely to be given in ounces, while in Europe it's grams.

In addition to using weight as an indication of quality, there are also practical aspects to choosing the weight of a garment. While you may want a suit with extra weight in winter to keep you warm, in summer you'll choose lighter weight material.

You can certainly combine weights of clothing, but you don't want the contrast to be too great. For example, you wouldn't wear summer weight linen pants with a thick wool sweater. Basically, you want to make sure the two fabrics are meant for the same season. So while you wouldn't pair heavy wool with linen, you can pair heavy wool with corduroy (see Figure 4-7). Use your common sense. The reason you wear these fabrics when you do is generally to keep warm in winter or cool in the summer.

Figure 4-7: A bad pairing (left) and a good pairing (right).

Pairing patterns

Don't be afraid to pair patterns. You can find many ways to make this work. The biggest key is to keep everything in the same color family. If you're going to wear two different patterns, the colors have to match (see Chapter 5 for more on color). The other thing to remember when pairing different patterns is balance. If one print or pattern is big and bold, make sure the other one is small. If you're just starting out, and not sure exactly how this works, start with something small: Pair a patterned blouse with a printed scarf and a solid pant or skirt. Just make sure all the colors in the blouse and scarf work together and that the pattern on one of the pieces is small, if the other is large.

It's a bit easier to see what to avoid when you examine extremes. Wearing two bold patterns, say polka dots with stripes, certainly risks causing a visual clash. But what about two stripes? It depends on the stripes. Do the colors compliment each other? Are the stripes the same size or is one set wider than the other? Do they go in the same direction? Obviously the combinations are endless, and I can't possibly go over all of them, so to some extent you have to develop your own eye and learn to trust it. But here are some rules that you can use to help you combine stripes:

- ✔ **Make sure they're not the same size, which creates too much tension.** If one stripe is a lot broader than the other, then they can work together, assuming the color combinations also work. If your patterns don't match, better to pair with a solid, as Figure 4-8 shows.

- ✔ **Keep everything else in your outfit simple.** If you're going to combine two stripes, anything else has to be simple and in neutral tones so as not to make the whole effect far too busy.

The same concept holds true for checks, with one caveat: Because checks are more intense, you have to be even more careful when wearing two different checks. Wearing two different checks of similar size is disorienting to the viewer's eye. But if you have one small check, like a houndstooth pattern, a larger check can work, though their colors would have to complement each other.

Figure 4-8: A mismatched outfit (left); a better alternative (right).

When it comes to combining patterns, like stripes and checks, it's best if one of the two is on an accessory item (see Figure 4-9). You can pair a jacket with checks, for example, with a striped scarf, as long as the colors complement each other. But you wouldn't want to wear a striped skirt with a checked blouse. Yikes! You also need to consider the scale of each pattern. Again, you don't want the scale and colors to match too closely because then the look is discordant. Instead, choose scales that contrast one another: If one pattern is small, like narrow stripes set far apart, then the checks can be more dense and larger.

If you're thinking of combining three patterns, don't. Unless you really know what you're doing, three different patterns can easily come off looking *way* too busy. For the most part, picking one pattern or item to accentuate is the way to go.

Figure 4-9: Two patterns working together well.

5

The Art of Color

Dress to be happy.

Betsey Johnson, Fashion Designer

"**W**hat's your favorite color?" How many times has your daughter, niece, or nephew asked you that question? No matter our age, we all have favorite colors. I love white and always gravitate toward a white dress, T-shirt, or jeans. But the truth is that your favorite color may not be what looks best on you. Your hair, eyes, and skin tone all play a part in selecting colors that belong in your closet.

This chapter explains how to use colors to highlight the parts of your body you love and camouflage the ones you don't. Also, if you're challenged in the what-colors-go-with-what department, I guide you through that as well.

Color Wheel Basics

If you've ever looked at a rainbow (and I'm sure you have), you know that colors appear in a natural order. This is called the *color spectrum*. Designers like to show the color spectrum in a wheel (like the ones shown in Figure 5-1). It turns out there's a practical reason for doing so: Not only are there visual effects when specific colors are compared to colors adjacent to them on the color spectrum, but there are also visual effects when a color is compared to the one opposite itself on the color wheel.

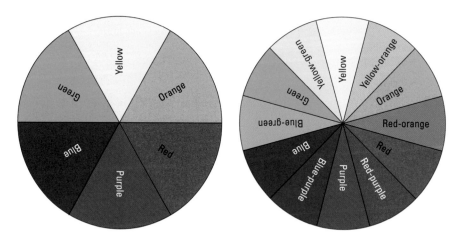

Figure 5-1: A color wheel with primary and secondary colors; another including tertiary colors.

You may think it's a coincidence that suddenly some colors are very in, but it's not. An organization called the Color Marketing Group pulls in experts from different fields — fashion, interior design, and so on — and decides what the popular colors are going to be two years from now.

Color designations: Primary, secondary, and tertiary

Colors fall into the following three categories (refer to Figure 5-1):

- ✔ **Primary:** The three primary colors are red, blue, and yellow.

- ✔ **Secondary:** When you mix the primary colors in specific combinations, you get the secondary colors: purple (red and blue mixed), green (blue and yellow), and orange (red and yellow). If the mixture is not exactly 50 percent of one primary color and 50 percent of another, you get shades of these colors.

- ✔ **Tertiary:** To make a tertiary color, you mix two colors adjacent to one other on the color wheel. If you mix blue with green, for example, you get the tertiary color blue-green; mix green with yellow, and you get yellow-green.

Analogous and complimentary colors

When it comes to fashion, you need to know how colors are perceived when they're together so that you can combine them correctly when you get dressed. For example, primary and secondary colors that are neighbors to one another are said to be *analogous.* So the colors analogous to green are yellow and blue. Orange's analogous colors are red and yellow. When worn together, analogous colors tend to subdue each other and therefore work well together.

Colors that sit opposite from each other on the color wheel are considered to be *complimentary* colors, so blue's complimentary color is orange and purple's is yellow. Complimentary colors make each other stand out more, so they appear bolder than they do when alone. Figure 5-2 shows how lavender (a lighter shade of purple) and pale yellow compliment each other in an outfit.

Analogous colors almost always go well with one another. Complimentary colors can also go together if you want to make a bold statement. Keep in mind, though, that complimentary color combinations (like red and green or blue and orange) can be more difficult to put together. Colors that may compete in their strongest hues can go well together in softer tones. Similarly, using shades of these colors, especially one darker and one lighter (baby blue with orange, for example) can work. If your skin tone is darker or you have a tan, you can get away with brighter colors.

 There really are no strict rules with this; you just have to try different versions of color combinations and see what works. Be adventurous if you have a knack for what looks good (running it by a friend you trust is also not a bad idea).

 If you mix complimentary colors, make sure you choose the right accessories to tie the whole outfit together. Neutrals are a good choice because they frame, but don't compete with, the strong colors in the outfit.

Figure 5-2: A good way to pair complimentary colors.

Black and white: The noncolors

So what about black and white? Technically, black and white are not really colors (even though many people call them colors). Black is the absence of color while white is the sum of all the color of light.

Because they're not actual colors, they can work well with each other, with any other colors, or by themselves. When using black and white, you really don't have to worry about whether two garments go well together because they almost always do.

The mandate to not wear white after Labor Day is antiquated. Basically different shades of white and ivory can work all year long, with each other, or mixed with other colors (although if you're going to wear all white, I suggest waiting until the warmer months). In the winter, a pair of white jeans with a bulky sweater and boots is fab. Black can work all year, too, even though in summer, you'll want to mix it up with some color. When wearing black, be careful to stay away from non-matching items. The shade of black should be exact when pairing them together.

Color Categories: Jewels, Neutrals, and More

Colors are often sorted into groups based on similar characteristics. Knowing what group each color belongs to helps you choose the right combination when putting together your outfit. For example, jewel tones are very rich colors; therefore, they're generally worn in the fall and winter. Neutrals, because they can be paired with just about anything, are perfect to wear with strong colors (to provide balance) or with other neutrals (to create a more subdued look). The following sections describe the most common color categories.

Jewel tones

Jewel tone colors, shown in Figure 5-3, are associated with various gemstones: emerald green, ruby red, topaz yellow, amythest purple, and sapphire blue, for example. Jewel tones have a high level of color saturation, making them very bold and lush. You're most likely to find jewel tones in stores in the fall and around the holidays. They're particularly appropriate during the holidays because they add a festive feature to your wardrobe.

If you want to wear jewel tones, keep these points in mind:

- ✔ **Be careful that you don't pair two jewel tones in the same outfit.** Because these colors are so strong, they are best on their own. Pair a jewel tone top with black slacks, dark denim jeans, or another dark neutral such as brown to balance out the look.

- ✔ **Make sure the jewel tone compliments your hair color and skin tone.** Brunettes and those with black hair can carry off jewel tones better than blondes and those with paler hair and skin tones. The vibrancy of jewel tones tend to make people with lighter hair and skin look washed out.

Ruby   Topaz   Emerald   Sapphire   Amythest

Figure 5-3: Jewel tones.

Neutrals

Neutral colors — black, white, brown, beige, and gray (see Figure 5-4) — are really shades without color, and they're the linchpin colors of a classic woman's wardrobe. When combined with other colors, neutral shades put the focus on the other colors and, depending on the combination, can serve to tone the other color down or make it stand out.

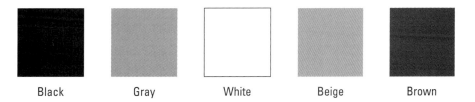

Black   Gray   White   Beige   Brown

Figure 5-4: Neutrals.

The following sections outline some of the attributes of the various neutral colors.

Black

Black is slimming. It's also sophisticated, elegant, and chic (yet another reason everyone should have the perfect LBD!). Black makes a good background color because primary colors really stand out when paired with it.

Gray

Gray is the most neutral of neutrals and goes well with any other color. Gray comes in various shades. Lighter grays work well with lighter colors, such as pastels. Darker grays work well with bolder colors like red and blue. You can also substitute darker gray for black.

White

White is pure and dazzling and goes with absolutely everything, just as black does. White and black are great together too. While black is slimming, white tends to show more of your body because of the way it reflects light, so keep this in mind if you're trying to camouflage a certain body part.

Brown

Brown is a warm, neutral color. As a neutral, brown goes well with all colors. You're more likely to wear dark brown in fall and winter, and a lighter brown in spring and summer. Browns can also be paired with each other in such combinations as camel and chocolate, tan and gold, and auburn and coffee.

Beige

Beige is the true neutral color and goes with anything. It has a bit of the warmth of brown and the coolness of white. Beige can warm up a color, like blue, without overpowering it. If you have lighter skin and want to wear a lot of beige, make sure you throw in an accent color to add a pop of life to your overall look.

Pastels

Pastels are lighter shades of basic colors: baby pink, light blue, lavender, pale yellow, and mint green (see Figure 5-5). Pastels work well with navy blue, kelly green, and white — colors that tend to appear in preppie wardrobes. If you have a lot of pastel pieces in your wardrobe, keep the following in mind:

✔ **They have a youthful quality.** Too many pastels can make you look too cutesy (after all, babies are often dressed in pastels).

✔ **They work well with neutral colors.** The best colors to match with pastels are those in the neutral family — camel, gray, beige, and tan. These colors give pastels an appearance of being stronger than they actually are.

- ✔ **They are more appropriate for spring wear.** Lighter weight spring clothing often comes in pastel colors.
- ✔ **If you're fair skinned and want to wear pastels, you need to pair it with a stronger color.** A light purple blouse with a deep grey skirt, for example, is beautifully chic. For a more casual look, a pair of dark jeans with a pale yellow polo is also classic.

Baby pink   Pale yellow   Mint green   Baby blue   Lavender

Figure 5-5: Pastels.

Earth tones

Earth tones, shown in Figure 5-6, are aptly named because they include the browns of the earth, from sand to dark brown (some people include other muted colors in the earth tone category, but I stick to browns in this discussion.) Earth tones are very common in clothing that has a bohemian style. They differ from the neutral colors, such as white, gray, and black, which tend to be cooler and more stark. Earth tones are softer and warmer.

Like neutrals, earth tones can be paired with anything. Since the undertones are the brown family, which is considered a "warm" color, they're flattering on all skin tones.

If you want another color in your outfit to stand out, pair it with a paler earth tone such as sand. If you want to balance and tone down a stronger, darker color, pair it with chocolate brown.

Ivory   Cream   Sand   Tan   Brown

Figure 5-6: Earth tones.

Dark colors: A busy mother's best friend

If you're a woman who gets up before dawn and doesn't stop moving until after dusk, I've got your number. If you have children, in addition to wearing comfortable fabrics (think terry or cotton), you probably dress in dark colors to avoid accidents (which likely occur throughout the day!) showing up on your outfit.

Well, you can still look good while managing busy schedules and babies that spit up. A dark jogging suit (provided it's a 10 — see Chapter 2) can take you through the day looking casually chic. Dark colors can also make a bold statement when

you finish your errands and are off to dinner. You can never go wrong with a little black dress, and combining darker colors definitely gives you a dramatic look.

Don't be afraid to combine black and navy, black and brown, navy and brown, or gray with black, navy, or brown. These color combinations are actually very chic. By discovering how to mix and match colors you wouldn't normally pair together, you can triple the number of outfits in your closet.

Choosing the right colors for you

You've all heard someone say, "That color looks great on you!" Well, there's a reason. Some colors work really well with your skin tone and even hair color. You can tell which colors best flatter you by just holding up a few different colored tops below your face to see which ones make you look brighter and which ones wash you out. Too many combinations of skin tones, hair colors, and clothing colors exist to cover them all here, so in this section I focus on the basics to get you started (see Table 5-1 for a quick list of flattering combinations).

Table 5-1	Recommended Colors	
Hair Color	*Skin Tone*	*Wear Tops and Blouses in These Colors*
Dark Brown/Black	Dark	Red Dark Pink Coral Yellow
Medium Brown	Medium/Olive	Brown Peach Medium/Light Pink Tan
Blond/Red/Gray	Fair/Pale	Green Light Blue Turquoise Lilac

Warm and cool colors

All colors are considered either *warm* or *cool*. Colors with red undertones are warm, and colors with blue undertones are cool. If you have darker or olive color skin, warm tones are going to be more flattering. So colors on the warm end of the spectrum like reds, oranges, pinks, peaches, and yellows (provided they don't have blue undertones) are better for you, as is anything in the brown family (see Figure 5-7).

Just because you have fairer skin doesn't mean you can't wear the colors on the warm end of the spectrum. You just have to be careful with the tone of the color. For example, a woman with fair skin can wear pink; it should just be a pink with blue undertones, as in Figure 5-8.

If you have fair, medium, or even pale skin, cooler colors are going to flatter you. Coolers colors — such as greens, blues, purples, and grays — are at the other end of the spectrum from warmer colors. Something like an ice blue top works well on someone with fairer skin (see Figure 5-9).

Figure 5-7: This outfit has warm, earth tones, perfect for darker skin.

Figure 5-8: Pink with blue undertones flatters fair skin.

Figure 5-9: Cool, pastel colors compliment fair skin.

Considering hair color and make up

The other thing to consider when choosing your clothing is hair color. If you have brown or dark brown/black hair, warmer colors are going to look better on you. If you have blond, red, or gray hair, cooler colors look good. For example, someone with brown hair looks better in red, while a blond or red-head looks better in green.

Most often, unless you dye your hair or wear a lot of makeup, people with darker hair tend to have darker or olive skin complexions and women with blond or red hair tend to have fairer skin. So accenting with warmer colors, like the warm pink scarf in Figure 5-10, works on someone with dark hair and dark skin.

REMEMBER

You can always use makeup as a tool to enhance or change your skin tone, and you can also change your hair color if you want to change your color palette as far as what you choose to wear. You're not locked in to specific colors, although as you get a feel for what looks good on you, you'll want to stick to the palette that's most flattering for you.

Figure 5-10: A warm pink accessory and earth tones flatter dark hair.

Making Your Color Choices Work for You

Your personality, body type, and personal style are going to determine what colors you choose to wear. As long as you understand which colors work together and how to use them to flatter your figure, feel free to experiment with combinations you may not have tried before. You may just find a whole new wardrobe right in your closet!

Pairing colors

The primary colors (red, blue, and yellow) in the brightest shades can be hard to match because their intensities are high in and of themselves. When you pair one primary color with another, the intensity is multiplied and the combination can be too much. However, the primaries, like all colors, have different shades. So where a cherry red may be hard to match with anything but a neutral, a brick red may be less overpowering (*any* muted primary color is less overpowering).

Following are some other examples of ways to use primary and secondary colors without being overwhelmed by the effect:

- **Yellow:** A bright yellow can be quite difficult to match, but a pastel shade blends nicely with most colors, both analogous and complimentary. If you're partial to bright yellow, use it as an accent color. Or if you want to use it as the primary color of an outfit, make sure that the rest of the outfit is more subdued (it's always safe to pair with white).

- **Green:** When it comes to the many shades of green, go with one that looks good on you. If you're not comfortable wearing bright green, try a subtler shade, like fir green or mint green, instead. A subdued green can go with many other colors, but I'd stay away from pairing it with red, regardless of the shade, unless, of course, it's Christmas (even then some basic rules exist; see Chapter 12 for tips on dressing for the holidays).

- **Purple:** Because purple is such a strong color, it works best when paired with a pale shade of another color. A lighter shade of purple gives you more leeway when pairing it with other colors. A pale yellow paired with a brighter purple, for example, can be beautiful during springtime.

✔ **Blue:** Blue is another strong color. For a bright, royal blue, you follow the same rules as with the other bright colors: Pair it with a neutral color or something more toned down. Because most denim clothing is blue, we tend to think it matches everything, but this is only true with lighter and darker shades of blue, as they are toned down already and can be paired with most colors.

So what goes with blue jeans? Almost anything you can name. The only thing that doesn't go with denim? *Denim.* I don't care what magazines say it's the latest trend; unless you're taking a time machine back to the 1980s, denim and denim (see Figure 5-11) don't go together. Ever!

Brighter colors and pastels tend to be worn in spring and summer, and the more muted and subdued shades are worn in fall and winter.

Combining colorful patterns

You *can* combine colorful patterns as long as you don't combine colorful patterns that don't match. Pairing patterns is tricky in and of itself. You can pair patterns as discussed in Chapter 4, but when you throw color into the mix, the color scheme *has* to match (see Figure 5-12). The items need to be in the exact same color family or one has to be a print in a neutral color scheme.

Figure 5-11: Don't wear denim with denim!

If each pattern has a dominant color, make sure those two dominant colors are the same. The colors must match *exactly* when pairing patterns. This pairing should look like it came together from the same designer. In fact, pairing items from the same designer is about the only way to ensure that all the colors and patterns aren't too busy. Plus, it's rare to find an exact match when pairing pieces from different designers' collections.

Using color to impact your mood

Studies have shown that color can have psychological effects. Yellow, for example, is said to help concentration, pink is supposed to make you seem more approachable, and red is an attention-getter.

It's also said that colors affect your mood. Wear too much black, for example, and you may find yourself feeling sad. Still, no scientific study has proved any such link between color and a particular effect, and because colors have different meanings around the world, these theories are far from proven.

Matching mood to color

While no scientific study makes a direct link between what wearing one color versus another may do for your state of mind, or how the color you wear influences those around you, simple observation tells you that a lady dressed all in red is going to draw the eye's attention first over someone dressed in muted tones. While not carved in stone, there are appropriate colors for certain situations:

Figure 5-12: Colors must match when pairing patterns.

- ✔ **For somber occasions:** Black is obviously acceptable. You can also wear navy, dark browns, and gray.

- ✔ **For serious occasions:** When you're going for a job interview, keep your color palette on the more subdued side even though the days of wearing simple black pant suits with a button-down blouse are over. A black pencil skirt with a classic sweater set and beautiful necklace (see Figure 5-13) is appropriate and highlights your personal style.

✔ **For celebratory events:** When you're attending an occasion that calls for celebration, like a baby shower or graduation party, bring out your bright colors. When attending an event that invites you to have fun, have fun — even with your clothing!

Getting a mood boost from your favorite color

To a certain degree, how a color affects your mood can enhance its ability to camouflage problem areas. You'd be surprised that black is not the only color that can hide a problem area. Some larger women, for example, tend not to wear red because they feel it attracts too much attention to their bodies. But red is also a color that exudes confidence. It's the ultimate power color. If red's your favorite color, find ways to wear it while still flattering your figure. For example, if you're a pear shape, wear a red top with a darker bottom. This combination attracts attention to your upper half, allows you to wear a color you love, and camouflages an area you want to minimize.

Get the best of both worlds. Combine the natural slimming effects of wearing dark colors with the brightening effect of wearing your favorite brighter colors. If you prefer a bright color but don't think it flatters your figure, use the bright color as an accent. You can use accents in so many different ways: shoes, belts, handbags, scarves, jewelry, and so on. Chapter 15 tells you how to accessorize.

Figure 5-13: Muted colors are good for job interviews.

Camouflaging with color

Creating color combinations that camouflage is an art form perfected by the military, but the traditional military pattern is not the only way to use color to camouflage. Many people who try to hide their problem areas turn immediately to black and for good reason. Not only is black slimming; it's also chic. But you don't have to wear *all* black *all* the time. It isn't the only color that you can use for camouflage. Consider these examples on how to flatter your figure:

✔ **Wearing all one color makes you appear taller.** A monochromatic outfit helps anyone — from petite to plus-size — project a longer, leaner look, which makes you appear taller and slimmer (see Figure 5-14).

✔ **Wearing colors that are in stark contrast to one another make you appear shorter.** If you're tall and want to appear shorter, wear contrasting colors on the top and the bottom. The two colors break up the one long line (see Figure 5-15).

✔ **Wearing any color of narrow, vertical stripes makes you look thinner.** The thinner the stripe, the more pronounced the slimming effect.

Figure 5-14: The same color on the top and the bottom creates a slimmer line.

Figure 5-15: Contrasting colors on the top and bottom make you look more petite.

Color meanings

The fashion world talks a lot about the psychological meanings of color. Here's what proponents of this theory hold to be true. First, colors on the red side of the color wheel are generally considered to be the warm colors, while those on the blue side are the cool ones. While psychologists differ on the importance of color, there's some agreement on the following points:

✔ Red depicts strength and courage.

✔ Blue is cooler and more intellectual.

✔ Yellow is the emotional color and gives off confidence and optimism.

✔ Green, because it's in the center of the color spectrum, is the color of balance and harmony.

✔ Purple is the spiritual color leading to introspection.

✔ Black is both sophisticated and menacing.

✔ White is hygienic, which can stand for good health or sterility.

6

From the Runway to a Store Near You

In This Chapter

- Following a design from an idea to a store near you
- Knowing the difference between haute couture, prêt-a-porter, contemporary, and mass-market
- Using this knowledge as you build your own style

Accessorize with pops of color! A simple, fun, inexpensive cocktail ring or bold-stone cuff can dress up an outfit. Or add a colored scarf or belt.

Tori Spelling, Actress

*L*ights, camera, action! Fashion Week in New York City is a twice-a-year extravaganza in the heart of the Big Apple. (There are also other "Fashion Weeks" that take place in cities like Paris and Milan.) Every fashion editor, fashionista, and celebrity is looking for a front-row seat to the hottest shows — not to mention a ticket to the chicest parties! Although much of what is unveiled during Fashion Week is just for show (the more dramatic the better), the events are still a great place for you to educate yourself on upcoming trends and get new ideas for how to put outfits together.

The designers try to catch the attention of the buyers, editors, and fashion media so the wilder and edgier the show, the more attention they get. For the most part, the clothing that actually gets produced is a toned-down version of what was seen on the runway. But that doesn't mean that you can't learn anything by examining these outfits. This chapter helps you take the looks from the runway to your closet.

From Designer to Mass Market

There isn't an article of clothing in existence that wasn't designed by somebody. It could be a creative individual designing for herself, or a professional designing for some segment of the market. Perhaps the design bears the designer's name, or perhaps it is someone designing for someone else's label. But even simple white T-shirts require the creative juices of a designer because someone has to pick out the exact cloth, choose the neckline, the length of the sleeves, and so on.

Getting any piece of clothing made takes a variety of steps, whether the garment is from a high-end designer or is mass produced. The process goes like this (see Figure 6-1):

1. **The designer comes up with an idea for a garment and creates a sketch, which goes to the pattern maker.**

2. **The pattern maker draws the actual pattern.**

3. **Materials are picked and a sample is made.**

   The sample is fit to a *fit model* and then scaled up and down in size to accommodate small, medium, large, and so forth. Colors and patterns are also decided, as are any embellishments or details.

4. **The design goes off to the showroom (and a runway show if the designer is high-end).**

5. **The buyers come to look at the merchandise and, if they like it, place orders.**

6. **The garment is sent to production.**

   The quantity produced is based largely on the number of sales already made and predicted reorders.

7. **The pieces are tagged and shipped off to a store near you.**

And you thought the clothes just appeared in the stores!

Figure 6-1: From designer to a store near you.

The following sections provide more specifics about these steps.

Even a T-shirt requires a careful design

You may think a T-shirt is just a T-shirt, but like every other item of clothing, a sketch, pattern, and sample has to be made for every single T-shirt style, too. You can't just produce a V-neck T-shirt from a basic crewneck sample, or a short-sleeve T-shirt from a long-sleeve one. Each type requires all of the steps outlined in Figure 6-1, which takes time and costs money.

The sleeve length has to be precise when you make either a short-sleeve or a long-sleeve T-shirt — no guesswork is allowed! — and the amount of material used determines how much of that particular fabric has to be purchased. All of this goes into the production costs and, of course, determines the shirt's cost.

Creating the design

During the early stages of a designing career, a designer works on every little detail with his or her own hands. Often, the higher the designer moves up the ladder of success, the less physical work he or she actually does. Instead, the designer has a staff to carry out the process of cutting, sewing, and so on. In addition, the very famous designers have other designers working under them, which means that once a designer reaches the top rungs of the ladder of success, he or she may never have to sketch out an idea again. (On the other hand some designers are very hands on, and for big celebrity events or weddings, many designers get extremely involved in the process.)

It isn't enough to just work on patterns and samples (or to direct other people to do so). The other trick to being a successful designer is to be ahead of the game. Designers create patterns and samples for *future* seasons. While their spring merchandise is just hitting the stores, designers have to have their fall lines ready to show to buyers and editors at Fashion Week. In other words, designers have already thought of, sketched, and produced their designs a season prior to when they'll come out. Many designers actually work about a year ahead, not just a season ahead. How far in advance they have to design depends on the designer, how big his or her line is, and the size of the overall enterprise.

Keeping their fingers on the public's pulse

In order to avoid designs that are out of fashion, a designer has to know what the competition is doing and what colors and fabrics are expected to be in fashion in the coming seasons. And because the ultimate buyer is the public, a designer also has to try to gauge what customers' moods and desires are going to be a few years from now. To do that, designers have to be up on the current trends in music, art, cinema, TV, and so on, as well as try to get ahead of those curves. So, for example, if a major motion picture about some historical era is being made, designers may try to capitalize on that by including one or two outfits in their collections that reflect that era on the off chance that the film becomes a big hit.

King Louis and his dolls; Napoleon and his edicts

Fashion has been an important part of many a country's economy, notably France. In order to publicize French fashions, King Louis XIV had life-sized fashion dolls made and sent to every court in Europe. Even after dress patterns became widely used, the dolls continued to be made up until World War I, and the mannequins seen in every department store have kept the idea alive even today. The French revolution badly damaged the French fashion industry, and when Napoleon became emperor, he issued many decrees in order to revive it. Among them, he ordered that ladies could not wear the same outfit twice to his court.

Following or bucking trends

The big question every designer has to answer is whether to follow the current trends or buck them. If hemlines have been inching up, then without a doubt they will head back down at some point, but does a particular designer risk lowering hemlines too early or wait until everyone else heads in that direction? A designer like the late Yves Saint Laurent was such a style setter that virtually every other top designer felt compelled to follow his lead. If Saint Laurent decided that the safari look was in, then almost all the other designers added one or two safari-inspired outfits to their collections.

Saint Laurent even influenced real estate, opening a store on Paris' Left Bank when the top designers were all based on the right bank and then watching as many others followed suit by also opening stores in the Left Bank.

An established designer can pave his or her own road, but for others it's a big gamble. Go too far afield, and you may get ignored. But be too conservative, and you stand no chance of breaking out from the pack. Fashion is an art form but also a business, and many a designer has failed because of an inability to cope with both.

Introducing the design

A fashion show is the best way for a designer to get his or her designs out into public view. So how do you score tickets to a designer's fashion show? It's not easy. These shows have limited seating, and the seats are primarily reserved for fashion editors, stylists, celebrities, and, of course, the buyers. The people attending the shows filter the information to you via the fashion magazines, celebrities wear the designs to events that are covered in the press, or eventually the buyers bring the designs to a boutique near you. If you want to get a head start, check out the shows online at www.style.com and www.elle.com.

On the runway

If there's one thought about the world of fashion that is shared by most people when looking at the fashions coming down the runways, it's "What normal woman could ever wear that?" And you'd have a hard time finding most of those items in a store if you did want to buy them. So why do the clothes displayed on runways end up being so outrageous? The basic answer is to satisfy the fashion media.

The major fashion magazines, *Vogue, Harper's Bazaar,* and *Elle,* can devote only so many pages to covering the fashion shows. Understandably, they show outfits that are eye-catching and innovative. Because it's vital for designers to get covered in the fashion media, they all know that some of the outfits they send down the runway are for show only. And don't forget, designers are also artists. Sure, they want to sell clothing, but they also want to express their artistic talents, and sometimes the two don't necessarily mesh. But that's fine, as long as you understand that what you're seeing walking down those runways is both fashion and art (see Figure 6-2).

Fashion Week, be it in New York, Paris, Milan, or wherever, is really more theater than anything else. The point is to get celebrities in the audience, photographers crowding behind the velvet rope, and cause as much buzz as possible. In fact, most of the buying isn't done at fashion shows at all, but before that in the showrooms.

Figure 6-2: Fashion Week in New York City is always an extravaganza.

In the showroom

The top buyers visit the designers' showrooms. The buyers then pick and choose what they think will sell best in the stores. Familiar with the most common sizes and most popular colors and styles, these buyers filter even further from the designers' collections and only buy what they think will actually sell. They place their orders, and based on these orders, the designers determine how much of each item to produce.

That's not to say that top designers don't also carry their higher-end apparel at their boutiques and high-end department stores. They absolutely do, and these clothes certainly have aspects of the more innovative designs that are shown on the runway, if not almost exact replicas.

That said, women still get a thrill from wearing the latest trends. So even if it isn't exactly what's shown on the runway, women want new clothes that incorporate the new and trendy. Designers know this, and they produce clothes that are actually wearable versions of the theatrical garments shown on the runway. In addition, savvy women know they need to stay true to their lifestyle and body type. Designers, therefore, produce basics, classics, and staples in addition to their current and trendy pieces.

Moving the design toward a wider audience

Other designers, whose names you may not be familiar with, take the same design elements and trends shown on the runways and come up with different lines that are more (or much more) affordable. Elements such as the quality of the fabric and the attention to detail usually determine at which level these clothes fall.

But that's not the end of the story. Not every garment ends up a big seller. If a particular style sits unsold for too long, it gets marked down in price, just like you see when department stores and boutiques have their big sales. And sometimes designers produce more pieces than they sell to the stores, and if there are no reorders on those designs, these articles can end up at discount outlets like Loehmann's, or even T.J. Maxx or Marshall's.

Even the designs themselves may have other lives. If a particular design sells well, you can almost bet that some other clothing manufacturer will make a copy of that design, perhaps using less expensive material and less costly manufacturing processes, and sell the item as a so-called *knockoff*.

Ranking Clothing: From Haute Couture to Mass Market

Visit a vintage clothing store and you'll quickly see that just as high-end cars hold their value, so do designer clothes. There's a real pecking order when it comes to clothes, and the designers fight to make it to the top of the ladder because along with the fame and adulation comes that pot of gold. The following list explains how to differentiate between the lines of designer clothing:

- **Haute couture:** This is the highest end. It's made-to-measure and costs thousands of dollars.

- **Prêt-a-porter:** This line is the next level down in a designer's collection. Prêt-a-porter clothing is still high-end and very pricey, but the pieces aren't one of a kind. The construction, materials, and fit are of impeccable quality. These outfits are shown on the runway, as are the haute couture pieces, and they're sold at the designers' boutiques or on the designer floor of the higher-end department stores.

- **Contemporary:** Designers that are mostly well known under their own labels design these pieces. These items are shown in the designers' own boutiques and are also sold in department stores on the contemporary floor. Contemporary pieces are less expensive than prêt-a-porter.

- **Mass market:** These are more affordable pieces that may or may not have a designer's name attached. They're not shown on the runway and are generally mass produced. Because there are a variety of mass market stores, ranging from stores like H&M to Walmart, the prices and the quality of their merchandise vary considerably.

Traditionally, when the term "designer clothing" was used, it meant high-end clothing, that is to say, clothing of limited quantity, high cost, and designed by somebody who, if not a household name, was at least somewhat famous. But beginning in the 1960s with Pierre Cardin, top designers began attaching their names to clothing meant for the masses, so that even babies could be dressed from head to toe in Calvin Klein or Ralph Lauren.

Haute couture

If you are Angelina Jolie and are heading to the Oscars to be photographed for the entire world to see, haute couture is appropriate! Haute couture dresses are made to order for a specific customer and are made from high-quality, expensive fabrics and sewn with extreme detail (see Figure 6-3). Making a haute couture garment is very time-consuming because these creations are hand made. The time and effort is worth it to the designer, though, because having a big celebrity wear a creation is a big coup and gives the designer an enormous amount of press and exposure.

What distinguishes haute couture from every other type of clothing? Most specifically, it's made for the person wearing it. A woman walks into the salon of a designer and sees various models, chooses one, and then selects exactly what fabric it will be made of. The dress is then hand-sewn to her exact size and specifications. (When this is done for a man, the term used is *bespoke*, which comes from Saville Row — the London street where the great menswear shops are located.)

A designer has to be designated as worthy of the appellation of haute couture. To do so, the French Ministry of Industry must decide whether the house meets certain requirements, including having a minimum of 15 employees and holding fashion shows twice a year, with each show having a minimum of 35 outfits for both day and evening wear. Surprisingly, not every one of today's most famous designers can use the term "haute couture" to describe its creations. Those who can include Chanel, Givenchy, Yves Saint Laurent, Christian Dior, and Jean Paul Gaultier.

Prêt-a-porter: The designer's ready-to-wear line

Haute couture is such a small niche in the fashion market because of its high price tag and the extravagance of the garments themselves. These pieces are mostly crafted for the art of fashion, the drama of the show, and the editorial exposure. They're not produced on a large scale, if at

Figure 6-3: A haute couture dress.

all. So how do these haute couture fashion designers make a living? Well, they sell their other line — the prêt-a-porter line, or in English, ready-to-wear. This line is at a much more attainable price for the general consumer. Don't get me wrong: Designer clothing is expensive, but the ready-to-wear line is much more wearable as far as design and much more affordable.

Comparing prêt-a-porter to other lines

What distinguishes prêt-a-porter from contemporary and so-called mass market clothing is that the fabrics are of better quality, some hand-sewing may be involved, and there is more attention to detail, all of which allows the designer to charge more. Where a haute couture dress may cost from $3,000 to $10,000 or more, a designer dress of the prêt-a-porter category probably costs between $500 and $2,500.

One of the biggest differences between prêt-a-porter and haute couture is in the design. Haute couture is not necessarily made to be worn by the average person; prêt-a-porter is (see Figure 6-4). And, even though prêt-a-porter is made in greater volume than haute couture, the quality is still top-notch. Make no mistake, when you're buying from a designer's ready-to-wear line, you're getting a high-quality garment made with the finest materials and using the finest labor methods. Some pieces may be hand-stitched or hand-beaded. Another major difference is that prêt-a-porter is *fully completed,* which is why a customer can go into a store, buy it, and wear it home. In many instances, some alterations have to be made, but because every store has the garment in several sizes, it may actually fit perfectly.

Ways to buy prêt-a-porter

Because prêt-a-porter is not inexpensive, such higher-quality garments are expected to last, both in terms of wear and tear and style. A two-year old dress may be out of style for a fashionista who feels she must dress on the cutting edge, but the quality should be obvious for many years. This gives women two avenues when it comes to purchasing clothing of the prêt-a-porter quality.

Figure 6-4: Prêt-a-porter.

✔ **Look for classics at discounted prices:** If you can find a high-quality item that didn't sell when it first came out, it may be deeply discounted. Yes, it may no longer be cutting-edge, but it certainly will still make a statement. The difference in price may make such a purchase very worthwhile. And because it is of higher quality, it will also last. So if you find a staple item, like a blazer or little black dress or charcoal wool skirt, that is greatly reduced in price, definitely consider its purchase. Especially if you consider that with a few alterations, like an adjustment to the hemline, it may actually be right in style.

✔ **Consider buying previously owned pieces:** Because prêt-a-porter items are more upscale, they most likely weren't worn very often. Many women don't like to repeat and will consign items to make money to buy more! See Chapter 7 for more advice on buying vintage clothing, but keep this option in mind when looking for higher-quality garments that may otherwise be out of your reach.

Contemporary

Contemporary designs may have recognizable names but are not considered as high-end as prêt-a-porter. These garments can be sold in the same department stores as the prêt-a-porter lines but are often sold on a different floor. These dresses generally run anywhere from $150 to $450 (see Figure 6-5). A mass market dress, on the other hand, can easily be found for under $100.

Mass market

If you think of fashion as a pyramid, with the haute couture clothes at the top, mass market forms the bottom, and because the bottom is the widest, it encompasses the most variety at the lowest price points.

Stores such as Nordstrom, Macy's, Kohl's, and Walmart are all big department stores, but the merchandise you find at each is different. Even though each of these stores is likely to have a selection of black dresses, you're unlikely to find the same dress, because the buyers for each of these chains has a different price point.

While finding 10s in the mass market category is certainly possible, as Figure 6-6 shows, you have to look a little harder to find the perfect item that also fits your style and body type.

Figure 6-5: A contemporary black dress.

You can thank Singer

Dressmaking was all done by hand until the middle of the 19th century when technological advances brought major changes. The year 1856 is the landmark year when the Singer Sewing Machine Company was born. The origin of the sewing machine stretched back more than 20 years prior, but when the Singer machine began to be sold in quantity, it was the beginning of a revolution. Tens of thousands of tailors would soon be out of a job, and while at first these machines permitted women to make their own clothes, eventually, as the machines became more elaborate, it spelled the birth of the mass market clothing business, and shops devoted to selling ready-to-wear clothes began to spring up.

Figure 6-6: When buying a mass market LBD, check detailing such as the quality of the stitches.

Building Your Fashion Awareness

Assuming that you're not going to rush out and buy an outfit in the category of haute couture or maybe even of prêt-a-porter, what does all this have to do with you and your fashion sense? Everything! If you're going to develop your personal sense of style, you have to have an idea of what's going on in the fashion world.

At the top is haute couture, and you can never go wrong wearing a designer dress of this caliber because it will be tailored to your measurements, made with exquisite care using the finest cloth, and be of the most cutting-edge design. At the next level, prêt-a-porter, you can be sure that the design is up to date, the fabrics are wonderful, and the manufacturing process is first class. The rest of the market is made up of contemporary designers and mass market merchandise.

Here's what fashion awareness lets you do:

✔ **Invest wisely in your clothing:** As you know so well, there's a very big difference in what you can buy at a department store and a dollar store. As you build your fashionable wardrobe, you have to decide which pieces are worth spending a little more on and which you can spend less on. My advice? Invest smartly in classic pieces and staple items that will stand the test of time as far as quality and style, and spend less on the super trendy items that'll be out of style before you can bat an eye. You'll never feel bad purchasing a few fun, trendy items to wear all season until they are "out" if you didn't overspend on them.

✔ **Create your own versions of designer fashions:** When you keep abreast of what the top designers are doing, you can create your own version of their designs, using merchandise that fits your budget (see Figure 6-7). Every designer, whether a household name or not, has his or her version of the latest trend. So even if you're getting your ideas from the high-end designers that grace the pages of the fashion magazines (tear out pictures of the pieces you like and take them shopping with you), you'll still be able to find items that work for you in your budget.

Figure 6-7: With the right accessories, you can dress up even an inexpensive LBD.

✔ **Be a savvy shopper:** Your goal is to be fashionable, *not* a slave to fashion! Raising your level of fashion awareness is going to make it a lot easier to buy clothes. You won't spend time guessing whether or not a particular outfit you see in the stores is fashionable or relying on a sales assistant who may have more incentive to push something that's not going to sell on its own. Instead, you'll be able to browse through the racks with confidence, selecting items that will let those around you know that you're someone who has good fashion sense.

What factors into something being trendy? The shape, hemline, neckline, color, type of material, and so on. How many times have you read that "X color is the new black?" If blue is the new black, for example, then maybe you want to add a little blue to your wardrobe this season.

If you want to be fashion conscious, you need to see what the top designers are doing. The reason is that so many of the designers who produce more affordable clothing will offer similar versions of the same trends the high-end designers produce. By seeing what the top designers are doing, you'll be able to spot trends that you can then imitate at whatever level comfortably suits your income. Even if you never purchase one of the gowns featured in the coverage *Vogue* gives to Fashion Week, by understanding what's being shown, you'll be able to select outfits in your price range that still reflect the latest trends.

Before you buy something because it's trendy, make sure it fits into your style and body type. If blue is the new black but it's not a color that you're comfortable in or look good in, then avoid it, regardless of the trend. If you're a women whose body type doesn't fit the latest fashion — if the latest style is low-waisted pants when you are long-waisted, for example — don't follow the herd. Be selective and wear only clothing that fits your body. This doesn't mean you can't be trendy. Accessories are very trendy items and are great ways to express your style and fashion sense without falling victim to unflattering hemlines, materials, and so on. Remain true to your style and your body type, and you'll look fabulous whatever you wear!

Part III
Stocking Your Closet without Going Crazy or Broke

The 5th Wave   By Rich Tennant

"Oh, quit looking so uncomfortable! It's a pool party! You can't wear a cape and formal wear to a pool party!"

In this part . . .

Different events, occasions, and situations require various outfits. Office parties, running errands on a Saturday, and the bedroom (ooh la la!) all call for different attire. Wouldn't it be great if you could make shopping your full-time job? Well, most of us can't, so in this part I share information on how to create a fabulous wardrobe that fits into both your schedule and your budget.

7

Building Your Wardrobe: Your What- and Where-to-Buy Guide

In This Chapter

- The must-have basics
- Where to shop and how to do so without busting the bank

I always ask the sales clerk of my favorite bargain stores (Filene's, T.J. Maxx, Loehmann's) what day they get their weekly big shipment in so I am one of the first to pick the "finds"!

Beth Stern, Model/TV Personality

*W*hen is the best time to shop? Hmmm...that's a tough question to answer, right? Here's the basic rule to follow (unless you're facing an extreme circumstance, and I mean *extreme*): Don't go on a shopping frenzy if you're feeling down, bloated, or bored. Although you may *think* these seem like the perfect scenarios to soothe yourself in a time of distress, they're not. If you're reading this while in a relatively calm frame of mind, you know where I'm coming from. With that said, for many of us, shopping does the trick when we need a lift, but then the focus should be on *what* you buy, not *how much* you buy.

This chapter explains what to do (and not do) to ensure that your forays into clothing shops leave you feeling good and owning items you need, want, look good in, and can afford. It also explains what items you should look for if your closet doesn't already have them.

Wardrobe Staples

There are some items that you absolutely need. These make up the basis of your wardrobe; they're the must haves, no matter what your style. I call them *wardrobe essentials*. To be considered a wardrobe essential, an article of clothing has to have several important attributes:

- **It must be versatile.** This is the most important quality of an essential piece of clothing. One key factor in versatility is color. Because wardrobe essentials have to go with lots of other clothing, they tend to be monochromatic and neutral in color. They also must work with different outfits. A blazer that you can pair with a skirt, pants, or a pair of jeans is a good example.

- **It has to be of good, perhaps even exceptional, quality.** A wardrobe essential makes a statement, and anyone looking should be able to tell that it's top shelf. High quality also means that it wears well — very important for a garment that you'll rely on again and again.

- **It should be in a classic style.** You don't want your wardrobe essentials to ever really go out of fashion.

- **It must be a 10.** These garments, like everything in your closet, should have all the qualities of a 10 (refer to Chapter 2), and because they form the basis of your stylish wardrobe, it's okay to spend a little more for these than you would other, less essential, items.

So what are the basic wardrobe essentials? Read on.

A lot of the items in the following list are black. Why? Because black provides a clean slate on which to build your outfit. Black garments offer many pluses: No one knows how often you wear them. Stains are difficult, if not impossible, to see. The color is flattering on every person and every body type. And with a black basic, you're free to add color in other areas of your outfit and have fun with prints or great accessories.

Little black dress (LBD)

Ah, the little black dress. It should be sexy, yet sophisticated. It should be well-made and fit like a glove. It should hide your flaws and accentuate your attributes. It should go from day (wear it to the office with a cardigan or blazer and a set of pearls and leather pumps) to night (take off the blazer or cardigan and add some makeup, jewelry, and heels). Really, the little black dress, shown in Figure 7-1, is so versatile, it can go anywhere and be appropriate.

Choose a LBD in the style that suits you, makes you feel comfortable, and looks most like *you*. It can be sleeveless, have cap sleeves, or have ¾-length sleeves. It can have a V-neck, boat neck, crew neck, or square neck. It can be knee-length, a little longer, a little shorter, or miniskirt length. Really, the LBD is both universal and individual at the same time. Find one that makes you feel fabulous and make the investment because this is one piece that really gives you your money's worth!

Black blazer

The black blazer is key in your wardrobe. Because it's black, it goes with virtually everything. You can change the look just by changing the accessories. (And, as I mentioned previously, because it's black, no one will notice how often you wear it.)

Although it doesn't need to be ridiculously expensive or high-end, the blazer does need to fit you perfectly and work with your body type. If you want to appear taller or longer, choose a blazer that's longer. If you want to accentuate your beautiful waistline, make sure it's fitted in the waist area. Also make sure it's current. Avoid one that looks like something from the 80s — oversized with enormous shoulder pads.

Figure 7-1: Pearls and pumps make the LBD simple yet chic.

Should you go with a double- or single-breasted blazer? My advice is choose a single-breasted one. You can wear a single-breasted blazer comfortably and fashionably either open or closed, and you have the option of wearing it over dresses or skirts, as well as pants. (Don't underestimate the power of a black blazer and jeans. As Figure 7-2 shows it's a classic look that can take you from day to night. It's my go-to outfit when in doubt!)

Don't be afraid to make the blazer your own: Add a favorite pin to the lapel if you want to jazz it up when the occasion calls for it. A black blazer doesn't have to be boring. Again, it's a basic that you can build your outfit around.

Crisp, white button-down shirt

The white button-down shirt should fit you well. Nothing oversized here. At first glance, your white shirt may look no different than the one your husband or boyfriend wears under his suits, but yours is made and cut specifically for a woman. It should be flattering and accentuate your best features. You can wear a white shirt on its own, tucked in or out, under a sweater, under a jacket, or as part of a suit. Keep the following things in mind as you decide on your white shirt:

Figure 7-2: You can never go wrong with a black blazer and blue jeans.

✔ **Style:** The more expensive shirts look a little dressier and need to be pressed (otherwise, they look messy), but if you're buying only one, a dressier shirt is the way to go because it's more versatile. You can dress it up for work under a suit or on its own with slacks or a great skirt. Or you can dress it down by putting it under a sweater or with a pair of jeans. Less fancy shirts are also an option if you're planning to wear the shirt only as casual dress. This type is good with jeans or tied at the waist over a bikini, for example. These shirts aren't as structured and don't need to be pressed.

If you have a great waist, buy a fitted shirt; if not, buy one that is cut straight.

✔ **Material:** Whether dressy or more casual, the white shirt is generally made of cotton. If you can, go for *combed cotton,* which means that longer fibers were used; these fibers are stronger and give the material a more luxurious appearance. Many shirts designed for office wear are made of cotton in an oxford weave. Although a comfortable type of cotton, these types of shirts don't wear as well, and tend to pill at the collar and cuffs. Cotton broadcloth is sturdier and resists soiling.

✔ **Construction:** Because your collar is usually at eye level, make sure it's sewn properly. Women's button-down shirts don't generally have actual buttons on the collar that button down to the shirt, so make sure there are no puckers in the material and that it lays flat.

Brooks Brothers (www.brooksbrothers.com) makes an iron-free, non-wrinkle shirt that you don't have to dry clean. You can throw it in the dryer and it comes out looking perfect!

Black trousers

A pair of high-quality, flat front, black trousers are a necessity in every wardrobe. Stay away from pleats because they only accentuate an area that no one really needs accentuating! If you can buy only one pair of trousers, select a length that matches the heel height you most commonly wear. And choose a lightweight wool that will work in summer or winter.

If you can buy another pair of trousers, ivory is great to have (even in the winter). I love winter white! It's such a refreshing change in the darker months, and it shows that you have style and are daring enough to let everyone know it.

Knee-length black skirt

Every woman should have a knee-length black skirt that fits perfectly and gives her a slim appearance. The particular style is up to you (and what looks good on your body type): It can be a pencil skirt or an A-line skirt (head to Chapter 9 to see a range of skirt styles). So that it can go from season to season, look for one that's a lightweight wool.

Think how much you can do with the basic black skirt. Not only is black always flattering, but the outfit possibilities are endless — a beautiful blouse, a gorgeous sweater, and high boots or pumps. You can pair a knee-length skirt with solids, such as a basic white cardigan set (see Figure 7-3) or with a fabulous print. If you keep the outfit simple, you can liven it up with great jewelry or a great bag.

Classic beige trench coat

The classic trench is a necessary staple because it never goes out of style and you can wear it in just about any season — spring, summer, fall, and, depending on the winter temperatures where you live, sometimes winter. If you stick to a classic trench coat, it will last you for years. When choosing a trench coat, follow these suggestions:

Figure 7-3: The basic black skirt and sweater set — always chic and classic.

✔ **Make sure the coat fits in the shoulders.** You don't want to be drowning in your coat. You should always be wearing your clothes; they should not be wearing you.

✔ **Choose a style and length that gives you the look you want.** Decide whether you want it to cinch at the waist or be looser fit. A belted trench flatters your waistline in contrast to your shoulders and the overall volume of the coat itself. If you plan to wear it over dresses and pants, make sure it's long enough that your dresses aren't sticking out the bottom. You can get away with a shorter trench if you are only going to wear it with pants or jeans (see Figure 7-4).

✔ **Make sure the coat doesn't overwhelm you.** If you're on the smaller side, pick a coat that's less busy, that is, has less going on with the pockets, lapels, buttons, and so on, and make sure it's single-breasted. If you're taller, you can carry off a more traditional looking double-breasted trench.

Because you'll probably buy only one trench coat, make sure it goes with everything in your closet and that it's a length to give you the look you want.

Black leather bag

You can look at a bag as something handy to carry your makeup, cell phone, and other necessities, or you can look at it as a great way to show off your sense of style. Or better yet, why not have both! Most women buy one great bag for the season and carry it everywhere.

A black leather bag is a perfect *everywhere bag,* a bag you can wear to work, to lunch, to dinner, and even shopping on the weekend. It goes with everything, and you'll feel comfortable using it with whatever color or prints you may be wearing. It should be medium-sized: large enough to hold whatever you need during the day but not so large that it looks awkward if you find yourself running straight out to dinner with it.

Figure 7-4: Make sure you wear the trench and that it doesn't wear you!

I highly recommend having several bags in your arsenal so that you can accessorize your various outfits, but as a go-to bag for every day, the black leather bag is key. You live out of your bag, so this isn't an item to skimp on. And just the way you notice every other woman's bag, every other woman will be taking notice of yours, so make sure it gives a good first impression of you!

Quality blue jeans

Everyone should have a pair of favorite jeans — you know, the kind of jeans that make you feel sexy, pulled together, *and* comfortable. These jeans should be current in style, and the cut should be one that flatters your best assets. The great news is that nowadays jeans companies are making jeans to accommodate every body type. So figure out what your body type is (refer to Chapter 3 for help), then pick the cut of your jeans accordingly. Some suggestions:

- ✔ If you have great legs, you may want a pair of skinny jeans.
- ✔ If you want to direct attention away from your waist area, choose a flared jean.
- ✔ If you have a great waistline and want to draw attention to it, go for a pair of high-waisted jeans.

Jeans can get a little pricey, but you can still get a great pair for around, or even under, $100. And always check the sale section because jeans do actually go on sale — a great price break if you can find your size. If you are only investing in one pair of jeans, go with dark denim. They are more slimming and more versatile. You can wear them totally casual during the day, and you can dress them up for night.

Pair of black pumps

Every woman needs a pair of "go to" shoes. Along the same lines as the little black dress and the black skirt, a pair of black pumps serves you well. Black pumps go with everything, they won't get too dirty, and they can also go from day to night. If you can afford only one pair of black pumps, go with a dressier pair; shoes are generally easier to dress down than to dress up.

When buying shoes, make sure they're comfortable! Don't expect them to "break in." You're going to spend some money on them because shoes tend to cost a bit more, so please, please, *please* make sure they fit right. For more on sizing shoes, head to Chapter 16.

White and black cardigan sweaters

Cardigan sweaters are great for those times when you don't know what the weather will be like or if it's the middle of summer and you get stuck in a ridiculously cold air-conditioned restaurant or office. If you get warm, you can always throw the cardigan over your shoulders and tie around your neck, and if you're chilly, you can wear it.

If you can afford it, get your cardigans in a light cashmere. If you can't afford cashmere, a great cotton does the trick! Whether cotton or cashmere, a good-quality cardigan sweater should last a very long time. You can find great cardigans at a store like Gap or Old Navy for a very reasonable price. (Target also has great ones.) You should be able to purchase a cotton cardigan for $50 or less.

Want more than black and white? Cardigans come in all sorts of other colors. Spring is a great time to buy cotton cardigans, which are generally a spring item and the stores will be well stocked. You can buy cashmere whenever; they generally have seasonal colors, too.

Set of pearls

A set of pearls can be a beautiful accent to any outfit. They're perfect for the office and for a formal affair. Obviously, real pearls are expensive, so if you can borrow from Grandma — lucky you! If not, you can buy fakes. Just play around with them.

Pearls aren't just for those who prefer classic styles. There are many ways to wear them, and a long strand can be worn with a funkier outfit. Remember, they don't have to look like your grandma's pearls if your outfit isn't like grandma's (see Figure 7-5).

You can get a nice strand of pearls that will do the trick at a good trimmings store. Try layering a few strands. M&J Trimming sells them for $10 each. If you're not able to visit the New York store, get them online at `www.mjtrim.com`.

Diamond studs, or shall we say cubics!

You definitely don't want to leave your ears bare, and diamond studs go perfectly

Figure 7-5: Pearls are not just for Grandma.

with everything. If you are heading to work in a suit and then out at night in jeans and a blouse, studs are the perfect complement. They're classy, and you can throw them on without worrying whether they go with what you're wearing because diamonds go with everything!

Don't have the money for genuine diamonds studs? Don't worry. Buy cubic zirconia instead; just keep them small.

Making the Most of Your Shopping Excursions

In real estate, it's location, location, location. In clothes shopping, it's focus, focus, focus. If you know what you want and how much you want to spend for it, every shopping expedition can work like a well-oiled machine. But if you shop with your eyes darting at every item that attracts your attention, you can be sure that you're going to wind up buying the wrong items for your wardrobe. The time to act like a kid in a candy store is . . . when you're a kid in a candy store.

Budgeting for your fashion wardrobe

It's possible to spend an almost unlimited amount of money on clothes. After all, Imelda Marcos, former first lady of the Philippines, left behind over 1,200 pairs of shoes when she had to flee the presidential palace. Throw jewelry into the mix, and she spent even more. But most of us don't have unlimited budgets. The trick is to dress fashionably within *your* budget.

To paraphrase Mick Jagger, you can't always get what you want, but if you try, you can usually get what you need. The first thing to do when putting together a clothing budget is to figure out what you need versus what you want. If you don't have a black blazer, for example, then that's a need. If you have a black blazer, but you'd like a new one by Ralph Lauren, that's a want. When you think about how much to budget, be willing to spend more on the must-have items because they need to last a long time. Consider these purchases investments.

The next thing to do is to determine how much you have available to spend. If you have enough to afford both what you need and what you want, lucky you. If not, focus on the needs. As explained earlier, they form the basis of your wardrobe and, because of their versatility, can be worn in a variety of situations and expand your wardrobe. What should you do with your list of wants? Write them down on a piece of paper that you keep with you when you go shopping, in case you see an item from your want list on sale.

Many people don't bother with a clothing budget, and that's a mistake. Using a budget — that is, knowing how much you can spend on an item and keeping track of when you spend more or less — allows you to buy more clothes, not less. If you know you saved money on a pair of black pumps, for example, you can add your savings to the money you're putting away for the diamond studs, and eventually you'll get them. But if you don't keep track, then those studs will always remain far off in the distance.

Figure out how much you can pay before looking for a particular article of clothing. By having a top price in mind while you're going through the racks, you can eliminate anything that costs a lot more, thus saving you time.

The following sections explain how to get the most for your hard-earned money.

Focusing on quality

When it comes to building your wardrobe, quality is more important than quantity for two basic reasons: One, better-quality clothing lasts longer. If you spend twice as much for a trench coat and it lasts you three times as long as a cheaper coat, you're actually ahead of the game. True story: The year I graduated from the University of Michigan, I used most of my graduation money to buy a black, Prada-belted raincoat that goes with everything. That was over ten years ago, and I still wear that same raincoat. The point? Investing in fine, good clothing is a bargain. I would rather you buy one fabulous item and mix and match it than ten that are just "eh."

So does that mean you should buy the $25 pair of plastic flip-flops rather than the 99-cent store variety? Absolutely not. Sometimes it makes sense to buy an item that is less expensive (when an item is trendy, for example, or when it's made of a material that doesn't shout out "This only costs $10!"). But more often than not, a quality item will be recognized for what it is, and it doesn't need a fancy label for that to happen. (I don't encourage wearing items that scream a certain designer anyway.) Even if people don't know exactly why one leather bag stands out more than others, they can still tell the difference. And trust me, you'll feel great every time you wear that great investment piece that you waited to buy.

Shopping to look, not to buy

In English, we call it *window-shopping*. In French, it's called *leche carreau*, which translates into "window licking" (when you think about it, it's an apt term for the fabulous windows in the Parisian fashion houses like Dior, Chanel, and Hermes that can easily cause you to drool when the prices may make it impossible for you to buy). But window-shopping serves a greater function than just being a way to spend a Saturday afternoon when you don't have money to spend. If you approach it as a learning experience rather than a shopping trip, it can be time very well spent. To get the most of your window shopping excursions, do the following:

- ✔ **Adjust your attitude.** When browsing, don't let yourself get frustrated because you can't plunk down the cash for everything that you see or try on.

- ✔ **Don't stay out of high-end department stores or boutiques because you can't afford to buy.** These stores shouldn't intimidate you, nor should you think that you shouldn't try anything on if you can't afford to buy. You *should* try on designer clothing if you fall in love with it. Doing so gives you an idea of what you're looking for, and perhaps you'll find a similar look in another store that *is* in your price-range. Knowledge is power, and if you see something you like, try it on! Trust me, the fashion police are not going to come and get you just because you had no intention of buying.

- ✔ **Comparison shop.** You know that you're eventually going to buy something, so think of window-shopping as preparation. You no doubt already comparison shop for big-ticket items. Not many of us buy the first car we see. Window-shopping gives you the same opportunity with clothing: It lets you make sure that you're getting the best item for your needs.

- ✔ **Understand how anticipation can increase the ultimate satisfaction you feel when you do eventually buy.** As you slowly narrow down your search (taking your time is important) and as the moment of purchase actually approaches, you'll feel more and more excited, and the purchase itself will give you that much more satisfaction — certainly more than if you just ran into a store, grabbed a few things, and took them home.

Choosing your wingman (or woman)

Sometimes you go shopping to buy a specific item, and other times you go shopping to, well, just go shopping. Some people like to hunt solo (which is totally cool if you are 100 percent confident in your judgment), and others need approval on every hair band purchased. Most of us fall somewhere between the two extremes. So what type of person do you need by your side when trying to find whatever you are looking for that day?

Choosing a friend

The best people to take shopping with you are the people who

- ✔ Make you feel secure
- ✔ Have your best interests at heart
- ✔ Give you his or her honest opinion
- ✔ Knows what you can and can't afford

If the person you are with fits these requirements, you are sure to walk out with only 10s for your closet.

In his comic strip, poor Dagwood is often shown shopping with his wife, burdened down with a mountain of packages. While a husband may make a good *schlepper*, most husbands, boyfriends, or partners may not want the role of the professional bag-carrier. So should you or shouldn't you shop with your significant other? If he (or she) does all the things in the preceding list, go for it.

Shopping with a sales associate

Whether you know what you're looking for or not, a sales associate can be very helpful to you. She knows what merchandise is in the store better than anyone and can direct you efficiently to areas that may be just what you're looking for. Sales associates also know what's trendy or current, and they can make your shopping experience a whole lot easier.

The thing to be careful of when working with a sales associate is overspending. If you stay focused, the salesperson can expedite shopping for you. But if you're aimlessly wandering and vulnerable to outside influences, especially if you're on your own, you could end up spending a whole lot more than you bargained for. Make sure that you shop in stores where you can return the merchandise without a problem.

Many times sales associates work on commission. Although you're looking for the approval of another person, it's hard to fully trust someone you know benefits from the sale. The best advice I can give is if you love an item, see if it is refundable, buy it, and then try it on at home or in front of someone you truly trust.

Keeping up the pace: Shopping tempo

As you may have observed, most retail establishments don't have clocks in clear view. Why? Because retailers know that if you feel rushed, you're likely to make fewer purchases. Which should tell you something about choosing your shopping tempo. Dawdle too long, and you're probably going to end up buying something that you'll later regret. Certainly you don't want to make mistakes because you were rushing around too quickly, but if you are back and forth about a certain item, chances are it is not a must-have. Remember, the 10s (refer to Chapter 2) should be obvious in the mirror when you try them on!

Having a hard time making up your mind? There's nothing wrong with leaving the store and taking some time to think about it. Almost every store will hold things, unless they're on sale, for at least 24 hours. If you leave the store and are still thinking about the garment the next day, chances are you really want it. If you haven't given it a second thought, then lucky you didn't buy it because you obviously didn't love it enough anyway.

Checking out the details

Okay, so you've found a fabulous must-have. Good for you! But before swiping your credit card, you need to take a few more steps:

- ✔ **Carefully examine the garment.** Check for any signs of damage. Make sure any closures, especially zippers, are in working order.

  If you do find a small defect, don't be too quick to put the garment aside. If it's small enough that no one looking at it could detect it, you may be able to show it to a floor manager, get a decent price reduction, and walk out with quite a bargain. If an item isn't perfect, 10 to 20 percent is a fair discount to ask for, depending on the damage. If the item is just dirty, stores often give you 10 percent off for dry-cleaning.

- ✔ **If you didn't actually try on the garment, make sure it wasn't mislabeled.** There may be a different size on the inside than is marked on the store label, for example.

Knowing Where to Shop

Many places try to get you to spend your hard-earned dollars in their retail emporium. Each type offers different advantages and disadvantages, and you should know what options are near you so that you can make an informed choice of where to purchase your clothes.

Department stores

Department stores offer you the biggest selection of clothes to choose from, which can definitely be a time saver. Many department stores are part of national chains, like Macy's, which because of their buying power, can offer attractive prices. A department store is also a one-stop shop, so that you can buy not only clothes, but also shoes, accessories, coats, and jewelry. But sometimes having so much to choose from can end up being confusing and make it harder to decide. And the sales help in a department store can be hit or miss.

Each department store is slightly different, some being more upscale than others. They all have sales, so you can save money on quality clothes if you're willing to be patient. It's also very easy to return clothes because even if you're not nearby the store from which you actually purchased the item, you can return it to a different branch.

Dressing room etiquette

The advantage of shopping in a store is that you can try on the clothes before buying them (duh!). That means going into a dressing room, which should be a straightforward enough activity, right? But there are rules, especially if you're shopping in a store you go to often. If you bring in a large amount of clothing, put the items back on the hanger after you're done trying them on. It doesn't have to be perfectly done, but leaving a mess in the dressing room is not proper etiquette, nor does it fit in with the fabulous new you. Also, don't be afraid to ask for bigger or smaller sizes, other items that you remember seeing, and heels (or flats) in your size to see how that particular outfit will look. At some of the less-expensive chain stores, you will not have the luxury of a tailor or shoe options to try on, but at department stores you should be able to reap many of the benefits. After all, if you're paying for something, you should get what you pay for.

Inexpensive and trendy stores

Let's face it — everyone wants a bargain, but no one wants to look like they're wearing hand-me-downs. Luckily, several chains offer the hottest clothes at really affordable prices. H&M, the Swedish chain that first spread across Europe, has landed in America and is quickly spreading itself from sea to shining sea. Forever 21 was founded in Los Angeles and now has over 1,500 stores across the country. Other popular chains include Wet Seal, Charlotte Russe, and Urban Outfitters.

These types of stores are great places to buy trendy items. While you may occasionally be able to find classic pieces in these places, their real forte involves fun jewelry, layering T-shirts, and look-at-me tops.

Fashion boutiques

Chain stores have buyers who shop for the entire chain. The buyers for boutique stores, often the owner, shop only for their boutiques. Although boutique buyers could choose the same dress that you'd find in Macy's, usually fashion boutiques offer items that aren't being sold everywhere else. Boutiques also generally have a much smaller quantity of merchandise, and, even if they do have the same dress that's in Bloomingdale's, it's probably at a higher price.

There are many more boutiques than department stores, and each one has its own personal vision. Most feature trendier items mixed with more classic pieces. The main advantage a boutique offers is service. The sales associate is both knowledgeable and helpful. And if you're a regular customer, she'll probably learn your tastes and may let you know when a new piece has arrived that she thinks you'll like. Boutique prices may be a bit higher, but your overall shopping experience will also be quite pleasant. If you don't have to worry too much about what you spend, a boutique could be the ideal place for you to shop.

Boutique shopping is a great way to help form your personal style. Most boutiques help you focus on what you like and are not as overwhelming as department stores.

Catalogues

The first mail-order catalogue was created by none other than Ben Franklin in 1744. Although he was selling academic books, catalogue shopping has been a convenient alternative ever since (even though online shopping is now giving catalogues a run for their money).

Since you can't touch or try on the clothes that you buy through a catalogue, you have to trust the catalogue company to do a good job in offering you quality merchandise. Many catalogue companies have thrived doing just that. Yes, you can send anything you buy back, in some cases even years later, but the repacking and mailing process is a pain. On the other hand, you can leaf through a catalogue while commuting or in bed.

The Internet

Shopping for clothes online can be very efficient, saving you the time it takes to get to the store(s), the cost of gas, and the wear and tear that a day of shopping takes on your body. Shopping online also eliminates having to fight your way through the crowds and increases your chances of saving a bundle of money because of the fierce competition between online markets. In addition to the savings, you get immediate access to the widest possible selection of merchandise, and you can shop whenever you want to, even at 3 o'clock in the morning. So why doesn't everyone shop online? Usually for these reasons:

- **You can't try on the clothing.** Of course, you can try it on after you buy it and (most of the time) send it back if it doesn't work out. But that can take days or weeks and you have to put in the effort of rewrapping it and going to the post office. If you were in an actual dressing room, all you'd have to do is put it back on the rack.

- **You don't get to feel the material and look closely at the way the garment has been made.** Chapter 4 has information on why garment construction is important.

    Do what many online buyers do: Go to an actual brick-and-mortar store to try on and touch the merchandise and then go home and look for the cheapest price online.

- **You may have to pay extra for shipping costs.** Many online stores these days try to lure you to make a purchase by offering free shipping. Just double-check that you don't have to pay for shipping if you have to send something back.

✔ **You have to pay by credit card.** Many people shy away from buying goods online because they're afraid of giving out their credit card number. Of course many of those same people gladly hand their card to a waiter who could easily write down the number as well as the security code. While online shopping is usually safe and millions shop online with their credit card every day, the possibility does exist for fraud; however, because of the Fair Credit Billing Act, your financial risk for unauthorized use is limited to $50.

Because the e-retail industry knows that this fear is holding many people back, retailers are coming up with various ways to increase the public's confidence. The buySAFE Web site rates over 300,000 e-retailers. Those that have passed its standards (which include examining each site's encryption procedures) are allowed to display the buySAFE logo (see Figure 7-6). buySAFE also has its own shopping portal which provides a $25,000 bond on each purchase and 30 days worth of ID theft protection insurance.

Another solution is to use PayPal. Your credit information is stored on PayPal's server, and PayPal pays the merchant, so your credit information remains in one secure place and is not given to the merchants. Not every online site accepts PayPal, but more and more are doing so. Another alternative is to buy a gift card, which both MasterCard and Visa offer. The gift cards do have limitations and fees, but as with PayPal, the company from which you're purchasing doesn't get to see your credit card number.

©buySAFE, Inc.

Figure 7-6: A buySAFE logo.

Where to look

Almost every major clothing store has a Web site where you can purchase everything featured in its stores, and then some. No matter where you live, you can shop online at any store across the country and around the world. In addition to Web sites associated with the big clothing stores, thousands of online stores aren't associated with so-called brick-and-mortar stores. These stores carry clothing that you can't find anywhere else. So the more important question when shopping online is not how broad a selection there is but how to narrow it down so that you don't get overwhelmed. There's no easy answer, but you can employ a couple different strategies:

- **Search by store.** Type names of stores you already know (like Macy's or Bloomingdale's) into your browser, then search the site for the item you're looking for. The downside of this strategy is that you'll see only what that particular store offers and you may not be getting the lowest possible price.

- **Let someone else narrow down the possibilities.** If you use Google Directory (www.google.com/dirhp), for example, and look under Shopping and then select Clothing, you get a list to choose from of every type of clothing, ranked by popularity (in Google). Just because a site is popular doesn't guarantee that you'll find anything you like, but it's a good way to narrow down the sites you visit. (Of course on the Web, "narrow down" is a relative term. At the time I wrote this, Google offered 324 sites under the women's clothing category alone. So while this strategy does narrow things down a bit, it's still a large selection, and one you couldn't possibly go through in one sitting.)

Mark your favorite sites so you can easily go back to them later. If you find a Web site that you like and know you'll want to go back to it, put it on your Favorites list or bookmark it.

Making allies online

While online shopping may tend to be a solitary pleasure, you don't really have to tackle this job all by yourself. There are two sets of allies that you can use to help you: family and friends (of course) and bloggers.

- **Friends and family members:** Let's say you just spent an hour checking out some new Web sites that sell clothes. Make a list of the places you visited and your opinions about those places ("good selection of shoes, not much in the way of plus sizes, and so on") and send that list to your allies in shopping. If they return the favor for sites they visit, you'll soon have a good list of sites worth visiting, as well as those to stay away from.

- **Bloggers:** While you may not have the time to visit a lot of Web sites, bloggers do. It's not hard to find fashion bloggers because most of them link to each other's blogs, so if you find one, you'll quickly be able to see who the other major bloggers are. They all have their specialties, and you'll soon learn which blogs you want to check regularly for sales and other fashion tips. If you love fashion, reading all these blogs can become addictive, so try to be selective.

To get started, go to Google (or your favorite search engine like Yahoo or AOL) and type in **fashion blog** to see a list. The ones listed at the top generally include sites that offer a directory of fashion blogs: www. apparelsearch.com/Fashion/Fashion_Blogs.htm and nymag. com/daily/fashion are two available directories as of this writing.

One easy way to see what's new on the blogs is to use RSS feeds, which are basically updates sent out by Web sites. You need a place to assemble these feeds, like Netvibes (www.netvibes.com). After you open an account, which is easy and free, you can create a fashion area and subscribe to the RSS feed on your favorite blogs. Then all you have to do is go to your Netvibes site to quickly see all the updates from the blogs you've selected. This can be a real time saver.

Vintage and consignment stores

When people clean out their closets, looking to give worn-out pieces to charity, they usually give to an organization like The Salvation Army. But vintage clothing takes quite a different path. Just like a boutique owner shops for items that she likes among the clothing manufacturers, the owner of a vintage store looks for used clothing that stands out. Now there are thrift shops that represent charities where people may donate designer clothing, and if you have one in your neighborhood, great. But keep in mind that shopping in a vintage clothing store is not something you do to save money (not everything in a vintage store is inexpensive; in fact, it can be the opposite), but because you expect to find unique items to help you define your own personal style.

✔ **Quality vintage clothing shops.** At these shops, you'll likely find original Dior, Chanel, and other very high-end designer dresses, blouses, skirts, and more. These pieces are great to have. Chances are there aren't any others like them still around, so you never have to worry about being in the same dress as anyone else at the party. These vintage pieces are also a great way to express your sense of style. They show that you're savvy enough to appreciate fine designer workmanship and bold enough to wear something different from everyone else. As far as cost, each piece is unique and is priced based on the designer, the workmanship, and the condition of the garment.

In some cases, you will be able to find a vintage designer piece for less than the original cost, but in others, the price could be very high. So don't go vintage shopping thinking that used means you'll get a bargain. In many cases the items have only been worn a few times, if at all. Just like classic wardrobe essentials though, a great vintage piece will stand the test of time, and if it's in your budget, it could be well worth the investment.

- ✔ **Thrift stores.** These stores are another option when looking for vintage clothing. Chances are good that you won't find the most high-end pieces there, but you never know what you may come across if you take the time to search through the merchandise.

- ✔ **Consignment stores.** People who drop off clothes to these stores expect to get money for them when the clothes are sold. The people running such stores only take clothes that are in good shape, so the price may be a little higher, as both the store and the owner expect to make some money. Still the selection is decent and the prices still very reasonable.

Sample sales

What happens to the designer wear that's made to be shown to buyers but doesn't get sold? Since they cost a fortune to make (because they're all hand-made), rather than let them go to waste, they're sold in what are called *sample sales*. While you may only know the very top names in fashions, literally hundreds of designers work in the fashion industry with their own lines, and they all have sample sales, so there can be lots to choose from, though obviously you can't expect to find a wide variety of sizes as these clothes were made to be worn by models.

To find out where the latest sample sales are being held, go to `www.topbutton.com`. This site is free, but you have to register. Otherwise, you can purchase a copy of *New York Magazine* or *Time Out New York* at the newsstand. You can also find sample sales in other cities like Los Angeles, Chicago, and Boston, but there aren't as many as in New York. Check `www.dailycandy.com`, which covers all the big cities across the U.S. and always has information on sample sales, boutique openings, and more.

You can even find sample sales online now. Certain Web sites have sales lasting for 48 hours or so for designer merchandise. The good news is that the merchandise for sale isn't just samples; the sites have excess stock, so you have a better chance of getting your size. A couple of good ones to check out are `www.hautelook.com` and `www.gilt.com`. After you register, you'll get e-mails about upcoming sales.

Controlling Your Inner Shopaholic

A *shopaholic* is a person who *needs* to shop and does it excessively. If you've got the time and the bank account to afford to use shopping as a form of entertainment or therapy, then more power to you. But most of us don't, and so allocating large chunks of both time and money to shopping for clothes poses dangers to those who get so caught up shopping that they leave reality behind and end up with bulging closets and skeleton-thin wallets. This section may not be able to help shopaholics lose their addiction to shopping, but it can help you improve your shopping experience and cut down both the time and money you spend to create a fashionable wardrobe.

Making a list and checking it twice

I know what you're thinking, "Does she really think that every time I go to the mall or my favorite store, I'm going to make a list of what I need and stick to it?" Well, that is sort of what I'm saying, but hear me out.

Most people make a shopping list before going to the supermarket, for several reasons, the most important of which is so that, when they actually return home, they have what they need. The same idea applies to clothes shopping.

Many of us shop as a way to blow off steam and brighten the day a little. And that's okay — sometimes. The key is that you have to be smart about it. Here's a strategy you can use to make your shopping trips more productive, without losing all the spontaneity and fun:

1. **With our list of "must-haves" in mind, take inventory of your closet (refer to the earlier section "Wardrobe Essentials").**

   When scanning your closet, make sure every item you keep is a 10 — meaning each of your staple items must be the right fabric, must fit you perfectly, and must look like you bought it at the start of the season (even if you didn't).

2. **Make a list of what you actually need in your wardrobe.**

   If you're into gadgets, feel free to make this list electronically.

3. **The next time you feel like just buying *something*, like so many of us do, buy something from the list.**

   That way, you still get the boost of a shopping pick-me-up and are productive at the same time, because in the process you got something you needed.

Having a wish-list of items that you want to save up for, hope for as a gift, or want in a less-expensive version is totally appropriate (and fun!). Some people have a folder of tear-outs from magazines of things they would kill for — and you never know when those items may go on sale. If you're one of these people, you may not need a tangible list (when you see it you'll know it), but it's good to have these items stored in the back of your head for those "you never know" times!

Spur-of-the-moment shopping without busting the bank

Now I know what you're thinking: You have a big party Saturday night, and you really want to buy something new to wear. Trust me, I get it! Before you run out and impulsively buy an expensive new dress, try this: Go into your closet and pick out the dress that already fits you perfectly and hugs you in all the right places. Then hit the stores with that dress in mind and look for a statement necklace or a pair of beautiful chandelier earrings to spice it up. Going in with this approach lets you add another dimension to your wardrobe, because not only will you have a knockout necklace for your big party, but next week, you can wear that same piece of jewelry with jeans and a white T-shirt! Often, you'll find that just buying *something* new gives you that natural high.

You can also look at sales racks. Because something is on sale doesn't mean it's of poor quality. Great pieces that don't move in a certain amount of time are forced onto the sales rack to make space for new inventory. When you scan the sales rack, keep the basics on your mind. That perfect pencil skirt is often waiting right there. The sales rack is also good for those impulse purchases. If you see a trendy item that you want but know won't last through the season, buy it on sale.

Electronic aids

Use electronic devices — digital cameras or phones with cameras, for example — to help avoid buying something you'll regret or don't need:

✔ **Take a picture of a top or skirt in your closet that you're looking to match.** This way when you are in the mall, you can refer to the picture while on your hunt.

✔ **Need a second opinion? Camera phones can help.** It's always a good idea to e-mail a friend who is honest if you are teetering on buying that perfect outfit (especially if it's not refundable!).

Many stores don't allow you to take photos of yourself in their clothing, but some don't make a fuss. Many high-end stores (especially boutiques) enforce this rule because they don't want people taking pictures of their items and then copying their designs. So if you try to take a picture and the salesperson tells you they don't allow it, just apologize and put your camera away. If the salesperson doesn't mind and thinks you're a serious buyer who's just getting reinforcement from a trusted friend, she may even take the picture!

8

Eliminating Fashion Confusion

In This Chapter

▷ Fashion consultants and what they can do for you

▷ Using the services of a personal shopper

▷ How fashion magazines, Webzines, and TV programs can help

Don't get stuck in a fashion rut. Try new things, experiment.

Cynthia Rowley, Fashion Designer

Keeping up with fashion is a full time job and you probably already have at least two of those! Luckily there are people who earn their living by keeping track of what Paris, New York, and Milan are producing, and in this chapter I show you who the best ones are and how to make use of their skills.

Calling In the Pros

Most professionals don't perform their respective service on themselves. Obviously there are many procedures that doctors or dentists couldn't do for themselves even if they wanted to, but even most lawyers seek outside counsel if they run into a legal problem. And the reason is that when it comes to a personal problem, your emotions can get in the way of your reasoning ability and cause you to make mistakes. (How many women hang onto their long hair when in fact they'd look far better with a shorter haircut? Check out the "Ambush Makeovers" I do every Friday on *Today,* and you'll know the answer is "Too many!").

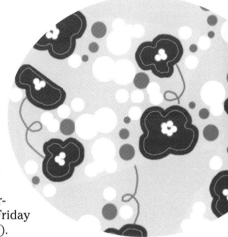

The point? When it comes to creating (or refining) your style, you can probably use a professional fashion expert. If you tend to look like the woman in Figure 8-1 when you try to get dressed up, maybe the time has come for you to consult with an expert. Fortunately, you have a few options to get the help you need.

The following sections describe what fashion consultants and personal shoppers do and explain where you can get help even if you're shopping online. To find out how fashion media can help, head to the later section "Fashion Media: Where to Look for Fashion and Style Help."

There are two basic services a professional fashion expert can offer:

✔ Teaching you how to dress in general, using the clothes you have and/or adding to your wardrobe

✔ Selecting what you need to wear for a particular event, which usually means going out to shop for you

In many cases, one person does both, but because you can hire a professional to do one or the other, you have to let them know what services you require.

Figure 8-1: Don't know which pieces work together and which don't? Time to call in the pros.

Using a professional consultant

If you have some money in your budget to spare, hiring a fashion consultant may be the route for you. When you pay for something, you tend to put more importance on it. If a friend tells you to stop wearing so much black, you may not heed her advice, but if a trained professional whom you're paying tells you the same thing, you are more likely to listen up! (The woman who wrote this book with us, Dana Ravich, is actually my consultant whenever I have a question about something!)

There are distinctions between a fashion consultant and a fashion stylist. A *fashion consultant* generally works with private clients, while a *fashion stylist* generally works doing photo shoots for magazines, television, and so on.

What a consultant does

A fashion consultant is going to look at you, ask you questions about your lifestyle, examine your closets and tell you what to keep and what to get rid of, and push you in the right direction when it comes to the way you dress. She may also put together outfits with items already in your current wardrobe (see Figure 8-2). And if you choose to take it further and decide to spend the money to add more items to your wardrobe, then the consultant will actually take you shopping. Or the consultant may go to the stores on her own, pick out several items, and then bring them to you — a more practical option if you need help with a specific event and not an overhaul of your whole wardrobe. Either way, if shopping is involved, in addition to the cost of the consultant, you'll also be spending money on items for a new wardrobe.

Figure 8-2: A fashion consultant helps you put the pieces of your fashion puzzle together.

Selecting a consultant

The best way to find a fashion consultant is by personal referral. You could look in the phone book, or go online to a Web site like www.fashion-411. com, but before you put your image in somebody else's hands, you want to make sure they know what they're doing. If none of your friends or family has ever used a fashion consultant, ask the owners of any boutiques in your area. They should be a reliable source.

When you've narrowed down the field, ask the two or three you like best to provide you with referrals and call them.

Before you choose any fashion consultant, do the following:

- **Get a referral.** Since referrals tend to be satisfied customers, you can't expect to get very many negative reviews. But ask the referrals how this consultant operated: Did she ask a lot of questions about their likes and dislikes, or was she dictatorial? You may be happy to just put yourself into someone's hands, but if not, you'd better know ahead of time. Also find out whether the store owners they visited knew the consultant well. Finally, ask questions to find out whether she was very busy: Did she leave the minute the time was up to go meet another client? (This could be a good sign, because it means she's talented, but it may also mean that you could become like Cinderella when the clock strikes midnight.)

- **Have a consultation with the person you're considering.** Check out the consultant's style. Is her personal style one you'd like to emulate? When you speak to her, does she understand your lifestyle and your personality? Even if your goal is not to look exactly like a professional fashion stylist, you should still expect to get help defining a style that works for you. You should also ask the consultant what her background is to get an idea of her level of experience.

What you can expect to pay

The cost of a consultant varies according to where you live (consultants in small towns usually charge less than those in big cities) and the consultant's experience. The consultant will charge in one of two ways:

- **By the hour:** Most consultants charge this way. The hourly fee can range from $50 to $300 per hour, and usually a minimum of three hours is required. At the mid-level price range (about $150 an hour), your minimum cost is going to be $450. (And that doesn't include the cost of the clothes!)

- **Day or half-day rate:** Stylists who charge this way, charge you a flat fee for the day.

In addition to the consultation rate, some consultants get a commission from the stores they take clients to. Some simply pocket that commission (and may push you to buy more clothes in order to fatten their wallets), while others offer you that percentage as a discount for your purchases. While the second option may sound like it's more to your advantage, if the consultant charges a higher hourly fee, it may not be.

Using a department store's personal shopper

Many major department stores allow you to come into the store and work with a personal shopper for free (ah, yes, I said free!) Saks Fifth Avenue for example, has the Fifth Avenue Club. You just call, make an appointment, give your sizes, and when you show up to shop, there's a room with all of your desired looks waiting for you! There is no minimum amount you need to spend and no fee; you just need to make an appointment. Call your favorite store to see whether it offers this service. Other department stores that have personal shoppers include Macy's (Macy's By Appointment), Nordstrom, Bloomingdale's, Belk, and J.Crew.

You're also likely to find a personal shopper in the smaller department stores in only one or two cities. These stores offer this service as a way to stay competitive with the larger chains. However, you won't find personal shoppers at lower-price stores, such as Target of Kohl's, because the prices are already so low, they don't offer this additional service.

If you use a personal shopper, keep the following things in mind:

- ✔ Using a personal shopper can be a time saver. If you pick something out that doesn't fit you, the shopper will go back to the floor to get the right size. And if she knows her merchandise, once she sees something on you and realizes why it works (or doesn't), she'll be able to get you other items to try that should work on your body.

- ✔ While a personal shopper is there to sell clothes, the stores recognize that if a personal shopper is too pushy, she'll turn away customers rather than make sales. So for the most part, your personal shopper will be as helpful as possible without seeming overbearing (though remember, she does get paid a commission).

- ✔ If you're going to ask the advice of a professional, be willing to accept at least some of it. If you walk out of a store with shopping bags full of clothes that you would have bought without anyone helping you, there's no point in using a consultant of any kind. You have to be willing to trust this person to take you out of your comfort zone. Just make sure everything you buy is returnable. That way you can afford to be a bit more daring when you shop.

✔ It's always wise to call ahead to make an appointment. You may go into a store and find that one of the personal shoppers has an opening, but they're usually busy.

✔ Since either a consultant or personal shopper is going to be right there in the dressing room with you, make sure that you're wearing underwear that you don't mind being seen in.

Fashion Media: Where to Look for Fashion and Style Help

The fashion media may not create styles, but if they decide to blow their collective horns about a particular designer, you can be sure that very soon people everywhere will be wearing that designer's creations (for a more in-depth look at the role the fashion media play in setting a trend, head to Chapter 6).

Print and online media

The Grande Dame of fashion media is certainly *Vogue*. Begun in 1892, *Vogue*'s current editor is Anna Wintour. While she's known for having her own style, a famous bob haircut (which she adopted at the age of 15 and never changed), and ubiquitous sunglasses, as an editor she's actually very much for change, always championing young, new designers. And while *Vogue* gives expanded coverage to designer wear, in a televised interview with Barbara Walters, Wintour admitted that "Jeans and T-shirts can be equally fashionable as an Oscar de la Renta ball gown." Figure 8-3 proves her point.

But any fashion magazine can help you when you're trying to figure out the current trends and, more importantly, what looks work for you. Buy one or two fashion mags a month, and check out the Web sites of the others, and you'll definitely be *au courant* (up to the minute!).

Many of the weekly magazines we all love to read also offer the hottest trends (admit it, you love to see what your favorite celeb is doing!). I work with *Us Weekly,* and every week you can find great buys and finds at every price point. To broaden your knowledge, check out some of these sources:

- ✔ **Women's Wear Daily** is the fashion industry's daily newspaper. Much of the information is on the business of fashion, which may interest you or not. While you may not want to pay to receive either the paper copy or get access to the full Web site, there's plenty of good information (including photos from the latest fashion shows) that anyone can access at www.WWD.com.

- ✔ **Burda** is the world's best-selling magazine for those who sew their own clothes. But even if you can't sew on a button, there's a lot of good information within the magazine's pages, or on its Web site (www.burdafashion.com). For example, you can learn a lot about fabrics through *Burda,* knowledge that will serve you well when checking out the clothes on the racks of your favorite stores.

- ✔ **Figure,** which bills itself as being for "Real Women," is for larger women. It includes lots of tips on how to dress if you're a size 14 and above.

- ✔ **More Magazine** is for women over 40. The magazine covers fashion along with many other areas of interest.

- ✔ **MaternityandStyle.com** is a good place to get ideas if you're expecting.

Figure 8-3: Chic can mean jeans and a T-shirt as long as it's the right jeans and T-shirt!

- ✔ **Magazines from other countries:** You can learn a lot by checking out magazines from other countries. Some will be in English, such as Canada's *Flare,* while others may be in a language you don't understand, but because fashion is a visual medium, you may still get some ideas, especially from the French magazines, such as *Jalouse, L'Officiel,* and *Madame Figaro,* since many styles originate there before crossing the Atlantic.

There are also magazines that don't have a paper version but are strictly electronic. Among the top Webzines for those interested in fashion are Hintmag.com, Fashion156.com, Glossmag.ca (which is a Canadian company), Unvogue.com, and Glam.com. Like their paper cousins, Webzines cover more than just fashion, but unlike them, you can find videos from the latest fashion shows and any late-breaking fashion news long before the print magazines can cover it. (Many of the women's magazines have deadlines of three to six months, meaning the stories have to be written that far ahead of time in order to make it into the magazine.)

TV goes high fashion

Though fashion was never off the radar of women, in recent years, it's been even more in your face with the advent of a multitude of television shows. It began with *Queer Eye for the Straight Guy* and exploded into more reality shows covering every aspect of the fashion business, and turning models and fashion professors into superstars overnight.

Many reality shows are centered around fashion. Here are a couple of my favorites:

- *The Fashion Show* (Bravo) will keep you glued to the TV. Fifteen professional designers compete in this series for a chance to have their creations sold in the retail market. Over $100,000 is also at stake! Designer Isaac Mizrahi and Grammy Award-winning performer and actress Kelly Rowland run the show. You really get to see what goes into the making of a clothing line.

- *What Not to Wear* (TLC) is also extremely entertaining and informative. The show teaches women how to find their personal style. Hosts Stacy London and Clinton Kelly take someone who dresses frumpy and give her a fabulous new look.

While some of these shows are more educational than others in that they focus on teaching you about how to dress, they're all fun. If you enjoy watching them, go ahead. (Just don't watch them instead of my fashion pieces on *Today*!)

Part IV
Dressing for Any Occasion

The 5th Wave   By Rich Tennant

"I have an interview with a law firm.
I hope to make an impression."

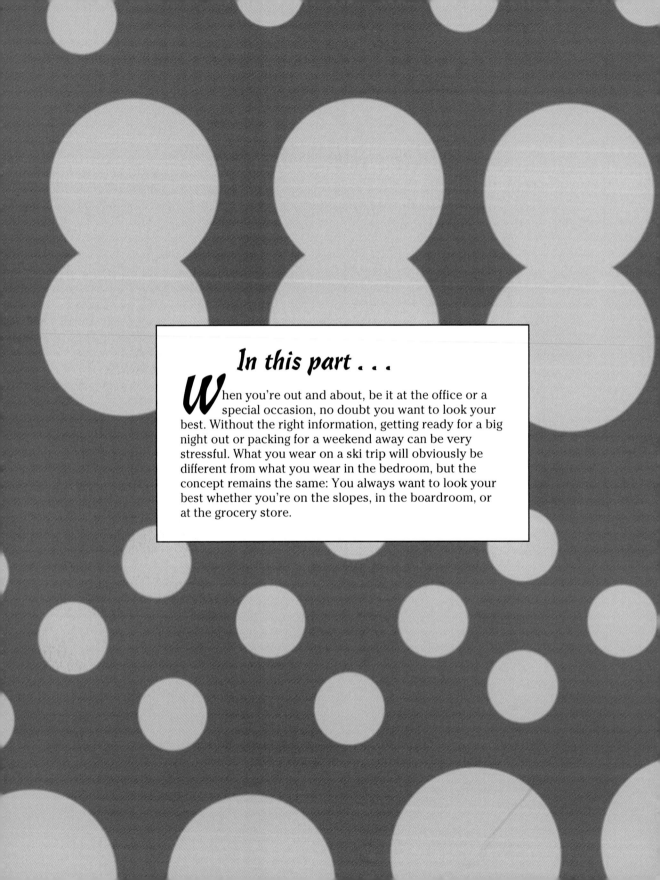

In this part . . .

When you're out and about, be it at the office or a special occasion, no doubt you want to look your best. Without the right information, getting ready for a big night out or packing for a weekend away can be very stressful. What you wear on a ski trip will obviously be different from what you wear in the bedroom, but the concept remains the same: You always want to look your best whether you're on the slopes, in the boardroom, or at the grocery store.

9

Dressing for Every Day

In This Chapter

- Knowing what to look for in blouses and sweaters
- Understanding skirt and dress styles
- Finding the perfect pants

I think every woman needs at least one pair of jeans that she absolutely loves!

Selita Ebanks, Victoria's Secret Model

Do you wake up in the morning, open your closet, and pull out the same pair of pants or skirt every time? My guess is you do. Well, that's okay. We all have pieces in our wardrobe that we just can't live without. And, for the most part, it's fine to wear those pieces over and over again, provided that they are 10s and as long as you mix and match them with a variety of different tops.

Before the late 1800s, women always wore dresses. Obviously, that's not the case today. Women nowadays have an overwhelming variety of clothing and styles to choose from: pants, dresses, blouses, skirts, and more. The key to being stylish is to make sure that each piece you put on works with your shape and the items you pair with it. This chapter lists the basic wardrobe pieces and explains how you can use them to express your style while remaining true to your personality and body type.

Tops First: Blouses and Sweaters

The right sweater worn with jeans can make for a very sexy outfit. So what's the "right" sweater? Depends on your body type. Different materials and cuts work better on certain body types. If you're larger on top, you can project a slimmer appearance by wearing a more fitted, longer sweater (bulky sweaters just make you appear larger). The same holds true for blouses: Just because you love a blouse you see in a store window doesn't mean that that blouse is the one for you. A beautiful blouse with ruffles draws attention to your upper half. If you're an apple shape, you'd do better with something simpler on top so as not to draw too much attention to an area you'd rather minimize. If you're a pear shape, a ruffled blouse accentuates your top half and draws attention away from your hips, which is the goal. The following sections explain what to look for to make sure your tops look and feel great on you.

A fitting start: Getting a good fit

You face a lot of choices when you go to buy a blouse — fabric, color, and pattern — but the number one reason to buy, or not buy, a blouse is fit. No matter how great the blouse looks on the rack, if it doesn't fit your body, then it won't look good on you.

How can you tell whether a blouse fits or not? Here are some guidelines:

The blouse is too big if

- You can grab handfuls of fabric.
- The neckline won't lie flat on your neck.
- The shoulders drop, causing the neckline to ride up.
- The sleeves are too long.

The blouse is too small if

- The button line pulls, especially across the chest area.
- It feels tight when you cross your arms.
- The sleeves are too short.
- You can't roll up the sleeves because it's too tight on your arms.

A shirt that fits nicely feels comfortable and allows you to move without making it look like you have no shape. In other words, it should make you look and feel like a 10 (refer to Chapter 2 for my 10 System)!

Buttons to the left or right?

You may have noticed that the construction of a woman's blouse is different than a man's shirt. The most interesting difference is the location of the buttons: On a woman's blouse, the buttons are on the left side; on a man's shirt, they're on the right. No one knows exactly when or why this change took place, but one interesting theory is that buttoning a blouse from the left made it easier for ladies' maids, who were responsible for helping the lady of the house dress, to get the buttons in the buttonholes.

Paying attention to cut

There are two ways to make a blouse or any article of clothing:

- **Draping:** You drape the cloth over a model, work to get the right fit, and then make a pattern from that one piece.
- **Flat cut:** You create the pattern first and then fit the pieces together.

It takes a lot more effort to design with draping, plus there's the added cost of the models, who can earn as much as $200 an hour. For that reason, blouses (and other articles of clothing) that have been draped are more expensive than those that have been flat cut. You can often tell whether a blouse was draped just by looking at it. If all the angles seem rounded, like at the shoulders, then it was draped. If it appears flatter, then it was flat cut.

In better quality blouses, you also find different cuts: classic, slim, and skinny. The classic cut is looser than the slim cut. The skinny cut is fairly tight. Which cut you choose depends on your body type, your breast size, and where you plan to wear it. If you're at work and need to move around, you're going to want a fit that allows you to move easily, such as the classic cut; if you're going out and want to appear a little sexy, then you may choose the slim or skinny cut.

Higher-end brands, like Ralph Lauren, designate their blouses as slim cut, classic cut, and so on. But not all manufacturers define the cut of their blouses. And not all manufacturers make all three cuts. If you try on blouses by several different designers, you can see which designer's line fits you best. When you find a blouse that fits you perfectly, see whether you're interested in anything else in that designer's line. Chances are, the designer's other items will also fit you well.

Style elements

For an article as basic as a woman's blouse, an incredible variety exists. Each area of the blouse — the collar, neckline, sleeve, cuff, waist, and length — can have many different iterations. When you combine them, the variety seems endless.

Collar types

Originally collars were a separate item attached to the shirt. Today all collars come pre-attached. Out of the more than 50 different collar types, the following are the most common:

✔ **Conservative collars:** The *classic* and the *round collars* (shown in Figure 9-1) are the most common and conservative, and they work with all body types. You really can't go wrong choosing this collar style.

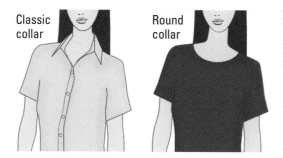

Figure 9-1: Conservative collars.

✔ **Feminine collars:** The *ruffle, sash-bow,* and *shawl collars* are the most girlie and feminine, and because they draw the eye to your neckline, they're perfect if you want to draw attention to your upper half. Any of these collars, shown in Figure 9-2, are perfect with a pencil skirt to give your look a little flair.

Ruffle collar	Sash-bow collar	Shawl collar

Figure 9-2: Feminine collars.

✔ **Youthful collars:** The *Peter Pan* and *sailor collars,* shown in Figure 9-3, tend to be on the youthful side. You see them mostly in little girls' clothes. If you want to be taken seriously as an adult with style, I suggest you avoid these collars altogether.

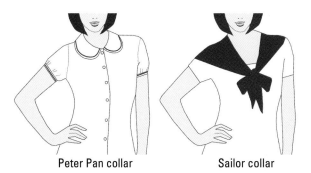

Peter Pan collar	Sailor collar

Figure 9-3: Youthful collars.

✔ **Other collars:** The *Mandarin* and the *Chelsea collars* are style statements in and of themselves, but they're rarely considered high style. The Chelsea is a very old-fashioned look and is rarely, if ever, seen; the mandarin collar looks a bit costumey. These two collars aren't necessary to have in your wardrobe.

The *button-down collar* is more of a man's shirt collar type. For women, stick with the classic collar. Figure 9-4 shows the Mandarin, Chelsea, and button-down collar types.

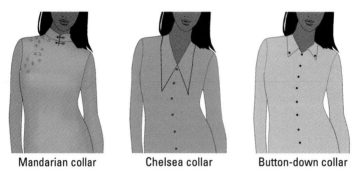

| Mandarian collar | Chelsea collar | Button-down collar |

Figure 9-4: Other types of collars.

Necklines

Not all shirts have a collar, in which case the neckline is what shows. Because some necklines may suit you more than others, they're an important factor to consider. The following list describes the most common necklines:

✔ **Conservative necklines:** The boat neck and the jewel neck, shown in Figure 9-5, are more conservative. The *boat neck* covers you to the neck, but because it opens wider at the shoulders, it makes your shoulders appear broader, which in turn makes your waist look narrower. If you're on the small side on top, have narrow shoulders, or want to minimize the waist area, this neckline is great for you. The *jewel neck* is a round, flat neckline that works well when you want to wear a fabulous necklace. The jewel neck works for every body type and won't draw attention unless, of course, you accessorize.

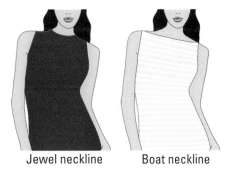

Jewel neckline   Boat neckline

Figure 9-5: Conservative necklines.

✔ **Feminine and flirty necklines:** The *halter, keyhole, one-shoulder,* and *off-the-shoulder necklines* are the most feminine and flirty. They expose your shoulders (or at least one of them), which is flattering for most women. (Shoulders are sexy, and bare shoulders are appropriate for any age.) The keyhole neckline exposes just a bit of skin, but makes the top fun and interesting. All of these necklines, shown in Figure 9-6, draw attention to your shoulder and neck area, thus minimizing the attention paid to your bottom half.

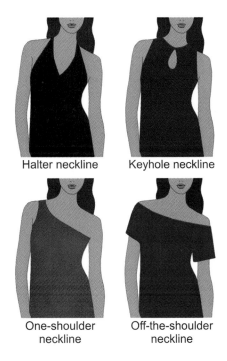

Halter neckline   Keyhole neckline

One-shoulder   Off-the-shoulder
neckline   neckline

Figure 9-6: Flirty necklines.

✔ **Necklines that expose your décolletage:** The *scoop, square, sweetheart, V-neck,* and *wrap-over* all expose your décolletage. The only difference is the actual shape of the neckline (as Figure 9-7 shows). If you like this area and want to show it off, these necklines do that. Again, an interesting neckline always draw attention to that area and away from your lower half.

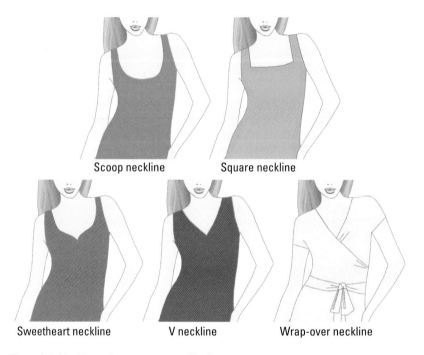

Scoop neckline   Square neckline

Sweetheart neckline   V neckline   Wrap-over neckline

Figure 9-7: Necklines that expose your décolletage.

Sleeves

Sleeves have less variety than other parts of a top, but finding the right sleeve is an important factor for many women. Obviously short-sleeves and sleeveless tops, as well as cap sleeves, are going to expose your arms (see Figure 9-8). If you have great arms and want to show them off, any of these lengths are good for you.

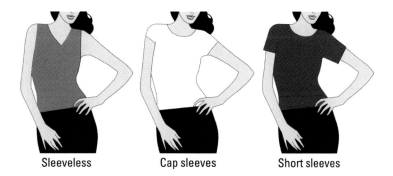

Sleeveless   Cap sleeves   Short sleeves

Figure 9-8: Sleeves that expose your arms.

Fortunately, if you don't want to expose your arms, especially your upper arms, you have other options. In addition to long-sleeves, you can try the *three-quarter length sleeve,* which ends anywhere from just below your elbow to the middle of your lower arm, showing off just the thin part of your arm. They're a classic, as well as a perfect way to keep cool in the warmer months.

The *bell sleeve* is another option. This sleeve gets wider and bells out toward your wrist. Just like flared jeans draw attention to your lower leg, this sleeve draws attention to your lower arm. If you're self-conscious about your upper arms, bell sleeves flatter you and make a style statement at the same time. Figure 9-9 shows the long, three-quarter, and bell sleeves.

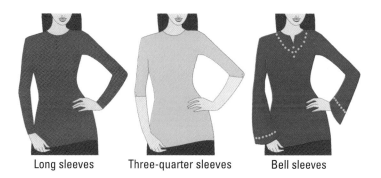

Long sleeves   Three-quarter sleeves   Bell sleeves

Figure 9-9: Sleeves that cover your arms.

The extended-shoulder and princess sleeves (see Figure 9-10) are all about shoulders and femininity. The *extended-shoulder* is an unstructured look that softens the appearance of broad shoulders (because there's no definition to where the shoulder ends and the arm begins). The *princess sleeve* has a puffy shoulder, a style that also softens the appearance of the shoulder area and gives the top some style.

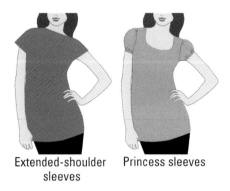

Extended-shoulder sleeves   Princess sleeves

Figure 9-10: Sleeves that soften the appearance of broad shoulders.

Shapes

The manner in which a blouse covers the upper half of your body is determined by its shape. In addition to length, here are some features that can alter the shape of a blouse (see Figure 9-11):

- **Darts:** Darts make a blouse more fitted and structured. If you have a thin midsection and you want to show it off, a darted blouse accentuates this area.

- **Peasant or camp style with front and back yokes:** This shape is a looser, unstructured cut, with more material around the midsection. It's soft and feminine and hides your midsection because it just drapes around it.

- **Shirred waist:** A shirred waist is gathered at the waist line. This look is great if you have a thin waist and want to draw the attention there.

- **Straight hem meant not to be tucked in:** This shape is cut straight down, so it doesn't accentuate your waistline, nor does it hug too tightly. If you are larger in the middle, this cut works for you because it doesn't look too tight but still shows that you have some shape.

Cute as a button

Most blouses have buttons that go all the way down the front or have several in the back near the neck to make the garment easier to put on and take off. Buttons in the front, back, or none at all are style choices you make when buying a top. In addition to providing a utilitarian or decorative purpose, buttons can clue you in on the quality of the blouse. The opening down the front is called the *placket*. If the stitching on the placket looks weak, or the stitches are far apart, then the garment is not top quality.

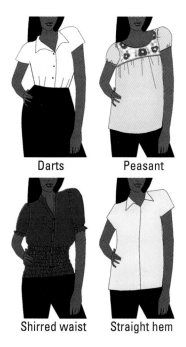

Darts   Peasant

Shirred waist   Straight hem

Figure 9-11: A variety of shapes.

Length is another factor that determines shape. If you have a narrow waist, you can show it off by wearing a shorter length blouse. If you prefer to camouflage your waistline in order to appear longer and leaner, then a longer length may be better.

A word about sweaters

Sweaters are tops made from knit material which, when used as a top and not an over-garment to add warmth, are generally tighter fitting and typically don't have collars. Sweaters that have buttons down the front are called *cardigans.* Others are *pullovers,* because you pull them on over your head (duh!), which is possible because their knitted material is more stretchy.

- ✔ **Fitted sweaters:** Fitted sweaters are generally on the simpler side and typically worn alone or over a very thin layer. They can be made from everything from cotton to cashmere, and they come with a variety of necklines: round, V-neck, or turtleneck. They're usually solid in color and are great to wear with jeans, corduroys, slacks, or even with a skirt. You can dress them up or down, depending on what you pair them with. Fitted sweaters show off your torso. If you want to show off your midsection, these sweaters are right for you.

- ✔ **Chunky sweaters:** Chunky sweaters tend to be very casual (they're best paired with jeans or cords) and, for this reason, they aren't really for work. If you're on the heavier side, a chunky sweater makes you look even larger. If you're on the petite side, a chunky sweater can overwhelm you.

- ✔ **Fancy sweaters:** If you want to wear a sweater out at night or to someplace dressier, look for one with adornments. Fancy sweaters are especially appropriate and readily available around the holidays. Many sweaters are decorated with sequins, paillettes, or rhinestones, which make them dressier and more appropriate for evening wear.

Sweaters by nature are clingy and show off your curves. If you are at all self-conscious about this, sweaters on their own may not be the right look for you. Try putting a fitted sweater under a blazer or layer a sweater over a blouse so that it doesn't cling as tightly.

Skirts and Dresses

Nothing is better than wearing a dress to work (or out!) that fits your body perfectly. Some women say that slipping on a dress is easy because there is very little thinking to do; just accessorize and go!

Dress styles

I wear dresses to the beach and to black-tie affairs. Dresses were once
considered formal, but now you can pretty much get away with a dress
anywhere, anytime. When choosing the right piece to wear, you must ask
yourself many different questions regarding length, style, and what you want
your overall look to be. You must make many choices before determining the
perfect dress for any occasion.

- ✔ **A-line:** An A-line dress (see Figure 9-12) is fitted at the waist and flares
out from the waist down. This style looks good on everyone. It's especially good for camouflaging your hips and thighs, so if you're a pear
shape or just want to hide this area, the A-line is the perfect choice.

- ✔ **Babydoll:** Short, flouncy, and with an empire waist (see Figure 9-12), a
babydoll dress may look more like a negligee than a dress. Even though
the neckline is usually more round than plunging, it *is* sexy. The empire
waist on this style camouflages your midsection by loosely draping over
that whole area. If you're trying to cover your tummy, a babydoll dress
will work for you. If you're apple shaped, be careful. The empire waist
accentuates your bust and upper body, causing you to look even more
top-heavy. This style is best for tall, thin types and tends to look very
youthful, so take your age into account if you try to pull this off.

- ✔ **Cocktail dress:** The cocktail dress encompasses many styles (including
the little black dress) and is appropriate at almost every occasion (see
Figure 9-13). You can dress it up or down with the help of accessories.
Cocktail dresses are generally around knee length — unless, of course,
they're *tea length,* which means they end mid-calf. They can be sleeveless, strapless, or have sleeves long or short. Because there are so many
styles, you can easily find one that's right for your body type.

- ✔ **Empire dress:** The waist of this style of dress is set above the natural
waistline, often just below the bust (see Figure 9-13). Similar to the
babydoll dress, the empire dress can be any length and doesn't have to
be flouncy. This type of waist is good for someone with a smaller bust
because it accentuates that area. It also takes your true waistline completely out of the picture. So if you have issues with your tummy, waist,
hips, or anywhere below the bust line, this dress hides all that for you.

Figure 9-12: From left: A-line and babydoll.

✔ **Evening gown:** For formal, black-tie occasions, most evening gowns are floor length (see Figure 9-13). Because they're not exclusive to one body type, anyone should be able to find an evening gown that flatters her body type. You just need to follow the body type rules and find one that works for you. Evening gowns can be very simple or have embellishments like lace or beading. It's really about personal style. My favorite evening gown is strapless, black, and simple.

Figure 9-13: From left: Cocktail, empire, and evening gown.

- ✔ **Jumper:** A jumper is a sleeveless dress designed to be worn over a blouse, T-shirt, or sweater (see Figure 9-14). Jumpers can vary in length, but most hit right at the knee, and they're often paired with pumps or high boots. This cut is pretty straight so anyone can wear it.

- ✔ **Mini:** Any dress that stops 2 or more inches above the knees qualifies as a mini, shown in Figure 9-14, though the actual style can vary from a sheath to a shift. Micro-minis are even shorter. The mini is best for someone — apples, this usually means you — with thin legs. Regardless of your shape, if you've got great legs, show them off. Keep in mind, though, that the mini is a youthful look.

✔ **Maxi:** The maxi was a counterpoint to the mini, bringing hemlines down after they'd crept up. A maxi, shown in Figure 9-14, is a full-length dress and works for those who want to cover up their bottom half. It also gives you the appearance of being longer and leaner because of the one, long line of material.

✔ **Sheath:** A sheath dress, shown in Figure 9-15, is very fitted (so it shows off your curves) but has no waist, thus creating a long line that has a slimming effect. Sheaths are usually sleeveless. If you'd prefer not to expose your arms, this dress style isn't right for you.

Figure 9-14: From left: Jumper, mini, and maxi.

✔ **Shift:** A shift is a straight-cut dress with no waist (see Figure 9-15). Shifts are a great choice for those who don't want something as fitted as a sheath but still want to wear a flattering dress. Again, because the dress has no waist, it creates a long, lean line in the torso; it's a good style for every body type.

✔ **Wrap:** A wrap dress, shown in Figure 9-15, wraps around your body and closes in the front. Diane Von Furstenberg made the wrap dress famous back in the 1970s. These dresses are classic and flatter every body type because they accentuate the neckline, and the line where it wraps creates a long appearance. You can also wrap the dress so that it's just the right fit — not too tight or too loose — which also is more flattering.

Figure 9-15: From left: Sheath, shift, and wrap.

Skirts

The advantage that skirts and blouses have over dresses is that you can mix and match them to get many different looks. Take a bold, fun-patterned skirt, for example, and match it with a plain white T-shirt for a chic look, or pair a beautiful silk blouse with a pencil skirt and be ready to go. It's all about how you mix and match.

If you're like most women, you like certain parts of your body more than others. Because women have so many likes and dislikes, designers have created a plethora of skirt styles to fit any body type. The trick is (again) knowing what your best parts are, highlighting them, and choosing with confidence clothing that works best on you. Take skirt length, for example.

If your legs are skinny, you want to wear skirts that have hemlines ending at the widest part of your leg (your thighs) — in other words, miniskirts. This doesn't mean you can't wear other types of skirts; instead it means that a mini looks great on you. If, on the other hand, your legs are heavier, your hemline should hit the skinniest part of your leg, which is most likely somewhere below the knee, possibly even below the calf.

In addition to skirt length, you have skirt style to consider. Here are some of the most popular varieties:

- ✔ **A-line:** A-line skirts are snug at the waist, barely touch your hips and thighs, and widen as they approach the hem (see Figure 9-16). Usually their length is below the knee. They're a good look for pear-shaped women who are heavier in the hips and thighs and not flattering to women without much of a derriere. However, a large pattern can make an A-line more suitable for thin women.

- ✔ **Flared:** A flared skirt is an A-line with more material so that it swings and swishes about your lower legs as you walk, adding to the slimming effect (see Figure 9-16). A flare with an uneven hem, especially in a light-weight fabric like chiffon, draws the eye away from your hips even more.

- ✔ **Circle or peasant skirt:** With lots of material, these skirts hide everything! They're full length and very loose and drapey, as shown in Figure 9-16, so you really can't see any shape underneath. So girls, whether you want to appear larger or smaller, this skirt does the trick!

Figure 9-16: From left: A-line, flared, and circle skirts.

✔ **Straight skirt:** In a straight skirt, the material falls straight from the hip (see Figure 9-17). Larger women should have more length in their straight skirts, while thinner women look better if the skirt is shorter. If you're tall, you can pretty much get away with a straight skirt being long or short, but if you're shorter, showing more leg makes you appear taller. If you want to show off your curves, choose a straight skirt in a material that clings, like satin. Vertical details on the skirt, such as pinstripes or stitching, can add to the slimming effect.

✔ **Pencil skirt:** Like the straight skirt, the pencil skirt's material falls from the hip but is more fitted to the body to emphasize the hips (see Figure 9-17). These skirts aren't ideal for those who need camouflage. If you have small hips, a high waist makes you appear more curvy. Generally pencil skirts are knee length, but the shorter your torso, the shorter the skirt should be to add length to your legs. Normally pencil skirts are plain and monochromatic.

✔ **Tube skirt:** The tube skirt is like the pencil skirt but longer, sometimes all the way to the ankle (see Figure 9-17). In fact, the only way you can walk in a tube skirt is if the skirt has a slit. This isn't an easy look for most women to pull off because it is very fitted and clingy and shows everything on your lower half except for skin. Not to worry though, you don't see many of these skirts around!

   ✔ **Wrap skirt:** A wrap skirt, shown in Figure 9-17, can be long or short. If
     you get one that's the right length to flatter your legs, this type of skirt
     can look good on any body type. Like the wrap dress, you can adjust it
     to fit you perfectly.

Figure 9-17: From left: Straight, pencil, tube, and wrap skirts.

Slacks

Many women think skirts are sexier than pants. Are they? The answer is, not
always. Although a great pencil skirt can show off your curves and give you
a sophisticated, classic look, the right pair of slacks can do the same thing.
Find out how to choose your pants wisely in this section.

Length

The most distinguishing aspect of slacks, besides the material (discussed in
the later section "Pant material"), is length. Women have the choice between
pants that are full length, ankle length, or capri style, which can reach
anywhere from the calf almost all the way to the knee, where they actually
infringe on the territory claimed by shorts.

Pant length is measured not from the top of the waist, but from the bottom
of the crotch to the bottom of the pants leg. This measurement is called your
inseam. It's hard to measure your inseam yourself, but if you get help and keep
it noted somewhere, it can be a very helpful measurement to know when buying
slacks. (For information on other key measurements, refer to Chapter 3.)

The zakkerz

Are you one of those women who wear flats to work and then change to heels when you get there? How many times have you worn a pair of pants and ruined the bottom of them because they are just too long for flats? Well, I have found the invention for you! The zakkerz (www.zakkerz.com) is an item that you use to temporarily hem your pants without using stitches! To use the zakkerz, follow these steps (it works, trust me!):

1. **Roll pant leg up to desired length.**

2. **Wrap the zakkerz around the bottom of pant, with one end of zakkerz inside the pant leg and other end outside pant leg.**

   The magnets bring the two ends of the zakkerz together and hold the roll-up in place.

©Zakkerz, Inc. www.zakkerz.com

In determining the best length, keep these things in mind:

> ✔ **The type of shoes you're wearing:** The biggest problem women have with pant length is that their height changes depending on the shoes they wear. If your pants are full length, you always want them to hit the top of your shoe or foot, if you're wearing a sandal (see Figure 9-18).

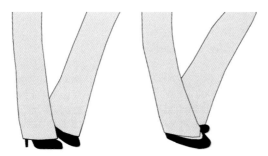

Figure 9-18: The correct hem length.

✔ **The area you want to highlight (for capris or pedal pushers):** Pedal pushers or capri pants are supposed to be short. But exactly where they fall can change your appearance. Ideally you want to show your legs off to their best advantage. If your legs are thin, your capris should end at your widest part, the middle of your calf, which adds breadth to your leg. If your legs are heavy, your capris should end just below the calf in order to highlight the thinnest part of your lower leg.

Pant rise

The *rise* of a pair of slacks is the distance between the crotch and the waist. Depending on your size, the rise for a normal pair of pants is usually around 10 or 11 inches. Low-rise pants (which have waists below the normal waist line) and high-waisted pants (which have rises higher than the normal waist line) have different rise lengths.

When you consider rise, don't be unduly swayed by the current fashion (such as when low-rise pants are all the rage). Instead, consider what looks good on your body type:

✔ **Short- versus long-waisted:** If you're a short-waisted person, you generally look better in a low-rise pair of pants, because they make your torso look longer. If you're long-waisted, a low-rise extends your torso even further — probably *not* what you want.

✔ **Apple versus pear:** Low-rise pants show off more of the belly. So the more belly you have (if you're an apple shape), the less appropriate a low-rise is for your shape because your goal is to minimize your midsection. (If low-rise is more comfortable for you to wear because it's less binding around the middle, by all means wear low-rise pants. Just make sure you wear a long top and/or jacket to cover and elongate the area.) If you're a pear and have a slim waist, you can wear low- or high-rise pants. Both accentuate your thin waist.

Pant legs

In addition to the height of the hem, the shape of the leg is also very important in determining what kind of pants look good on you (see Figure 9-19).

✔ **Straight leg:** A straight leg drops straight down from its widest point, which is the part that touches the hips. This look is flattering for every body type. The straight line doesn't accentuate the top or the bottom of the leg, nor does it attract the eye to any particular area.

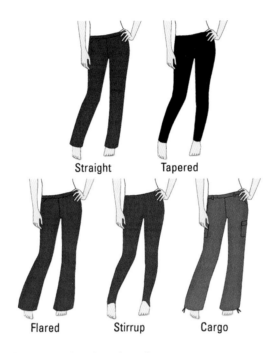

Figure 9-19: A variety of pant legs.

✔ **Tapered:** Tapered pants have a slight narrowing below the hips, all the way down to the ankle. Skinny pants are a style of tapered pants. The difference is that they hug your legs from top to bottom. These pants are better for those with skinny legs because they draw the focus to the legs, but because the pant leg gets narrower at the bottom, it accentuates the waist. If you don't want to accentuate your hips or waist area, avoid this style.

✔ **Flared:** Flared-leg pants widen toward the bottom. A slight flare is called a *boot cut,* meaning you can fit a tall boot under your pants. When the flare is extreme, it's called a *bell bottom.* This style is great if you're hippy or bigger in the waist area, because the flare draws attention to the lower leg. The width of the flare balances out the waistline and minimizes its appearance.

✔ **Stirrup:** These pants have a piece of elastic that extends under the foot. Originally for people who rode horses (the stirrup stops the pant leg from riding up), stirrup pants are also used in other sports, like skiing, where the same thing may happen.

✔ **Cargo pants:** These pants are especially popular as an alternative to jeans. Although traditionally they're not very dressy and are best meant for play time, some versions have been made in dressier materials and can be worn as such. Cargo pants have pockets on the side of the legs and are best suited for women with skinny legs, because the pockets tend to make you look wider.

Pant material

Pants can be made from any material, but certain materials have become closely associated with pants more than tops, mostly because of their durability. Pants get more wear and tear than tops, so they need to be able to stand up to all the activity.

Denim

The most ubiquitous pant material is denim, particularly blue denim. Blue jeans, originally made by Levi Strauss in the 19th century, started out as work pants and the material was made as sturdy as possible so that it would last. In the 1960s, jeans became part of the uniform of young people and then morphed into a piece of apparel that was worn by everyone.

Jeans have their own look, and people of every size and shape wear them. They are a great staple, and so many styles are available that you can definitely find a pair that suits your body type and flatters your figure. Styles include low-waisted, high-waisted, straight leg, skinny leg, flared leg — just make sure you get the right size (measured by waist size and inseam length) and choose the style that suits you. Jeans tend to be form-fitting and show off your legs. If that's not what you want, you probably won't choose jeans for every occasion. Most people, though, feel comfortable in them. Even if your jeans are for casual wear only, having a pair that fits you really well is a good idea.

If you're going to go with only one pair of jeans for the season, pick a pair of dark denim, boot cut jeans. Dark denim is the most versatile kind, and boot cut is a safe choice because it fits most women and can go with most looks.

Khakis

Khakis, or *chinos,* are made from a yellowish brown cotton twill fabric (refer to Chapter 4 for information on twill and other types of weaves). Khaki pants can range in color from olive green to a light tan. Like jeans, khakis have become a separate entity unto themselves. They're very preppy and can be worn to informal occasions and also to work. The same rules apply to khakis as to any other slacks: Choose a style that works for your body type.

10

Dressing for Success

Confidence is key.

Tommy Hilfiger, Fashion Designer

*E*ven though I consider myself a put-together person, whenever I do a segment on television, I am even more aware of what I look like and what I'm wearing. Of course, the content and the information I provide to viewers is the most important thing, but what I look like is also important. If I look disheveled, how on earth are viewers (including you, hopefully!) going to be able to concentrate, let alone trust, what I say? The same holds true in any profession. People who look put together give the impression that they have things under control and know what they're doing.

When you look put together, your overall confidence improves, and that in turn helps you be more successful at work. Makes perfect sense, right? A recent survey conducted by careerbuilder.com offers support: Of the employers surveyed, 41 percent said they tend to promote people who dress professionally. In this chapter, I discuss not only hemlines, but also how to help your bottom line.

Deciphering Office Dress Codes

You can wear various types of clothing in a business environment, but the key to climbing the ladder of success is understanding which style in your place of business makes that climb go smoothly and quickly. The following sections outline the different categories for business dress.

Business casual

With business casual, you have the freedom to be a little more stylish and a lot less conservative. Instead of the traditional business suits, you can wear pants, blouses, skirts, and dresses. These selections make business casual more comfortable and give you the opportunity to inject some more of your personal style.

If you're the slightest bit confused about what to wear as far as business casual, take a cue from the men in your office. If they're wearing khakis and polo shirts, you can use that as the standard, even though you don't want to wear exactly that. Your goal is to distinguish yourself in a way that makes you look both stylish and feminine. So instead of khakis, try sharp wool gabardine slacks or a pair of linen pants, and instead of a polo shirt, put on something more fitted that shows your curves without revealing any extra skin. Of course, if you do decide to wear khakis and a polo shirt (a preppy look), make sure the fit on each is a 10: The shirt should be fitted and in a feminine color (pink or another soft pastel), and the khakis can be capri length to show off your legs. Don't forget a great pair of shoes (ballet flats are always chic yet comfortable). Figure 10-1 shows how a pair of khaki pants and ballet flats can be a stylish yet comfortable outfit for work.

Dealing with some of the challenges

Business casual may be one of the most common forms of dress these days, but with no exact definition, getting dressed in the morning can be complicated. When you just had to choose from one of the five suits you owned, the limitation made choosing your outfit for the day a lot easier (shopping was a lot easier, too). Now that you have a lot more options (pants, blouses, skirts, and more), the selection process can be tricky. Following are some tips to help you adapt your business casual wardrobe when the need (or desire) arises:

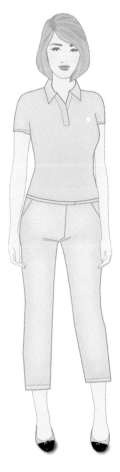

Figure 10-1: Business casual: Put together *and* comfortable.

> ✔ **Keep a few items in your office to throw on when you need to.** These items include a cardigan of neutral color and/or a scarf. Suppose you wear something to the office that's a little on the edgier side and you have a meeting with a client late in the day and need to tone it down.

You can throw on the sweater or tie the scarf around your neck for a more conservative look.

Keep a perfect pair of black pumps and a perfect pair of black flats at work, too. You'll be glad you have the flats if your feet are killing you, and if last minute plans come up, you can dress up your outfit with the black heels.

✔ **Even if your place of work doesn't require you to dress formally, show up decked out from time to time.** You'll feel great when people say "Wow, you look nice today!" It also helps people see you in a different light, which never hurts. And when people ask why the change (which you know some inevitably will), just say with confidence, "I felt like getting dressed up today."

✔ **You can be playful, but make sure it doesn't turn from playful to too sexy.** If you're wearing a tight skirt that rides up when you sit and you're in a business meeting, part of you will constantly worry about how much of your legs are showing instead of the subject matter being discussed. While you're tugging at your skirt, you could be missing an important point, and others in the room may notice that you're distracted. Plus any type of fidgeting often can be misinterpreted as anxiety or lack of preparedness. Why chance it?

Figure 10-2: Adding flair to business casual.

Accessorizing to add flair

Aside from wearing more comfortable clothing, business casual dress is an opportunity to wear clothes with more flair. A scarf, earrings, and a nice pair of sandals can totally transform your work look (see Figure 10-2).

Accessories can be a quick fix when trying to make an outfit pop. If you're wearing a simple outfit, you can use statement jewelry to express your personal style. A chunky necklace or chandelier earrings can dress up any outfit, but don't wear both — choose one or the other! Also don't underestimate the power of a belt. An outfit that is simple or even a little roomy around the midsection can be totally transformed with a great belt. Play around with it. If you do go the belt route, make sure you don't over accessorize. Earrings or a bracelet (or even a small necklace) is fine. But just one is likely enough!

Casual

From business casual we move to simply casual. The distinction between the two is slight, but important: Business casual doesn't incorporate jeans; casual can bring denim into the mix.

How casual you can go depends on the attitude of the office environment and the industry in which you work. In the fashion industry, a lot of the fashion PR companies tell their girls to dress casually. They want stylists to feel comfortable and relaxed when they walk in, so I often see women in jeans and funky tops, like the one shown in Figure 10-3. When I walk into a more corporate office environment, the look and feel is a little more formal and conservative.

In casual work situations, jeans have become the go-to item. Obviously, jeans come in countless varieties. Some jeans scream casual; others can be chic and appropriate. A beautiful pair of nicely fitted, dark denim jeans are always appropriate in a casual work situation. Try them with a sophisticated blouse or sweater set for the office. Faded jeans with holes in the knees, on the other hand, are an entirely different story. Save those for the weekend.

If you dress casually every day, invest in a few great pairs of jeans and quality blouses and sweater sets. With these basics in your closet, you can make jeans fashionable yet appropriate for work. A fabulous sweater with a great scarf or a statement belt (or even a bold cocktail ring) paired with jeans not only makes you stand out in

Figure 10-3: Done right, casual attire can be quite stylish.

the office, but it can also take you from day to night in a flash. Furthermore, if you're wearing jeans and casual clothing to work, make sure you have a few great pairs of heels and at least one fabulous work tote. These items help pull an outfit together and make you look "done."

Going casual without overstepping the bounds

Casual clothing can be very tricky for women, especially during hot weather. Baring too much skin can become too sexy and provocative, which can create problems that can affect your work and work environment.

Are shorts ever okay? That's a tough question. The easiest answer is a simple no, but there may be times when shorts are okay. First, never wear shorts to work unless you work in a very (and I mean *very)* casual environment. Second, if you're going to break this rule, wear a pair of tailored shorts that hit right above the knee and pair it with a sweater set or blouse (see Figure 10-4).

Because shorts tend to be a very casual look, you can wear them with ballet flats or flat sandals, or, if you want to take it up a notch, you can wear them with heels.

Most firms that allow casual clothing do have some restrictions. Even if the policy is "anything goes," you must remember to always dress appropriately. Take cues from your co-workers. Often your supervisor sets the tone. See what the appropriate level of dress is in your office, and add your personal flair to those clothes. For general expectations about any work attire, head to the later section "Universal rules for all kinds of business dress." It's always better to be a little overdressed than underdressed. You can never go wrong if you follow this advice. In fact, people will end up looking to you to set the standard.

Figure 10-4: Long, tailored shorts paired with a blouse and heels can be casual yet chic.

Business conservative

Conservative business attire for women is a variation on the suit and tie requirement for men. You may wonder whether pant suits are as acceptable as suits with skirts. The answer is yes. A suit in almost any color (I would stay away from white in a work setting) paired with a blouse, camisole, or shell always looks professional and put together.

Be sure to put your own style into this look. If you love jewelry, try adding a bold necklace or earrings. Make sure your necklace lays properly and falls in the right place and doesn't compete with the neckline of your top or suit jacket. And keep the earrings on the smaller side or just wear studs (you don't want your earrings to make you look like you're going out for a night on the town).

Getting that polished look

Business formal for the woman who wants to look fashionable means being both professional and polished. To accomplish that, do the following:

- ✔ **Buy nicer quality suits.** You may not want to spend a fortune on the suits you wear to the office, but you do spend a huge portion of your time at work and in those suits. For that reason, spending a little more money to feel and look great is a good investment.

- ✔ **Stick with suits in darker colors.** You can tell more easily the quality of the material when the color is lighter. So if you're buying a suit that's not of the highest quality, it will be less noticeable in a darker color, which is why most people default to buying black.

- ✔ **Make sure that whatever you wear fits properly.** If you need to, spend a little more to get your suits altered.

- ✔ **Keep your suits in great condition.** Dry-clean them whenever necessary (do both jacket and pants or skirt together to keep the colors on both pieces looking the same) and possibly invest in a home steamer for last minute touch ups. You don't have to dry-clean every time you wear a suit. I recommend just steaming it for the second wearing. Depending on how grueling your work days are, you can usually get away with wearing a suit two to three times before dry-cleaning it.

- ✔ **Make sure that every item you wear complements the other items.** Haphazardly throwing together your bag, blouse, and shoes projects an overall look of disorganization. Everything you wear from your coat to your scarf to your shoes, must (in some way) work together.

- ✔ **Make sure your coat and briefcase (or work bag or tote) are as polished and refined as you are.** What you look like when you enter and leave the building can leave a lasting impression. Nothing is worse than a fabulous woman in a great suit with the wrong outerwear. It's like a great present with the wrong wrapping.

Being prepared for emergencies

To keep up your polished appearance, be prepared for emergencies because accidents do happen. If your hose or tights catch on your desk and rip, make sure you have another pair on hand so that you can dash to the ladies room before that big meeting. (Nail polish or hairspray also prevents a run from spreading.) And because winter time means static, keep static guard handy in case your skirt clings to your legs. A lint remover is another handy thing to have close by. For clothing rips, a piece of tape on the inside can keep you going for the rest of the day.

A convenient and relatively inexpensive way to be ready for any accident is to buy a Shemergency Survival Kit (see Figure 10-5). It holds mini-versions of everything you need in the event of a fashion emergency: folding hairbrush, hair spray, emery board, nail clipper, nail polish, nail polish remover, static remover, breath freshener, safety pin, shoe shine wipes, dental floss, pain reliever, double-sided tape, deodorant wipes, tampon, adhesive bandages, facial tissues. Can you believe it — all these items fit into this hand size pouch and the whole thing costs only $20! You can find one at www.msandmrs.com.

©Georgette Kaplan, Shemergency Survival Kit™ by Ms. & Mrs.

Figure 10-5: The Shemergency Survival Kit.

Letting your style stand out

Even if the attire is more formal at your place of work, you can still dress appropriately while expressing your personal style. To dress up a suit, a sweater set, or a simple blouse and look sharp and stylish while still maintaining a more formal look, use the following suggestions:

✔ **Wear statement jewelry:** Statement jewelry is a great way to make a simple suit stand out (and it can also work as a talking point). If you wear a bold necklace, bracelet, ring, or earrings, someone is likely to say, "I love that! Where did you get it?" This may strike up a conversation with a co-worker you've never had interaction with before. It may sound silly, but that's how relationships start sometimes!

✔ **Wear something other than pumps, if allowed.** If you're in a conservative environment, pumps are definitely the safe way to go, but if you have some leeway, sandals are a great way to express your style. If you're required to wear hose, wear a closed-toe shoe, no matter the season. Look to the women in higher positions to see what's acceptable in terms of shoes and hosiery. (For more on these topics, head to Chapters 14 and 16.)

✔ **Have fun with your hair.** Changing your hairstyle every so often can give you a new look without having to go out and buy a new wardrobe. Just always make sure your style looks clean and neat.

If your hair covers your face or your bangs get in your eyes, your hair will be seen as an encumbrance to working most effectively. Need a stylish solution? Put your hair back in a sleek low ponytail or loose bun (see Figure 10-6).

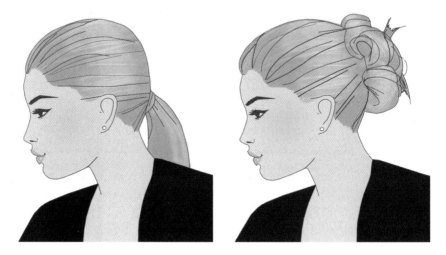

Figure 10-6: Two perfectly acceptable hairstyles in any office setting.

You always want to feel and look your best, but remember to keep your audience in mind. Your goal is to wear what you're comfortable in and also make the person or people you're meeting with feel like you're on the same page. In a work situation, you want to make the people you're meeting with feel confident in your abilities. The way you look has a huge impact on how they perceive you before you even say a word. So if you're meeting someone who's on the more conservative side, dress more conservatively. If you're meeting with someone you know is on the trendier side, grab that trendy bag (or pair of shoes) you've been dying to wear.

Universal rules for all kinds of business dress

Understanding exactly what a business's dress code is (and consistency in enforcing such a code) would certainly take some of the guessing out of what to wear to work. But some types of dress don't fly in most offices. In the same careerbuilder.com survey, 64 percent of employers said they banned flip-flops, 49 percent said no to miniskirts, and 28 percent didn't allow jeans.

Whether dress code rules are written down in your office or not, certain guidelines are pretty universal:

- ✔ **Whatever you wear to work, make sure it's neat.** No wrinkles or tears. If you have a pair of capri pants, but you're not sure they're appropriate, try ironing them. Being crisp and neat may put them over the edge from unacceptable to acceptable.

- ✔ **If one part of your outfit may be pushing the envelope, pair it with something conservative.** A sleeveless blouse, for example, can be acceptable when you wear it with a conservative skirt.

- ✔ **Stay away from showing too much cleavage or wearing something too revealing.** Tops made of translucent or wispy material are inappropriate, unless you wear a tank or camisole underneath it. And if you find yourself wondering, "Is this too much cleavage?" it's too much. While showing cleavage can be sexy and appropriate in the evening, it's unnecessary and distracting in the office. Worse, it can undermine the impression of professionalism you want to exude. That doesn't mean you can't wear a blouse with buttons or a V-neck, just err on the side of more conservative in the office.

Dressing for Off-site Work Events

Some people travel all the time — the road warriors — while others rarely leave the office. If you're going on a quick jaunt that doesn't require an overnight stay, your challenge is to try to keep your clothes looking fresh after you've been on the road for a few hours. On longer trips, you have a variety of challenges, like what to wear on the plane, what's appropriate attire for the various activities and venues you may be at, and how to pack everything you need.

Looking stylish en route

You may be tempted to wear just any old thing on the plane (or bus or train) and change at the hotel, but I advise against it. First, lost luggage or a delayed flight can end up causing a problem. Second, you should always look your best while flying because you never know who you may meet (yes, I know I sound like your mother). The trick for dressing for the flight is to find clothing that is stylish, comfortable, and resistant to wrinkles. Some materials that fit the bill are

- **Wool and silk:** These fibers (refer to Chapter 4) have natural elasticity, which helps keep them from wrinkling.

- **Synthetic fabrics:** Fabrics such as nylon and polyester are less prone to wrinkling.

- **Fabrics that use finishing agents designed to reduce wrinkles:** Textile manufacturers began to add finishing agents to their cloths that change the chemical structure in such a way as to make fabrics that once wrinkled easily, like cotton, wrinkle free. When purchasing garments for travel, look for pieces that say they're wrinkle resistant *and* still 100 percent cotton. Some wrinkle resistant garments aren't all cotton, but cotton polyester blends.

- **Knits:** Knits wrinkle much less than woven fabrics, so anything that's a cable, ribbed, tricot, or jersey knit will remain wrinkle free. If you roll knits instead of folding them when you pack, they come out of your suitcase wrinkle and fold free.

The Donna M clothing line (www.bbydonnam.com) sells something called the 5 Piece Wardrobe (see Figure 10-7). Most of the items are under $100, and you can mix and match them hundreds of different ways. The pieces are comfortable, don't wrinkle, and will take you from day to night in a flash. I wear them whenever I fly.

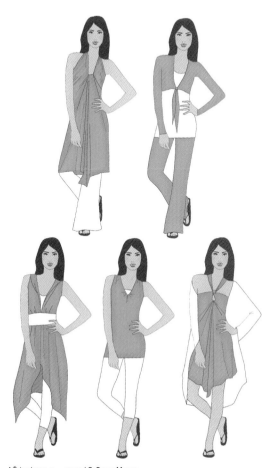

b® *by donna.m — www.bByDonnaM.com*

Figure 10-7: The Donna M 5 Piece Wardrobe is perfect for travel

Wrinkles can get you coming and going. So pay attention to how you look from the rear as well as the front. If your pants are creased in the back or the label on your blouse is sticking up, you may make a good first impression but a lousy parting one. So check both the front and back in a mirror before you head to that meeting.

Daytime casual

Daytime casual varies from industry to industry and from state to state. What you may wear to a luncheon in New York among people in finance is different from what you'd wear to a meeting in Los Angeles with people in the film industry. Most businesses have their own definitions of daytime casual. Unless you've been to a particular event or a place many times before, play it safe and slightly overdress. Better to feel a little uncomfortable because you're slightly overdressed than to feel very uncomfortable because you're underdressed.

One way to handle this type of dilemma is to dress in layers or use versatile accessories. If you're wearing a jacket and no one else is, simply take the jacket off and you'll fit right in. A silk scarf worn around your neck can make an outfit seem more formal. If it makes you seem *too* formal, you can simply take it off.

When you're away from the office, sharing a meal with your colleagues is very common. If you know ahead of time where you're dining, check out the restaurant's Web site to get an idea of how formal or casual it is. That way, you're prepared for each scenario.

If you travel for business, you'll probably try to pack as few clothes as possible so that you don't have to check your luggage. Convenient, yes, but it means you won't have a spare blouse or skirt to change into if the one you're wearing gets stained. Some materials are more stain resistant than others, and for those pieces that need more protection, you can use Scotchgard. Taking such garments on trips can be a good form of stain insurance. A quick and easy alternative, though, is to use a Tide Stain Stick, which removes stains on the spot. (I use my stain stick all the time!) Simply take off the cap and press down on the tip to release the stain fighter directly onto the stain. (Use caution depending on the material and item you're wearing.)

Daytime conservative

Some business trips or events require you to get dressed up. Perhaps you're a lawyer going to court or pitching a new business to a firm. For men, the decision of what to wear is fairly easy because the key word is *conservative*. For women, dressing conservatively is a bit more vague. While dressing more conservatively used to mean wearing a skirt rather than pants, that's no longer the case.

A suit (pants or skirt) always works well. Alternatively, a pencil skirt paired with a blouse or sweater set and accessories works in almost any setting. What about a dress instead of a suit? Yes, as long as it's a simple dress (especially with a blazer over it) — no cocktail or sexy dresses! It doesn't need to be black, but it should be conservative in color; a conservative print is fine, too. Even a sleeveless dress that hits below the knee is perfectly okay.

Each situation is different, but the old way of thinking — that a woman must wear a suit for a presentation or big meeting — is antiquated. The key is to know your audience. And if you don't, you're better off being as conservative as possible. No one will fault you for being too conservative, but if you're not conservative enough, someone may immediately judge you as a person who doesn't "get it"— a group you never want to be in!

Feeling confident is so important, and finding the right mix between dressing appropriately and dressing with confidence is the ultimate goal in any situation. Even if you have to dress conservatively, it's sometimes fun (and appropriate) to switch it up. So pack a colorful scarf and some dangly earrings, and if it seems like you can get away with standing out a bit, go for it.

Evening casual

It's always good to feel like you're wearing the right thing from the second you walk in, but evening casual gets a little tricky. A cocktail party could be at the fanciest hotel in town or a pub down the block. A trip to a ballgame could be in the stands or in a company box with a waiter in a tux. Following are some suggestions:

- ✔ **The little black dress (LBD):** You can rarely go wrong with the LBD (see Chapter 7) and a pair of perfect pumps. It's the perfect solution if you know you're going out after work straight away. To work, wear the dress with a blazer, pumps, and work tote; for evening, simply take off the blazer, switch out your shoes and bag, and add some dressy jewelry (see Figure 10-8).

- ✔ **Statement jewelry:** Adding bold jewelry is a great way to make your outfit more exciting.

- ✔ **A suit with something pretty underneath:** An outfit like this takes you from day to night and is the perfect solution if you know you're going out after work straight away. If you wear a pant suit with a pretty blouse or tank underneath, you can go from your business meeting to a cocktail party simply by removing the jacket.

Figure 10-8: With the right basics, you can easily go from work wear to social wear.

Of course the final decision about what to wear depends on the activity involved. Dinner at a barbeque restaurant obviously rules out your LBD. There is nothing wrong (by the way) in saying to a co-worker you trust, "What are you wearing tonight?"

Evening fancy

A business black-tie affair is not a wedding or a party with friends, where you may want to show off your fabulous back or beautiful cleavage. Leave that look for your next big *social* event. At a business event, even one where you need to dress to the nines, keep your outfit stylish but work-appropriate at the same time (see Figure 10-9). Following are some guidelines:

✔ **Don't wear anything too revealing.** "Too revealing" is anything that implies sexy, especially when it comes to cleavage, though in some situations, you also want to make sure your upper arms and back are covered, too. If you decide to wear something that you have in your closet already but that may be too revealing on top, a wrap is always a great solution. It covers you up a bit while maintaining a pulled together and, depending on the wrap, dressy look. Many kinds of wraps are available, some with beading, that are perfect for evening wear.

✔ **Choose an outfit that's relatively easy to put on.** You may not have a lot of time to change. If you have business meetings during the day, the meeting may run longer than expected. If you don't have a female associate with you to zip you up, you'd better wear something that you can get in and out of on your own.

Figure 10-9: An outfit that's elegant without being too sexy.

✔ **Make sure whatever you take looks great once it comes out of your suitcase.** A great trick to get rid of wrinkles is to turn your shower on hot and close the bathroom door. The steam from the shower helps take out any wrinkles and generally freshens up your outfit.

Your gown should be modest but it doesn't have to be dowdy. Take advantage of embellishments like beading, embroidery, rhinestones, velvet, and metallic pieces to give your look some sparkle. Make sure that you have a matching evening clutch because, again, everything should be fabulous like you. Buying a great silver or gold clutch to keep in your wardrobe is always a good idea as it can work with many different outfits.

All these warnings don't mean that when you go out with co-workers, you can't show a different side of yourself. Business black-tie affairs are prime opportunities to let co-workers see glimpses of what you're like outside of the office (which is often interesting and fun). But you have to walk a fine line. If you have any question about whether something will work, don't wear it. It's better not to test the water until you know for sure.

If you don't have a great work-appropriate formal dress and you're just finding your personal style, a black cocktail dress is always a safe bet and works well for many occasions. Choose one with a conservative neckline that doesn't show cleavage. Some good options include a basic round neck, a square neck, or a boat neck (Chapter 9 describes the different kinds of necklines). Sleeveless can work if you pair it with a shawl or shrug that you can remove if appropriate.

Packing for a Business Trip

When you pack for a vacation or a weekend getaway, you usually have the luxury of packing more than you need. If you can't decide between the strappy sandals and sparkly sling-backs, you can pack both and decide later. Packing for a business trip is an entirely different thing. Your goal is to pack the most functional clothing into the least amount of space because if you can avoid having to check your luggage, all the better.

You've seen the road warriors. They travel differently than everybody else. First, they're usually carrying around a lot of electronic equipment, heaviest of all being their laptop computer and battery pack. Second, they almost never check their luggage (see Figure 10-10). They manage to fit everything into a carry-on.

Yes, packing everything you need into one case is a challenge, but it's a must for an overnight trip. And it's completely doable. Here's how:

✔ **Wear the clothing that's going to take up the most room in your luggage.** If a blazer is required, wear it on board. You can probably hang it up once you're on the plane. If you're flying from a warm climate to a colder one, wear your overcoat and stick it in the overhead compartment when you get on the plane. If you absolutely need two pairs of shoes, wear the one that would take up the most luggage space (which are hopefully the ones that are more comfortable).

✔ **Roll, rather than fold, your clothing.** As I said earlier, knits make great travel clothes because they can be rolled up without wrinkling. In fact, any type of clothing generally accumulates less wrinkles when rolled. Clothes made with spandex or polyester blends throw off wrinkles no matter how you pack them. (These fabrics are good not only for packing, but also for sitting in long meetings.)

Figure 10-10: Ready for a business trip.

✔ **Make sure everything you take can be mixed and matched.** If you're going for two days, you need to pack only one and a half outfits rather than two. Black is an especially good color to wear because it doesn't show any stains that may splash your way.

✔ **Choose things that you can wear multiple times.** If you have a pair of straight-legged black pants and a black pencil skirt (which has less fabric so packs easier) and a pair of black pumps, all you need are a couple of monochromatic tops and you can go for quite a few days that way.

✔ **Choose lighter rather than heavier clothing.** Because it may be cold on the plane and many airlines no longer give blankets, a cardigan is a good idea because it can also substitute for a jacket. Instead of bringing jeans to lounge in your room (if you don't plan to wear them when you're not working), take along a pair of lightweight sweat pants instead. They take up less space.

Though more companies are cutting their travel budgets these days, business travelers will never completely disappear. If you find yourself one of them, don't allow being on the road make you any less fashionable.

Très Chic: Threads for Special Occasions

"The sexiest thing on a woman is a little black dress."

Tyson Beckford, Model/TV Personality

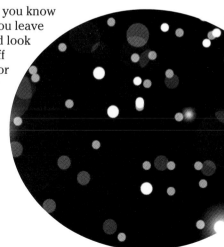

If you've been reading this book straight through, you know by now that I want you to feel like a 10 anytime you leave the house. When you head to the market, you should look put together in your sweats or jeans. When you're off to work, you should look and feel like you're ready for a productive day. And when you're getting ready for a special occasion, well, the fabulous *you* better be ready for a fabulous night out!

In this chapter, I explain the differences between white tie, black tie, and cocktail attire; how to dress for holidays and weddings; and how to shop for whatever else you may have coming up that falls in between!

Evening Wear

How many times have you received an invitation in the mail and said to yourself, "What am I going to wear to *this!?*" Well, we've all been there, excited for an occasion but less than thrilled about deciding what to wear to it —

especially when you don't quite know the fashion rules that apply to the different types of events, be they white tie, black tie, cocktail, or something in between. It can be confusing and the rules are a bit subjective, but I steer you in the right direction in this section.

In real estate, the key phrase is location, location, location. When deciding what to wear for an evening out, the same phrase applies. When picking out your attire, you have to keep in mind *where* you're going and who your audience is.

Dressing for a cocktail party

Cocktails anyone? Now we're talking my language! A cocktail party can celebrate many different occasions. Some people hold cocktail parties just for the fun of it while others center this type of party around birthdays, anniversaries, promotions, and so on. A typical cocktail party usually starts somewhere between 6:00 and 9:00 p.m. and lasts for a couple of hours. Light food — a selection of hors d'oeuvres, for example — is served, but not a sit-down dinner, hence the name *cocktail party!*

What should you wear to a cocktail party? This type of event is much more casual than a black-tie event but dressier than a dinner out with friends. The following can clear up any confusion you have about cocktail attire.

Figure 11-1: A dress that hits right below the knee is always a safe bet for a cocktail party.

✔ **Dress length:** If you wear a dress, cocktail length is the way to go (obviously). That means that your dress should hit your leg right below the knee, as shown in Figure 11-1. But because there are no strict rules when it comes to a cocktail party, if you have fab legs, feel free to wear a shorter dress. How short should you go? With a cocktail party, you have a lot of leeway. How short you can go depends on a few things. Is it business or purely social? When it's business, it's still safe to wear something above the knee as long as it's not a mini, but if you have doubts, always err on the longer side. If it's purely social, use your judgment. In this case you can get away with something shorter.

For cocktail parties, you aren't limited to cocktail dresses. If you feel more comfortable in a two-piece outfit, go that route. For example, a sequin skirt paired with a beautiful cashmere sweater is perfect cocktail attire (see Figure 11-2). You can also go with a beautiful pair of slacks and a dressy blouse. Wear what you look best in. "Cocktail attire" is a looser term than "black tie." You've got room to play around, so play!

✔ **Color:** What is the appropriate color to wear to a cocktail party? Well, that depends on where the function is and on what day of the week. A little black dress always works. But if you're always in your LBD, try to get away from that. If you're heading to a work cocktail party at 6:00 p.m. on a Tuesday, I suggest sticking with more neutral tones in a fabric, like wool or silk, that's not shiny; avoid the red strapless satin dress. If, on the other hand, you're going to your best friend's home on a Saturday night for a soiree, go for it! No colors are off-limits, as long as you're season appropriate. (See Chapter 5 for more on color.)

✔ **Accessories:** Obviously, the accessories you choose depends on what dress you decide to wear. I love wearing simple dresses and switching up my accessories. Bold statement necklaces or chandelier earrings always complete an otherwise plain-looking dress. If your

Figure 11-2: Cocktail dresses aren't required at cocktail parties.

dress already has a lot of embellishment, go simple with the accessories. Fun, fun, fun. This is the type of event where you can really express your personal style, especially with the right statement piece.

If you question what to wear, don't be afraid to ask other women whose style you trust and who are attending the same event. Other partygoers may offer some clues as to what is the most appropriate thing to wear. Maybe one of them has been to this venue or knows the crowd better than you do and can give you guidance. For example, if the event you're going to involves a more mature crowd, you may want to dress a bit more conservatively. If you're heading to a soiree with a crowd you know well and are comfortable with, your outfit can take a sexier turn! Remember, if someone is inviting you to a cocktail party, they want you to have fun. So have fun!

If you have a lot of cocktail parties or other events coming up and are on a tight budget, buy one classic dress in a neutral color. You can switch up the shoes, accessories, and clutch and create many different looks. Also, don't forget the power of a shawl. A beautifully made, adorned wrap can take a dress from simple to sizzling in a flash! Figure 11-3 shows how a dress can take on a different look.

Figure 11-3: Changing accessories and adding a shawl can change the look of a dress.

Attending a black-tie affair

So you're heading to a black-tie affair. Should be fun, right? Is someone getting married? Are you attending a bat or bar mitzvah? Is your loved one being honored for being fabulous? Whatever the occasion, I assume you know it's black-tie, because, well, the invitation says so.

Men are lucky when the invite says "Black Tie" because they pretty much know what to wear: A tuxedo of some sort is the *dress du jour.* The only big choice a man has to make is what tie or cummerbund to wear! Women, on the other hand, face a multitude of choices. Do you wear a floor length, tea length (one that hits mid-calf; see Figure 11-4), or cocktail length dress (one that hits just below the knee). Do you choose a black dress or take a chance with a bright color? Do you wear your hair up or let your hair down (so to speak). Time of day, location, and the nature of the event are just a few of the factors you must take into account when deciding on the *big* pick.

Don't stress out yet! Here's the good news. When an invitation says "Black Tie," the person or people throwing the party are pretty much telling you how they want you to look. They want you dressed to the nines! A long dress is the safe choice for an affair of this magnitude, but going shorter (as I mentioned) is no longer a faux pas. Similarly, wearing that fabulous long black number is totally appropriate, but it's also acceptable to redefine, within boundaries, what black tie looks like. While I'd advise against whipping out that sexy dress from New Year's Eve, you can, for most black-tie occasions, choose a dress with color or adornments that highlight your personal style. Next time you're perusing the racks for that perfect dress, keep these ideas in mind because you *are* allowed to have fun when dressing up — I promise!

Here are some pointers for choosing an outfit for a black-tie affair:

✔ **Know your audience.** If the person or people hosting the event are more conservative, follow suit. You can never go wrong with a simple, floor length dress when attending a black-tie affair.

Black-tie attire can range from conservative to whimsical. For example, a couple I'm close with had a black-tie wedding on a Saturday night, and I debated what to wear to it. The couple is very edgy and far from conservative, so I knew I could play around with my black-tie look. I chose a cocktail length, midnight blue dress — did I mention my fab accessories? I loved it. It was perfect for *that* wedding.

Figure 11-4: Show your personal style when picking what to wear to a black-tie event.

- ✔ **Pay attention to the event's timing.** A black-tie event on the weekend is often dressier than a black-tie event held during the week.

- ✔ **Have fun!** Make sure your personal style shows when you saunter into your event. Confidence is key!

If you plan to wear that long black dress you have already worn to an occasion with the same group of people, switch it up: Buy a big statement necklace or earrings to serve as the centerpiece of that look. If First Lady Michelle Obama can repeat an outfit, so can you!

Tuxes for women

Yves Saint Laurent was the first to show women in tuxedos. The year was 1962, and since then, many designers have shown women in either full tuxes or outfits with a tuxedo motif. But it's definitely a daring selection for most occasions. My advice? Unless you know your audience is one that is on the edgier side, and you feel totally comfortable in one, stay away from the female version of tuxes! True, megastar Rihanna did get a lot of play for wearing a black Dolce & Gabbana suit to the Met Costume Institute Gala in 2009, but, hey, she's Rihanna!

White-tie affairs: The most formal of all

A white-tie affair is the most formal event you can attend. State dinners at the White House and similar high status locations distinguish themselves by being extra formal — that is, white tie. Most people never attend an event of this stature (I never have). But knowing what's expected is important, just in case your invitation comes in the mail!

White-tie events are more formal than black-tie events, and a long gown is always a must (see Figure 11-5). As I said, many white-tie events are state dinners, when the head of state of one country visits another. But other occasions may also call for white-tie dress, such as fancy balls or cotillions. And of course, any group that wants to be very formal can host a white-tie event (although this is very rare).

Because of the formal nature of these events, there are certain expectations regarding attire. The dress for a white-tie evening is not only an evening gown, but a rather modest one. Bare shoulders are generally not acceptable, and women often wear opera length gloves (reaching up the arm just past the elbow, usually made of satin). Silk or satin shawls are usually worn as well. One exception: A woman from a foreign country attending a state dinner may wear the dressiest clothing representative of her country, such as a sari for a woman from India.

If you find yourself with an invitation to a white-tie affair, bring me as a date! Seriously, if you're heading to this type of affair, there is no room for error. Rules must be followed.

Figure 11-5: Attending a white-tie affair? Follow the strict dress code.

Dressing for the Holidays

There are two schools when it comes to dressing for the holidays. Some people like to wear items to commemorate the season: Santa Claus sweaters, socks with dreidels, and other items with a seasonal feel. Now I don't want to sound like the Grinch, but if you're going this route, I suggest you do it minimally (especially if you're leaving the house). The only way to pull off this look in style is to pick one gimmicky item and make it the focal point of your outfit. Everything else you wear should be a solid color and nothing else should have details.

Another way to commemorate the holidays is to go in a subtle direction. You can wear seasonal colors and materials that give off a holiday vibe. This section shows you how to be the life of the party without looking like the centerpiece!

Wearing holiday colors

A great way to celebrate the holidays is to wear the season's colors. You can still look the part without shouting out the particular holiday you're enjoying by doing the following:

Figure 11-6: Sequins can give you holiday style without the gimmick.

- ✔ **Mix holiday colors with neutral ones.** Pick one color (red or green for Christmas or, if you celebrate Chanukah, blue or silver) and pair that color with a complementary one. For Thanksgiving, maybe try a top in the pumpkin or cranberry family. No matter your faith or the type of holiday you're celebrating, the goal is the same: Stay festive while remaining stylish.

   If you don't look good in the colors of the season, don't wear them. Stay true to your style, your color scheme, and your body type.

- ✔ **Try accessories.** An alternative to wearing a color representative of a particular holiday is to pick an accessory that gives you the same feel. Chandelier earrings that sparkle will put you right in the mix with other partygoers. For more on accessories, head to the section "Accessorizing holiday-style."

You can get a dressier holiday look by wearing a sweater or dress with sequins, beading, or paillettes, which give you the sparkle and the festive feel without the gimmick (see Figure 11-6). These choices are sophisticated and appropriate for everything from a holiday dinner to the office holiday party.

Holiday dress styles

What dress styles are acceptable for the holidays? Good question! As always, your LBD is acceptable, as is your favorite cocktail dress. But you have other alternatives to play around with, too.

If you love your shoulders, try an asymmetrical or strapless dress. If you love your legs, try a shorter dress with a higher neckline. If you want to show a little cleavage (and I stress *a little*), try something with a plunging neckline. Whatever your preference, just pick a dress that's made with a winter-like material and in a color that's seasonally appropriate. Now of course "winter-like" material is different depending on what part of the country you're in. If you live in New York, go with velvet or satin. If you're spending winter galli-vanting in Miami (lucky you!), you can wear a silk-satin or chiffon number.

If you choose to go the short route, make sure you don't push the envelope. If you have any doubt that your dress is too short, it is. Always err on the longer side. Sexy is *really* sexy when only one part of your body is on display. If you're showing a little cleavage, don't wear a short dress. If you're wearing a short dress, don't wear something low cut. You never want to be the girl in the revealing dress that everyone is talking about for all the wrong reasons.

Choosing materials that give a holiday vibe

Delving a little deeper into materials appropriate for the holidays, certain fabrics make you think "party" as soon as you see them. For example, a blazer with satin lapels is understated yet celebratory because of the extra shine provided by the satin. Velvet and cashmere give you that same holiday feel because they provide an added sense of luxury. I go skiing for the holidays. After a day on the slopes, my favorite thing to do is lounge around in my cash-mere sweater and pants (which I invested in eight years ago and still have) and drink hot chocolate. Cozy, right? What's great about wearing materials that are holiday-like is that you probably have many items sitting in the back of your closet that, when paired with the right things, will work perfectly.

During the holidays, you can wear an outfit that's a little more dramatic. For example, a black velvet pant suit may be too much to wear to just any old event in the winter, but at a holiday party, the same pant suit paired with a simple tank and fun jewelry makes you queen of the night. Any other night you'd put the blazer with jeans or the pants with a blouse. Bottom line: It's all about how you put your outfit together.

Patent leather is another holiday staple (in fact, the material is so versatile it should be in your closet year round). Patent leather shoes, handbags, and belts are all items that make an outfit pop. The trick is to pick one piece to add to what you're already wearing. For example, if you plan to wear a velvet blazer with jeans, grab a white button-down shirt, silver chandelier earrings, and a pair of black patent pumps, and you're instantly holiday chic (see Figure 11-7).

Patent leather shows scuff marks more readily than other materials, so avoid the lighter colors where scuffs are more obvious. Bad shiny shoes can ruin even the most stylish outfit.

Accessorizing holiday style

A way to look chic without wearing holiday-obvious clothing is to shimmer with metallic accents. A great way to do this is with silver and gold jewelry. The good thing is you likely already have pieces that you can combine to make a holiday statement. Here's some advice based on questions I get all the time:

- ✔ **"Does brown (or black or any other particular color) go with gold or silver earrings?"** Here's the deal: Any solid color can go with yellow gold, silver, white gold, or platinum. You run into a problem when you get into a top or a dress that already has embellishments. Almost 100 percent of the time (and I say "almost" because there are *always* exceptions in life), you should wear an accessory that matches what is highlighted in the dress. If your dress has gold paillettes around the neckline, a simple gold hoop works best.

- ✔ **"Is it okay to mix metals?"** The answer is yes, yes, yes! Don't be afraid to mix your gold and silver necklaces. Different length chains (and even ones with charms or lockets), when mixed correctly, can be chic and festive. Experiment with what you have. You'll be surprised how you can reinvent jewelry you've had for years.

Figure 11-7: A sophisticated, festive look.

Jewelry is not the only way to accessorize for the holidays. A shawl with metallic accents is very chic. So are metallic colored shoes and handbags. Again, the key is to not overdo it. If you're wearing all black, try pairing gold sandals and a gold clutch with your outfit. (Metallics are considered neutral, so use them instead of basic black to spruce up your wardrobe.) I'm also a huge fan of *small* hair accessories! (Did I say "small" in a strong enough way?) I often wear low buns with a very small studded bobby pin on the side. You almost don't see the bobby pin, but when you do, it becomes a conversation piece. Another trick is to take a festive brooch you've had forever and pin it to a clutch. I also do this with jean jackets (on the pocket).

Open-toe shoes in winter — yes or no?

It's perfectly fine to have your feet exposed during the winter. Here's a little guidance to help you determine if open-toe is the way to go:

✔ **Let common sense be your guide.** If you think you'll be outside for an extended period of time, go with a shoe that keeps you warmer. But if you're out in the elements only long enough to get in and out of the car, you can wear a sandal during the holidays whatever the climate.

✔ **When you wear open-toe sandals in the winter, stick with darker colors that have more of a wintery feel.** Keep brights, pastels, and light colored shoes packed up until spring and summer come around! Black, gold, and silver are acceptable year round.

✔ **If you wear an open-toe shoe or sandal, go sans stockings.** For more on hosiery do's and don'ts, head to Chapter 14.

The holidays are a time that you should really have fun with what you wear. Don't forget you can make a statement with any article of clothing you put on your body. If you're set on wearing that little black dress, how about pairing a great pair of heels with it? Nothing says "Happy Holidays!" like a great pair of red stilettos! Have fun, don't be too theme-y, and be sexy! No matter your age, when you feel great, you'll enjoy yourself more — trust me!

What to Wear to a Wedding

Chances are you've opened a wedding invitation, seen the requested attire, and said to yourself, "I have nothing to wear to this!" Well, you're not alone. Nowadays, with all the different types of weddings, who can keep up? When it comes to a wedding, many variables affect what you should and shouldn't wear. The following sections go into more detail, but it all boils down to these two key factors:

✔ **The couple whose wedding you're attending:** Take into account the bride and groom's personality and adopt their vibe into your personal style. If the bride wants you to look "hot" because she has a great friend she wants to fix you up with, then opt for a sexier dress. If the couple is more conservative, better to err on that side and go with a more conservative dress. If the couple is more relaxed, you can get away with having some fun with your look. Bottom line: Respect the couple hosting the affair and choose something that expresses your style while staying within the boundaries of what's appropriate.

✔ **The location of the wedding:** Consider the location and setting of the wedding. If you're heading to an outdoor barbeque in the summer, you can never go wrong with a nice sundress and flat sandals. A formal wedding in a cathedral requires something more formal.

The following sections go into more details.

Type of attire specified on the invitation

Many invitations specify a type of attire, but even when you open the envelope and the invite spells it out for you, you're still left wondering, "What am I going to wear?" The following helps you decipher what is what when it comes to wedding wear:

✔ **Casual:** An invitation that says "Casual" clearly indicates the couple is planning a more informal wedding and requests casual dress. An informal wedding can be anything from a barefoot beach wedding to a barbeque where flip-flops are the requested footwear. Because of the variation in what constitutes casual dress and what any particular couple envisions, figuring out what to wear can often get tricky. As I mentioned earlier, think about the couple whose wedding you're attending and, if you need to, feel free to ask them what other people are wearing.

✔ **Cocktail:** If the wedding invitation says "Cocktail Attire," a cocktail dress is most appropriate. I recommend staying away from wearing a floor length dress, which for the most part shouts black tie (if they wanted you that dressed up, they would have said so). See the earlier section "Dressing for a cocktail party" for advice on choosing an appropriate cocktail dress. And remember, cocktail attire generally means cocktails are in the mix, so get ready to have some fun!

✔ **Black tie:** If the invitation says "Black Tie," you'll see a lot of floor length dresses, but don't be afraid to wear a cocktail dress if that is what looks best on you. You can be elegant and formal and totally appropriate without wearing a floor length gown. For almost every black-tie event, a dress that comes right below the knee is totally appropriate (for weddings, I wouldn't go too short — no more than an inch above the knee, tops). The earlier section "Attending a black-tie affair" offers more advice on black-tie attire.

Figure 11-8 shows types of attire for weddings: casual, cocktail, and black tie.

Figure 11-8: Different styles of wedding attire, from left: casual, cocktail, black tie.

If you're at a loss, don't be afraid to ask questions. E-mail or call the bride and ask what most people are wearing. If you don't have that kind of relationship with the bride, ask a mutual friend who is attending as well. Between that, the invitation, and the advice in this section, you have all the info you need to pick the perfect dress!

I know I've said this before, but I'm saying it again: It's always better to be slightly overdressed than underdressed — always.

Time of day

Knowing the time of the wedding is a huge factor in helping you decide what fabulous dress you're going to choose. Fortunately, you only have to look at the invitation to get this info! The key thing to know is that nighttime weddings are, for the most part, dressier than those held during the day. Here are the details:

✔ **Daytime weddings:** Typically, daytime weddings are informal or semi-formal. A shorter dress is fine, as is a suit. If you go with a suit, don't wear one in a Wall Street pinstripe or anything that looks too corporate. Feel free to wear something in a lighter color. And if any part of the wedding is going to be on grass or sand, remember to leave the heels behind. If you want to wear two pieces, keep it on the dressier side, such as a satin A-line skirt paired with a dressy blouse. For the most part, you also want to stay away from black if you're attending a daytime wedding. Weddings are fun and festive, and black, although dressy, tends to be more conservative and serious. So while you can get away with black at night (as long as you dress it up with fancy or statement jewelry), during the day it's more appropriate to wear something happier.

Don't feel you can go ultra casual just because the wedding is during the day. You're still going to a wedding. Whether it's 11:00 a.m.or 11:00 p.m., it's still the bride's most important day, so dress up for it! When my friend Pam got married at 11:00 a.m. on a Sunday in Miami, I wore a long sundress and some people even wore cocktail length dresses.

People always ask me whether it's okay to wear sunglasses for a daytime wedding held outdoors. The answer is yes. You want to be able to see the ceremony without squinting!

✔ **Evening weddings:** Woo hoo! Dress up time! Evening weddings almost always have a dress code. "Cocktail Attire" or "Black Tie" will likely be nestled in the corner of your invitation. This type of affair calls for a cocktail or black-tie dress. For everything you need to know, see the earlier sections "Dressing for a cocktail party" or "Attending a black-tie affair."

The setting

Where the wedding takes place certainly plays a part in what's appropriate attire. Different venues call for different types of attire. A wedding that's held in one of the top hotels in a big city is going to be more formal than a wedding held at a local restaurant in a small town. If you're going to a country club wedding, expect people to be dressed up; if you're off to a night club type of venue, the outfits will be edgier; and a beach wedding is more casual. Location is definitely one of the key ingredients when figuring out what to wear.

If you're going to a wedding at a venue you're familiar with, the dress is easier to predict. Never heard of the venue? Then let Google be your friend! Type the name of the venue into the search field to find out what the venue's like.

If the ceremony is outdoors where you'll be walking on grass, sand, or cobblestones, here's a great invention to put on your heels to keep them protected: SoleMates (see Figure 11-9). These plastic heel covers are intended to keep your slim sticks from sinking into grass, grates, or other tough-to-manage surfaces. Check them out at www.thesolemates.com.

©Jeffrey Weir, thesolemates.com

Figure 11-9: SoleMates let you walk comfortably on uneven surfaces.

A wedding that takes place in a house of worship generally means that you need to dress in the manner appropriate to that location. If you're unsure, the simplest solution is to ask the bride, or you can call ahead to the house of worship, though their guidelines may be stricter than the ones the bride will provide. In any case, you can rarely go wrong if you bring along some sort of wrap just for the service.

Have a great dress that's perfect for the reception but not quite as conservative as you want it to be for the wedding ceremony itself? Pair it with a shawl. With a shawl, you can transition your dress seamlessly from sexy to conservative. A wrap can also be good to have on hand if the reception hall is very well air-conditioned or if the air temperature drops as you swing from late afternoon to evening.

General rules for all weddings

While no two weddings are exactly alike, most weddings follow the same basic pattern. For example, usually a religious ceremony precedes the reception, and that means you have to take the rules for dressing in a house of worship into account as well as the party afterward. The following are some other basic guidelines:

✔ **Don't wear white.** One wardrobe no-no when it comes to weddings is *never* wear white, ivory, cream, or any color in that family to a wedding, or even to a rehearsal dinner for that matter. White is normally reserved for the bride.

✔ **Stay away from the color the bridesmaids are wearing.** It's a little awkward if you're the only non-bridesmaid in peach. You'll look like a wedding party wannabe.

How low can you go? The neckline dilemma

When it comes to plunging necklines, there's always the question of how much is too much? To arrive at the right answer for a wedding, consider the following:

✔ **How well-endowed you are.** If you stick with the theory that less is more, bigger busted women may want to opt for a dress that is not low cut. A sweetheart neck (see Chapter 9) or strapless dress would be flattering and appropriate choices. If you're smaller around the bust area and want to wear a dress with a plunging neckline,

you can. Just make sure that nothing that shouldn't be exposed is exposed. (If necessary take precautions like using double-sided tape.) As long as you can be comfortable and move around and not worry about falling out of your dress, you should be fine.

✔ **Whose party you're attending.** If the couple is more conservative, it's more respectful and appropriate to dress on the more conservative side. As much as you'd like to be noticed for your taste and style, you don't want to stick out like a sore thumb.

✔ **It's okay to break out the dressier accessories.** Weddings are certainly the occasion to wear those special pieces that you normally don't get the chance to wear. This goes for jewelry, a fancy clutch, or dressy heels. (But be careful not to over accessorize; see Chapter 14 for details.)

If you're someone who buys something and then waits to wear it for that "special" occasion, listen up! I want you to feel special all the time. So in addition to wearing that jewelry to your next big occasion, try to incorporate some of it with a more casual outfit. Your good things should be worn, not stored!

Shopping for Evening Attire and Clothing for Other Special Events

Regardless of your budget, when shopping for clothing for special events, make your first stop a store that carries high-end designer gowns and dresses. Why? Because you'll learn the current trends and see what's hot at the moment. With this info in mind, you can then head to the stores that fit your budget and find dresses that are of a similar style to the more expensive ones. So once you get the lay of the land, begin searching more seriously elsewhere (unless you happen to find the perfect designer dress on sale — lucky you!).

Next, look for a style that is most flattering for your body. For example, in 2009 asymmetrical necklines were all the rage at the awards shows, but if you don't have fabulous arms, this isn't a trend you should adopt. Instead, pick the body part you like most and accentuate it. If you love your bust line but hate your hips, a plunging neckline is the answer. If you carry most of your weight in the lower half of your body, try picking a dress that has patterns or embellishments on the upper half of it.

Whether you're a size 8 or a size 18, I want you to feel fabulous! That means highlighting the parts of your body you're confident about and choosing clothing that helps camouflage what you consider your flaws. Here are some specific pointers:

- **Don't shy away from color; just wear it the right way.** As a general rule, darker colors are more slimming. But don't feel like you have to buy black every time you go shopping. If you carry most of your weight in the lower part of your body, for example, choose a dress with a plunging neckline or a top that is detailed or ornate. This way you draw the attention to the upper half of your body.

- **Find a feature you like that you can focus on.** This is all about being real and honest with yourself (not to mention giving yourself a break). If you look in the mirror and say, "I hate my stomach, thighs, tush, and arms," you're going to have a hard time finding a dress. But if you look and say, "My arms are good, but I don't love the way my hips look," you have enough to work with to find the perfect outfit. In this case, buy a sleeveless A-line dress, which will show off your arms and camouflage your hips.

- **Think about the material the dress is made of.** Some gowns are made of heavier fabrics and others are made of very wispy ones. You have to know which type works best for your own shape. A more structured dress made of a heavier fabric gives you more support and camouflages more, whereas a flowing, wispy dress is more likely to be made of a thinner, possibly sheer material and more revealing. You can find more detailed information on how to accentuate your attributes, no matter what your body type, in Chapter 3.

When you try on dresses, make sure you look put together so that you can envision, at least to some degree, what you're going to look like. If you plan to wear your hair a certain way, try to wear your hair in that 'do. No, you don't need to go to the salon before you go shopping. Instead, fake it! Simple hair clips that pull your hair away from your face, for example, may give you a more formal look. Also don't forget to wear shoes with about the same heel height as the shoes you'll be wearing. Everything helps when making a significant purchase.

12

The Four Seasons: Dressing for Comfort and Style

Clothing serves as a first impression, as well as a form of self-expression.

Michelle Smith, Designer, Milly Clothing

For those of you who live in a tropical climate, shopping for one season is hard enough. Imagine having to rotate your wardrobe for four seasons! Fortunately, you can stock your closet with items that transition you from season to season, which means you do *not* need four different wardrobes to get you through the year. The trick is choosing wisely and buying right.

Winter: Staying Warm and Stylish

Nothing is quite like cozying up in front of a fire with someone you love, right? Well, that is the picture-perfect view on winter. But if you're someone who views the colder months with a frown because of the bulky clothing you have to wear, this section is for you.

Layering for winter

If there's one distinguishing characteristic of the clothes worn in winter, it's weight. Heavier fabrics like woolen tweeds and corduroy help you retain body heat and stay warm. If not worn correctly, however, they can also make you appear heavier. That's where the art of layering can come to the rescue. The trick is to layer your outfit in a way that enables you to remove a layer or two when indoors and still have something fabulous underneath.

Just because you need the added warmth, don't assume you can't wear your lighter-weight clothes in winter. You may be surprised how smart layering lets you stay warm without looking bulky:

- ✔ **Layering tops:** A natural tendency when layering is to add layers on top, like putting a heavy sweater over a blouse. But if the look you're going for is the blouse, not the sweater, layer a silk camisole beneath the blouse to get an added layer of warmth without the bulk. If you choose to wear a thin, fitted sweater (one that's meant to be worn on its own and not over a shirt), try a long-sleeve silk undershirt. These undershirts don't add bulk to your appearance, but they do help you retain body heat (see Figure 12-1).

- ✔ **Layering bottoms:** If you don't want to wear thick wool slacks, wear a pair of tights under pants made of a thinner material. You can even wear tights under your jeans. Just make sure the pants aren't tight (otherwise, the extra layer underneath shows). Also, a pair of boots that go up to your knee gives you another layer of warmth on your legs.

Figure 12-1: A silk undershirt can keep you warm without adding bulk.

Choosing coats and jackets

Outerwear is just as much of a fashion statement as the clothes you wear beneath them. In fact, in the colder months, it's the first thing people see on you when you show up to work, dinner, or a party — so select a coat or jacket that really expresses your style.

One difference between a coat and a jacket is length. Coats are generally longer, giving you more coverage and protection from the cold, and jackets are shorter. Another difference between the two is weight. Coats tend to be heavy and too warm to wear inside. A jacket is an item that you may wear inside or out. In other words, a coat typically has one purpose: to keep you warm and protect you from the elements (keeping in mind that a great-looking coat makes a fashion statement, too). Jackets, on the other hand, are a bit more versatile. They're perfect for warmer temperatures or transition weather, and you can use a jacket much the same way you would a cardigan or a wrap — to keep yourself warm in an air-conditioned office or restaurant without looking like you have one foot out the door.

Coats and jackets can be pricey, particularly the good-quality ones. They also take up a fair amount of closet space, so you want to be especially careful when buying one. The criteria for the perfect outerwear? Your piece needs to be stylish, fit you properly, and most of all, keep you warm. Most likely, you won't have a different coat or jacket for every day of the week, so pick versatile ones. As you shop for a coat or jacket (or evaluate the ones you already have), keep these things in mind:

- ✔ **Choose a length that complements your body type.** If you want to appear longer and thinner, a long coat is a great option. If you're on the taller side, opt for a shorter one. When considering length, think about what's most practical. If you're always getting into and out of a car (as mothers of young children tend to do), the shorter one may be more practical and the longer one may be too cumbersome. Many lengths between the full-length coat and the short jacket are available, which means you absolutely can find one that suits your body type.

- ✔ **Analyze your body before you make any big investment purchases such as a winter coat.** Coats come in a variety of styles and lengths, ranging from fitted pea coats and belted trench coats (which are generally on the shorter side), to the less fitted A-line and unstructured poncho-style coats, to the full-length coat. If your hips are wide, you don't want the coat to end in the middle of your hips, making the overall appearance even wider; choose a longer coat instead. If you're on the thinner side, buy a fitted or belted coat, which allows you to show off your figure. And if you want to camouflage your bottom, get a wider body coat with some swing to it. An unstructured coat that drapes, rather than clings, camouflages any body part you'd prefer to keep under wraps. (For more on body shapes, see Chapter 3.)

- ✔ **Keep your coats and jackets in the neutral color range.** Because few women have the budget or closet space to have a different coat for every outfit, make sure the ones you do select match most of your wardrobe.

The following sections describe the different kinds of coats and jackets you can choose from.

If you're buying two pieces of outerwear, buy one down jacket to keep you warm and that you can wear when it snows or rains. Make the other one a pea coat or full-length coat that you can wear to work and out at night. A good place to find designer jackets for less is Burlington Coat Factory. I got a jacket last season for under $50, and it was a two-in-one. The sleeves zippered off and it became a cute vest!

Down outerwear: Dressing for warmth without looking bulky

Down outerwear is called a *parka*. Parkas come in short, sporty jacket lengths (see Figure 12-2) and in full-length coat style. They're very warm and very light, and if they have a Gore-Tex or other microfiber shell, they also protect you from the elements. Fortunately, you don't have to look like a marshmallowman when you wear a parka. You can find chic ones that have minimum bulk. (I live in mine for work and play.) Although big, puffy down parkas are out there, you can also find very stylish and trendy brands (like Marmot, The North Face, and Bogner) that can keep you warm and looking fabulous. Here's how to choose a down coat that looks good on your body type:

- **Apples:** If you've got an apple shape, choose a down coat that creates a waist. Look for one with a belt or an inner draw string (make sure that you pull it tight).

- **Pears:** If you're pear-shaped, go with an A-line jacket, which emphasizes your top while maximizing coverage around your hips.

- **Plus sizes:** A three-quarter-length coat is the right choice because this length keeps the coat from being too short (which would probably cut you at the wrong spot) or too long (which would just be too bulky).

The underbelly of the camel: Camel hair coats

The camel hair coat is definitely a classic (see Figure 12-3). Warm and never out of style, these coats are worth the investment because they can take you from day to evening and are just as appropriate over jeans as they are over a fancy dress. Camel hair coats come in the traditional camel color, as well as a variety of neutral colors such as black, navy, and gray.

Figure 12-2: This jacket is perfect for après ski or après Starbucks!

The original camel hair coats were worn by polo players and were actually made from the under-belly hair of the Bactrian camel. Today's "camel hair" is more likely to be a combination of wool and cashmere dyed to look like camel hair.

Camel hair coats come in different lengths; the longer the coat, the longer your profile. If you're trying to appear taller or leaner, a longer coat may be a better investment. Also, for evening, longer coats are more elegant. Plus, if you wear a skirt or dress they extend past your hemline. However, if a shorter jacket looks better on you and still serves your wardrobe needs, invest in a shorter one.

If camel hair coats have a drawback, it's that they can easily get dirty, especially in slushy conditions. To solve this problem, either buy one in a shorter length to avoid splash stains or choose one in a darker color.

Wool coats

Wool is a very popular fabric for winter coats because it's a very good insulator. Wool coats come in a variety of lengths, from the shorter pea coat style to the full-length coat, and in the basic neutral colors as well as bright colors like red. The following are some suggestions that can help you find a wool coat that fits your body shape:

Figure 12-3: The camel hair coat fits in anywhere.

- ✔ **If you have narrow shoulders:** Pick a coat with wide lapels to accentuate your upper half while balancing out your lower half. Epaulets serve the same purpose and give your coat a little flair. Figure 12-4 shows how lapels and epaulets can provide balance.

- ✔ **If you've got curves or a thin waistline:** Pick a coat with a belt to emphasize your waist.

- ✔ **If you're tall:** Try a shorter coat to cut your long line and show off your legs.

- ✔ **If you're petite:** Wear a fitted coat so you don't look like your coat is overwhelming you. Keep it in close proportion to your size.

✔ **If you're heavier on top:** Choose a long coat to provide balance between the top and bottom halves of your body.

✔ **If you're a little wider in the midsection:** A long coat gives you a longer, leaner line.

Figure 12-4: Wide lapels (left) or epaulets (right) provide balance for women with narrow shoulders.

Pea coats

The pea coat remains a classic. Originally designed for sailors, it's double-breasted (the extra flap of cloth over the chest adds warmth), usually three-quarter length (which allows sailors to swab the decks without problem), and has slash pockets. Traditionally made of wool, these coats also come in inexpensive versions made of synthetic fibers (but these aren't very warm). These days, pea coats don't have to be in the traditional Navy blue, yet they still look best in the basic neutral colors, such as camel or black.

The classic double-breasted pea coat doesn't work well for women who don't have a waist or who have a large bust. If you have a large bust and want to wear a pea coat, choose the single-breasted variety, which draws less attention to the bust area. Figure 12-5 shows both single- and double-breasted pea coats. (As this figure shows, not all pea coats have to be navy blue, either.)

A double-breasted pea coat doesn't look good on *anybody* if it's left hanging open and unbuttoned. If you're going to wear a pea coat in situations where you won't have it closed all the time, such as commuting or while at the mall, consider getting the single-breasted style.

Figure 12-5: Two pea coats, one single-breasted (left) and one double-breasted (right).

Leather coats

If you take the hide of a cow or pig, without the short fur on these animals, you're left with leather or suede. Although leather coats and jackets are usually considered more appropriate for the transitional seasons because they're not very warm, they can be lined with fur, wool, or a synthetic liner, and then they can be used in winter. A leather coat can be a bomber jacket style (which is not very flattering or feminine and probably best avoided), or it can be a fitted blazer-type jacket (which can be very fashionable).

Fur coats

Fur coats remain a classic and elegant look. Designer fur coats can cost tens of thousands of dollars, and even the most modest run into the thousands. Fur is light and warm, but a lot of controversy surrounds wearing fur. Some groups, like members and supporters of PETA, the animal rights organization, think killing animals to wear their fur is wrong. Designers who are supportive of this stance have come out with fake fur options. Fake fur is a great way to keep up with the trends while being kind to animals.

Whether you're choosing fake or real fur, keep these style elements in mind:

- ✔ **Length:** Just as with all coats, fur comes in a variety of lengths. Before you make the investment, decide what looks good on you and where you plan to wear the coat. For a more casual look, a short fur or faux fur jacket may be more appropriate. If you're buying a jacket to wear out at night, a long coat may work better because it's dressier.

  If you're petite or on the smaller side, choose a coat that doesn't look like it's wearing you.
- ✔ **Color:** Real fur and faux fur come in a variety of colors. Choose one that best matches what's in your wardrobe.

Sheepskin, in which the skin is used in addition to the wool, is another type of fur. Coats made of sheepskin are not as expensive as many other furs, but they are quite warm. And of course, fake fur is always a great option — to save money and the animals.

Adding a shot of color

Winter clothing and coats can be drab, and wearing dark colors all the time can definitely take a toll on your mood. I know, I know — the last thing you want to do is put on your favorite ivory slacks when it's sleeting outside. Fortunately, you don't have to risk ruining your prized pieces of clothing to add some color to your winter wardrobe. If you're wearing charcoal gray slacks, try pairing them with a sweater set in a bright color.

The same rules apply for coats. If you're wearing a black coat, pair it with a colorful scarf, a great bag, a pair of boots, or even a great hat. Use accessories to draw attention away from the coat itself and express your sense of style. However, if your coat, boots, and bag are all of impeccable taste and quality, a dark monochromatic look is very chic and elegant, not drab at all.

Summer: Looking Good When You're Wearing Less

Ah, summer. Picture yourself sitting under a palm tree drinking a margarita getting fanned by a cute cabana boy. Okay, enough daydreaming! The truth is, many women don't look forward to a season where they may have to wear lighter or less clothing. Never fear, you can dress for summer without feeling too exposed.

Fashion rules apply in summer just as they do in any other season: Find summer clothing that accentuates your attributes, while camouflaging anything you don't want to show. How much skin you show is completely your preference. If you prefer to keep covered, simply choose the right fabric and color.

Summer fabrics

Keeping cool in the summer doesn't mean you have to wear less clothing. You just have to be smart about the fabrics you select. Natural fibers like cotton, rayon, and linen are better for hot weather than manmade fabrics like polyester because natural fibers allow your skin to breathe. Your skin — the human body's largest organ — keeps you cool by sweating. As sweat on your skin evaporates, it removes heat. Clothes that promote the free flow of air allow sweat to evaporate more easily. Summer clothes should be not only lightweight and made of fabrics that breathe, but also loose so that the air can get under the material and aid in evaporation.

Some modern fabrics also add an element of protection from the damaging rays of the sun. These fabrics, with brand names like Solarweave and Suntect, have actual SPF ratings, just like suntan lotion, and can help protect you against sunburn. Of course, they only protect the body parts they're actually covering. They also make hats with these treated fabrics, some of which have a piece that hangs down to protect your neck. ***Note:*** Most dermatologists will tell you that wearing SPF-rated fabrics shouldn't stop you from wearing suntan lotion as well.

Cool colors for summer

In addition to the fabric fiber and weight, another factor to consider is the color. Darker colors absorb light and heat, while lighter colors reflect light and heat. That's why people wear more white and other pale shades in the summer.

One of the most popular pieces of summer apparel is a pair of white pants or jeans. You can wear white on the bottom and look and feel fabulous if you follow these pointers:

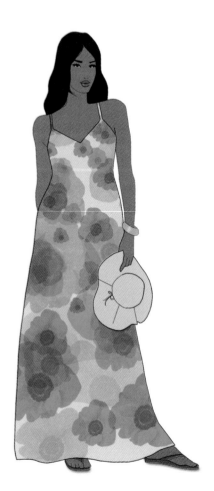

Figure 12-6: Loose clothing helps you keep cool.

- ✔ **Don't throw out the fashion rules for your body type just because it's hot out.** Everyone should be able to pull off an outfit with white pants or jeans. If you're apple-shaped and love to wear white, pair some white linen slacks with a longer tunic-type blouse, which elongates your upper body. And if you're pear-shaped, belt your top to draw attention to your waist.

- ✔ **White pants reveal everything (panty lines, the tucked in parts of your blouse, and more), so be careful!** Make sure you look at yourself from every angle. If you look only at your front, you'll miss the view that everybody else has as you walk away.

✔ **If you wear less-expensive white pants, be careful of the pockets (both front and back).** If you can see them through the pants, they detract from the clean look you want (see Figure 12-7). A great idea is to have them removed altogether. You really aren't going to use them to hold anything (that's what your great purse is for), and the look will be much cleaner and more flattering. (***Note:*** Having pockets in white jeans, however, is totally acceptable. Denim is a heavy fabric, and often the pockets are part of the design.)

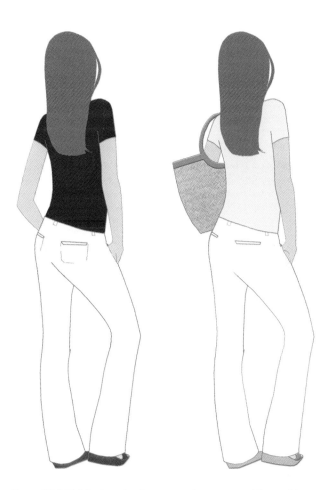

Figure 12-7: Think about having any pockets removed from white pants.

When it comes to other white items like tops, skirts, and dresses, draw people's attention away from your problem areas by adding splashes of color. You can wear colorful scarves in a variety of different ways to spice up any outfit; you can even tie a brightly colored scarf around your waist or wrap your hair in one (head to Chapter 15 for different ways to swear scarves). In addition to color, black is a great accent with summer white. A black patent leather belt can brighten up a white outfit, and a bold black-and-white floral or geometric pattern on a dress or skirt serves to dazzle the eye and keep whatever's underneath camouflaged. For further help, use the right undergarments. Flesh-colored body shapers will hold you in and smooth you out, and won't allow anything you don't want seen to show through.

Summer styles

Sure, summer wear is more casual than that of other times of the year, but that can lead some people to forget all sense of fashion. You can still be very fashionable, even with the least amount of clothing. Even bathing suits, covered in the later section "By the sea," can be fashionable. Just remember to keep in mind what works for your body type.

Who wears short shorts?

Shorts come in a variety of lengths. Find a pair that looks good on your body type.

- **Short shorts:** Very short shorts belong on young teens or women with really skinny legs. If you're an apple shape and have great legs, short shorts can be a great way to draw attention to your assets. But if you don't have very thin thighs, short shorts cut you at just the wrong place.

- **Mid-thigh shorts:** These shorts are less revealing and more appropriate for women who are no longer in their teens or twenties.

- **Bermuda shorts:** These very fashionable shorts come to just above your knee and work on women of all ages.

If shorts are flattering to your legs, go for it. If not, try a skirt or dress. You'll be just as cool, while remaining true to your look and sense of style.

Skirts and dresses

Skirts and dresses are a great way to keep cool and fashionable in the warm weather. They feel lighter and cooler than pants and give you the opportunity to really express your personal style. So many options are available, from the structured pencil skirt to a flowy dress.

Wrap skirts and dresses, which are a classic look and never go out of style, can be very flattering because the diagonal line makes you appear taller and keeps the eye from focusing on any one part.

Capris

Three-quarter length capri pants are another great option for summer. You can mix and match them with tops and shoes to your heart's content. You can even make them part of a suit if you want. Again, just be careful about what is most flattering to your legs. If you want to make your legs appear longer, capris may not be right for you. For more on capris, head to Chapter 9.

Summer tops

T-shirts aren't the only summer tops. You can find so many types of blouses in a wide variety of materials that are cool and great-looking, from peasant tops to silk blouses to longer tunic tops. Another popular look these days are babydoll tops with an empire waist. They're very youthful-looking and go well with jeans.

By the sea

Summertime is bathing suit season, which some women can't wait for and others dread. Don't dread it. The fact is that everyone has flaws. You just need to figure out a way to accentuate your attributes and camouflage whatever you don't want exposed. Hiding flaws is obviously more of a challenge in a bathing suit, but it can be done.

One piece or two?

The first decision is whether to wear a one-piece or two-piece suit. What you choose depends on what you're comfortable in and what body part you want to show off or hide. Get a one-piece suit if your belly is an area that you don't

feel comfortable revealing. Many one-piece suits come with tummy control. And *ruching,* shown in the suit in Figure 12-8, is one of the many tricks you can use to camouflage your body even while baring so much of it. If you like your back, then look for one that covers your front but is cut-out in the back. Go for a two-piece bikini if you have a great waist and want to accentuate it. If you like the ease of a two-piece, but still want to cover your tummy, try a *tankini*. The tankini is a two-piece that looks more like a pair of underwear and a camisole, so you get the coverage you want without having to be in a one-piece suit.

When buying a two-piece suit, buy separates if you can. This way if you're large on top and small on the bottom, you can get the appropriate size for each part and a better fit all around. This is true for all body types. If you can't buy separates, try to get a top that adjusts in as many ways as possible so that you can make it work for you.

Figure 12-8: Ruching on a bathing suit.

Look for bathing suits with built-in control panels that hold you in while you frolic in the pool or ocean. (www.drreyshapewear.com)

Here are some tips to help you choose a suit style that fits your body type:

✔ **Small-busted:** The bandeau top or triangle top, shown in Figure 12-9, looks great on you (and many suits now come with padding if you want an extra boost!). Also, a cute suit with ruffles on top helps accentuate the chest area. Any detail on top helps give the illusion that you're more curvaceous. These tops are available in either a one-piece or two-piece style, so you can choose which look you prefer.

Figure 12-9: A triangle bikini flatters the smaller-chested woman.

Figure 12-10: Small as they are, bikinis can still provide the support a fuller-breasted woman needs.

✔ **Large-busted:** If you have larger breasts and want to wear a two-piece suit, try ones that have more supportive straps. The bra-style bikini top is a very good choice for you (see Figure 12-10), as is the halter top suit. These both flatter and support you in the chest area. If you prefer to wear a one-piece suit, look for one with straps that provide the support you're looking for.

✔ **Bottom-heavy:** Play up your top in order to even out the proportions. Choose either a one- or two-piece suit with a top half that attracts all the attention. Separates, where the top has thicker straps or a colorful print and the bottom half is a dark solid that flatters and still matches the top, are always a good choice. Or try a color block one-piece with lighter colors on the top and darker ones on the bottom, as

in Figure 12-12. Avoid boy short bottoms, which emphasize and attract attention to your derriere.

Accentuating your cleavage is a good way to divert attention from other areas.

✔ **Short legs:** Choose a suit that's cut high at the hip to make your legs look longer. A plunging neckline also creates a more vertical look (see Figure 12-11). Vertical stripes serve the same purpose.

Figure 12-11: A high cut suit gives the illusion of longer legs.

✔ **Long torso:** Go for horizontal stripes. A two-piece suit breaks up your midsection. If you wear a one-piece, try one with cutouts, which break up your torso. And don't be afraid to add splashes of color to keep eyes from looking at you in a straight up-and-down manner (see Figure 12-12).

✔ **Thick waist:** If your hips and waist are about the same size, wear a two-piece with bright colors so that there's a clear definition between your two halves. Choose bottoms that sit low on your hips (these add a lengthening effect), and try to find a suit that has some bows or other adornment at the hips to differentiate your hips and waist. In a one-piece, look for a suit that has a sash in the middle or a horizontal color block stripe to accentuate the waistline.

✔ **Plus-sized:** Dark colors are best. A streamlined one-piece in a dark color makes you look longer and leaner. Try an interesting neckline, maybe one that's deeper rather than rounder, as it creates more of an illusion of length and draws attention to your chest area (which is most likely an attribute).

Figure 12-12: By mixing colors, you can create an assortment of effects.

Cover-ups

If you want to be a little less exposed when you're not in the water, another option for looking great while hanging out by the pool or at the beach is a cover-up. These can range from sarongs to caftans, depending on the amount of coverage you desire. The great thing about a sarong is that you can use it in several ways, depending on which parts you want to cover (see Figure 12-13). Tie it above your chest, like a bath towel, and it covers you entirely without being too hot or looking out-of-place. If you just want to cover your lower half, tie it at your waist. Sarongs are so easy to put on and take off. You can even use it to lie on at the beach when you take it off!

Figure 12-13: Adjust a sarong to give you the amount of coverage you desire.

Spring and Fall: The Transition Seasons

For those of us who live in climates with four seasons, spring and fall are usually the favorites because they don't offer any temperature extremes. What these transition seasons lack in extremes, though, they make up for in variability. No wonder there's so much confusion about what to wear during these times. Really, the trick is just to layer so that no matter what the day brings, you'll be dressed appropriately.

Slipping from season to season

One way of slipping from one season to the next is to make some subtle changes. When the weather starts to get a little warmer in spring, for example, ditch the boots and dark tights for jeans and peep-toe shoes. You may still need a coat to fight that nip in the morning air, but by late afternoon, you can slip off the coat and feel like you're actually at the edge of summer. Other changes you can make are to go from heavy sweaters to lighter knit cardigans. Or put a camisole under a blouse, so if the day turns a lot warmer, you can just take the blouse off. In the fall, you transition your wardrobe the opposite way: Start with switching from open-toe to something like a ballet slipper before you dive into the boots. Add a jean jacket or a wrap over your top; during the warmer part of the day, just take it off.

Green leaves and spring flowers or fall foliage aren't the only colorful additions to these seasons. As the next sections explain, your wardrobe should make the transition from winter to spring or summer to fall by using the appropriate colors as well.

Figure 12-14: Add a touch of color to your spring wardrobe.

In the spring

You may not be ready to give up black altogether, nor do you have to, but you'll feel a lot more spring-like if you begin to add some dashes of color, as shown in Figure 12-14, and even a few bold prints. Eventually you'll be able to substitute lighter-weight coats for those that have to hold back those March winds. A spring coat in a lighter color is a good transition piece. It can still be neutral so that it matches most of your wardrobe, but you have a little more freedom from black, navy, and other dark colors. If you can afford more than one coat, try a fun spring color to start you on the way to lightening up your wardrobe. Scarves can also make a good bridge accessory. Put your wool scarves in the closet with mothballs and pull out the silk ones in a wide array of colors.

In the fall

When the weather starts to turn cooler in the fall months, you can begin to add layers. Begin by slipping a cardigan over a summer dress, and then go to wearing long sleeves and lightweight wool under a jacket. Finally, resort to pulling out your gloves and hats.

Fall is a good time for vests, which allow you to slowly ease into the idea of requiring all that clothing to keep warm. It's also a great time to break out those fabulous boots from last season that have been stored away all summer (see Figure 12-15). And, yes, the cooler temperatures mean it's okay to start wearing black again.

Transitional outerwear

During the transitional seasons, you need outerwear that provides enough warmth to combat the low temperatures, but it also needs to be light enough that, when left open, it won't make you sweat if the sun starts to warm up the atmosphere. And between April showers and the cold fall rains, you also want your outerwear to be waterproof.

Vests

For mid-range weather, vests are a great option (see Figure 12-16). They keep you warm, especially if they're down (refer to the earlier section "Down outerwear: Dressing

Figure 12-15: Ah, fall, when you can start wearing your favorite boots again.

for warmth without looking bulky") and still show off your arms, so you're not too hot and you get to see a little of your body. They're a little tougher for apple shapes because they accentuate your top half, so use your judgment when trying them on and deciding whether or not they flatter your shape.

Shawls, wraps, and sweater coats

The most versatile item for transitional weather is the shawl or wrap. Sometimes, just adding that one layer warms you up enough when it's chilly. Obviously, the cooler it is outside, the weightier your shawl or wrap should be, and vice-versa. You can also pair a shawl or wrap with other outerwear. If you're wearing a light-weight jacket designed for both indoor and outdoor wear, you can better fend off the cold by throwing a colorful wool or pashmina shawl over your shoulders. And voilà — you're all set!

A sweater coat is a longer version of a sweater that doesn't close in the front but hangs open like a cardigan without the buttons. Sweater coats, which come in lengths ranging from just below your rear to knee length, are knit and cling in all the right places. Most of them even have belts that you can tie. If you want to show your curves, a long knit sweater coat may be just what you need.

The trench coat: A transitional superstar

If there's one piece of outerwear that you're going to wear the most, it's a trench coat — particularly if it has a zip-out lining. Depending on where you live, a trench coat may even get you through an entire winter. Because you'll wear your trench coat so

Figure 12-16: A vest is perfect for transition weather.

often, it's definitley worth spending a little extra if you find the perfect one. And because you'll wear it in many different seasons, stick to the classic neutral colors — those in the beige or gray family. Be careful if buying black; it can look heavy in spring.

Is it worth spending $800, $900, or even $1,000 on a Burberry designer trench coat? It all depends on your budget, of course, but you have to look at this as an investment in style and function. A trench coat is an item you can proudly wear for years and years, and the satisfaction it will give you every time you slip it on will definitely make the price you paid five years before seem to be a bargain. Look for good quality brands that don't force you to empty your wallet. Who says you have to buy yours at the most expensive retailers? Visit a place like Burlington Coat Factory or Loehmann's for a great deal on a trench coat.

Slickers and jackets

Although you can still buy a yellow slicker based on the polyurethane raingear worn by fishermen and almost identical to the one you wore as a child, today you can also find slickers that are much thinner, though just as waterproof, and that don't come down to your knees. These shorter, more fashionable lengths, when paired with the colorful rubber boots, such as the popular classic brand Hunter (`www.Hunter-Boot.com`), help you look stylish and remain dry.

Jackets made from fiber instead of polyurethane are not as waterproof, unless they have a Gore-Tex lining. But if you're not backpacking and you're packing an umbrella, it really doesn't matter if your jacket isn't entirely waterproof. In fact, if you don't expect the temperatures to drop too much, you could just put on a simple blazer. On the other hand, if you're going to be outdoors for an extended time (maybe you're watching your kids play soccer through an October drizzle), having outerwear that has a microfiber lining like Gore-Tex is your best bet at staying dry.

Should your slicker or jacket be long or short? That depends on your body type. If you prefer to keep your bottom and hips from showing, then long is better, and an A-line or swing coat serves your needs best. If you don't mind showing off your derriere, then go with a short jacket. (And a reminder to all you pears: Make sure it doesn't end at your hips.)

When purchasing a jacket, especially for cooler temperatures, be sure to pay attention to its design elements, which also serve a purpose. Although you may not care that much about the pockets on a jacket that you only wear indoors, that's probably not true for one that you plan to wear outdoors. If you want to be able to stick your hands in the pockets if a sudden chill descends, make sure the pockets allow you to. You may also want to have the option to turn up the collar for added protection from the wind, so look for one with a collar as opposed to one without.

Can you wear a spring jacket in the fall and vice versa? Obviously there's nothing stopping you, but each of these seasons announces the coming one, which is why a spring jacket would normally be in a lighter, brighter color while a fall jacket, like one in black or brown leather, is more appropriate for the fall months. Of course, if the jacket is in a neutral beige or gray, or mid-range blue or red, it can definitely be worn in both spring and fall. A denim jacket is a great spring-to-summer *and* fall-to-winter option (see Figure 12-17).

Figure 12-17: A denim jacket knows no season.

13

Dressing for the Bedroom

In This Chapter

▷ Picking the right pajamas or nightgown

▷ Taking a look at sexy sleepwear choices

▷ Choosing a robe

Add some zest to how you dress at home and you'll add a spark to your love life.

Dr. Ruth Westheimer, Psychosexual Therapist

Whether you're sleeping alone or with someone special, you always want to look, and more importantly, *feel* confident and beautiful. So this chapter pertains to everyone — single, married, dating, or divorced, whatever your status on Facebook says! (For the record, I'm single. Know anyone?) You're probably rolling your eyes and saying to yourself, "She really wants me to dress up when I go to bed?" No, I don't want you to dress up like you're going to a black-tie affair, but I do want you to feel fabulous and comfortable at all times. It all goes back to my 10 System (refer to Chapter 2).

Let me explain: I have a great T-shirt that I got as a freshman at the University of Michigan. It's 100 percent cotton and, because I've worn it over and over again, feels perfect every time I put it on. My goal in this chapter is to help you keep only the sleepwear that is 100 percent *something* — 100 percent comfortable, 100 percent sexy, or 100 percent special. So ditch those ratty T-shirts that aren't your favorites and do away with lingerie that no longer makes you feel great. Everything you own, including your PJs, needs to have a reason to be in your closet.

Sleepwear 101

Obviously you should be comfortable when you go to bed, and sleepwear manufacturers (successful ones at least!) are well aware of how important that is. But there are different levels of comfort: cozy-comfortable, cute-comfortable, and sexy-comfortable. You just have to choose one and go with it. Your final outfit of the day should be as put together as you want to feel when you get up the next morning.

Just as you may wear a skirt one day and a pair of pants the next, you can alternate between nightgowns and pajamas and maybe even nothing at all! There's nothing wrong with switching it up according to your mood or the season, and the best thing about sleepwear is that you get to experiment in the comfort of your own home.

Pajamas

The word *pajamas* comes from *pyjamas,* traditional loose pants held up by a string tied around the waist worn in Southeast Asia. The colonial Brits, who paraded around in the blistering sun all dressed up in uniforms or ties and jackets, eventually understood the advantage of the native dress and brought this style back to England toward the end of the 18th century. They added a jacket and found it to be a comfortable sleeping outfit and a nice replacement for drafty nightgowns during their long, cold winters.

Although the basic design of pajamas is pretty set, that doesn't mean you can't make a fashion statement in them. Ever since women adopted this particular style, pajamas have come in a greater selection of fabrics, from cotton to flannel to satin and silk. You can even find some made out of eco-friendly bamboo. As to styles, you can choose from a large variety. In winter, you may want to get as much coverage as possible (and throw on a pair of socks to boot). As the weather heats up, you may prefer shorter sleeves and legs. With all the variety available, your PJ pants can go from full-length to capri-length to shorts, and your tops can shrink from full sleeves to short sleeves to no sleeves.

If PJs are your sleepwear of choice, keep these suggestions in mind:

Figure 13-1: PJs can keep you cute *and* cozy.

- ✔ **Stick to natural fibers.** Synthetic fibers like nylon or spandex may keep you too warm or may be too constricting.

Although it's a natural fiber, I don't recommend wool. Although very warm, it can also be scratchy — not so much fun in bed! If you're especially cold, better to add another layer of cotton (in the form of thermal underwear, for example) rather than switch to wool PJs.

- ✔ **If you sleep on your stomach, look for PJ tops that pull over your head.** Traditional pajama tops generally button down the front, which can be uncomfortable for tummy-sleepers (like me). If you fall into this category, try a pajama top that pulls over your head, such as one in the T-shirt or cami style (see Figure 13-1).

Why not just sleep in any old T-shirt and sweats and avoid the whole button-down-the-front dilemma? Because PJs, which are usually a matching set, help you look pulled together. It all goes back to feeling put together and fabulous, even when you're just heading off to dreamland.

✔ **Limit the number of gimmicky pajamas you have.** Pajamas run the gamut from conservative solids (see Figure 13-2) to the most ridiculous prints. Seriously, you can find everything from animal prints to crossword puzzles. These tend to be a very popular gift, especially around the holidays (if your friend likes golf, pajamas with golf balls is a no-brainer). Although it's okay to have a couple pairs of gimmicky pajamas, you don't want to look like you belong on the lunch box of a first grader all the time.

✔ **Look for pajamas that suit your style.** PJs can be sexy or conservative, less material or more, sheer or opaque, camisole or long sleeves. Make sure you select only those that fit you perfectly and are in a style that represents you. Material is also key — choose a fabric that makes you feel comfortable and cozy. Suffering through a formal affair in high heels is one thing; the last thing you want is to be uncomfortable in bed.

✔ **Choose PJs that work best for your body type and accentuate what you want to show off.** If you have long legs, for example, try a set with shorts. If you're on the short side, a design with a vertical stripe elongates your appearance. And if you prefer to keep your partner's eyes away from your bottom, keep the top button or two of your top undone. (Woo hoo!)

Figure 13-2: A basic pajama set is a perfect look for bedtime.

Nightgowns: Naughty or nice

Before there were pajamas, everyone, both male and female, wore nightgowns to bed. The preference for nightgowns had to do with comfort: They didn't constrict you while you slept, and they allowed couples to be intimate without having to take all their clothes off on a chilly night. Today, night-gowns are still very popular among some women.

If you're really concerned with camouflaging some body parts, even in the bedroom, a night-gown is your best bet. The flowing style of a nightgown covers up pretty much everything because it doesn't cling to the tummy or hips or behind. (Nightgowns can be found in plus sizes, so don't allow anyone to tell you that these outfits aren't for you if you're above a certain size.) You can shop for all this sleepwear online, a great solution if you're too shy or uncomfortable shopping for this kind of clothing in public!

Because nightgown styles vary from conserva-tive (those that totally cover you up) to super sexy (and revealing), you can definitely find a gown that fits your comfort level and sense of style.

- ✔ **The traditional nightgown:** Traditionally, nightgowns served two purposes: cover-ing up in the interests of modesty and keeping warm. If that's what you want in a nightgown, flannel is a good choice. It retains heat, is comfortable, and because it's opaque, is totally concealing. If, on the other hand, you want your nightgown to silhouette what's underneath, silk would be your first choice (see Figure 13-3).

- ✔ **Negligees:** Negligees are nightgowns designed to be seductive. These usually have more frills (lace and bows, for exam-ple) than traditional nightgowns and are made of sheer or semi-transparent mate-rial. They also generally reveal more skin. Although you may want to wear a negligee

Figure 13-3: Even though you're fully covered, a silk nightgown is still sexy.

for your husband's or boyfriend's benefit, you need something to cover it up outside the bedroom, especially if other family members are in the house! Luckily, most negligees are sold in sets with a matching *peignoir* (see Figure 13-4). For all intents and purposes, a peignoir is a robe, only much sexier and fancier.

Traditionally, a peignoir was the garment a noble woman wore as her personal maid combed her hair (the word peignoir, in fact, is from the French word *peigner,* which means "to comb hair").

✔ **The babydoll:** As women became less modest in their outerwear, the trend followed suit in the bedroom, and along came the babydoll. The babydoll is a negligee, except it's much shorter in length and is generally sold with matching panties (see Figure 13-5). To raise the bar on the sexiness factor, you can wear a babydoll with a thong or a G-string. Figure out which bottom is most flattering for your backside and go for it!

Figure 13-4: Most negligees come with a special robe, called a peignoir.

Color is another factor in the level of sensuality in a nightgown. A white negligee conveys a mixture of innocence and seduction. A negligee in black or red conveys out-and-out seduction, no matter how many little bows it may have! And if you really want to turn it up a notch, try a negligee in some type of animal print or one that is totally sheer.

Figure 13-5: A sheer babydoll is very sexy.

Teddies and other things

In the 1920s, the original name for a teddy was *camiknickers,* because it was a combination of a camisole top and knickers bottoms. It was intended to be worn under shorter skirts. Because the shape reminds one of a teddy bear, the nickname "teddy" eventually stuck.

Women wearing pants in the factories during World War II adopted the teddies to wear under their work clothes. Although some teddies are still sold because of their utilitarian value as a one-piece undergarment, most are made to be highly suggestive. They don't leave much to the imagination because they're see-through and have openings pretty much everywhere. So, ladies, if you're looking for another option when you want to look seductive in the bedroom, look no further.

It's a good idea to have some type of sexy sleepwear in your repertoire. You may not wear it every night, but you want to be able to express your different moods with your clothing. Figure out which style, color, and material best suits you and go for it! You'll be amazed at how sexy sleepwear makes you feel, not to mention how happy it will make your partner!

I once dated a man who told me that the sexiest thing I ever wore for him was his white button-down shirt. You can make your partner's clothing work for you, too (see Figure 13-6). Be creative. A woman can be sexy in many different ways; all *I* needed to do was go shopping in my boyfriend's closet!

Figure 13-6: A simple button-down shirt (from his closet) can be as sexy as lingerie.

Robes

A robe is generally used to add a layer of warmth to whatever you're wearing underneath, if anything. Robes designed to keep you warm come in all types of fabrics, and with heating bills going up, there will surely be more and more people putting on their robes right after they lower their thermostats. Today you can buy robes in fleece or microfiber, and they do an excellent job of retaining heat while not being too heavy. The following sections detail the different kinds of robes.

Bath robes

Bath robes are usually made of terry cloth or are at least lined with terry cloth so that when you step out of the shower or bath, you can quickly wrap yourself up against any lurking drafts (see Figure 13-7). You can then step out of the bathroom and head for your bedroom to get dressed knowing that you're amply covered.

If you prefer robes to sweaters when lounging or working at home, give some thought to how you look. Make sure you choose a robe that flatters your shape. Because robes add an extra thick layer, they can leave you looking very bulky, especially terry cloth robes. As an alternative to terry cloth, try a robe made of silk or cotton. If you have great legs, a shorter robe will flatter you. And keep in mind that darker colors are always more slimming.

Figure 13-7: A terry cloth robe.

Silk robes

A fine silk robe not only gives you a slimmer appearance, but the feel of silk is also very sensuous. Silk also lends itself to many types of imprints (because silk originated in China, many silk robes have an eastern motif). Of course, you can get a solid color silk robe and just bask in the look and feel that simple silk offers. (By the way, woven silk is softer than knit silk, and so better for a robe.)

To reduce the cost of using real silk, some manufacturers offer silk blends or use fabrics that have the appearance of silk but are made entirely of synthetic fibers (nylon or rayon, for example). These synthetic silks don't have the same luxurious feel of silk, nor do they hold up as well, but they're still an option.

Kimonos

A kimono is a form of silk robe. Because silk was first woven into cloth in China, the most beautiful silk robes still come from the Far East. Kimonos, which have Chinese or Japanese designs (see Figure 13-8), are elegant and quite beautiful. The more elaborate the design, the higher the price, of course. Traditionally, kimonos were one-size-fits-all garments and were cut on the small side; today, plus-size kimonos are readily available. When selecting a kimono, make sure that the decorative pattern matches your body type. If you have full hips, for example, make sure the design is mostly around your top, drawing the eye away from your hips.

Housecoats

An offshoot of the robe is the housecoat, which is basically a robe meant to be worn during the day, as opposed to the traditional robe which is associated with evening lounge wear. Housecoats are a cross between a dress and a robe. For that reason, the material generally has more of a pattern than does a robe. Although younger women usually put on their jeans or sweats to do household chores, older women sometimes put on a housecoat.

Figure 13-8: A silk kimono is both chic and comfortable.

Housecoats are functional and allow for more freedom of movement than jeans do. As long as you don't decide to live in a housecoat 24/7 or let anyone see you in it, they can be an appropriate mode of dress around the house. (They're definitely *not* appropriate outside the house, even if you're just running to the store or the salon.) Really consider how you look and feel before deciding to wear a housecoat. Don't wear one if it makes you feel dumpy, no matter how practical it may be. Other options are available that will make you feel like a 10.

Vintage sleepwear

Society today is a lot less formal than it used to be; so many people simply sleep in their underwear, sweats, or nothing at all. (However, I hope this chapter has inspired you to give a little more thought to your nighttime wardrobe than that!) Fifty years ago, however, the nighttime regime included slipping on a complete outfit designed for going to bed. Because the demand for sleepwear was so much greater back then, people had a lot more to choose from. So if you really want to get fancy, or you're looking for sleepwear or loungewear that is special and unique, try shopping for something vintage.

You may not want to wear someone else's old pair of flannel pajamas, no matter how many times it's been washed. But when it comes to robes, silk pajamas, and negligee and peignoir sets, you can find fabulous, one-of-a-kind items that will bring the height of glamour to your evenings at home. Even if you don't want to wear them for sleeping, putting them on to lounge around the house can make those few hours between work and sleep extra special.

These items were usually well cared for, if even worn at all. If you shop carefully, you can find some in impeccable condition that will make you look sensational. A set that is really fancy and in perfect condition can set you back quite a bit (more than you'd normally spend on sleepwear), but if it's really special and makes you look and feel great, it can be worth the price. Just remember to take good care of them in order to protect your investment!

Part V
Finishing Touches

The 5th Wave   By Rich Tennant

"Maybe a shower curtain wasn't the best thing to try to make into an evening dress, but the embroidery looks great."

In this part . . .

The wrong bra can ruin a smashing outfit and let's not even go into what horrendous panty lines can do to a dress! In this part, I show you a few tricks to mastering the undergarment world so that you can avoid fashion calamities. I also delve into accessories and their importance in every outfit. You may be asking, "Where does the shoe portion of the conversation come in?" Right here! Flats, heels, and sneakers — I break down how you can make your footwear look fabulous with any outfit.

14

It's What's Inside That Counts: Undergarments

It doesn't matter what body type or size you are. Wearing the proper undergarment makes you look better in your clothes.

Sara Blakely, Founder, Spanx

Double Spanx!

Nancy O'Dell, Access Hollywood host,
on getting red carpet ready

*H*ow many times have you seen a woman in a great outfit and said to yourself, "I love that dress, but how could she let those bra straps hang out like that?!" Here's the deal: You never want to be the girl in the great outfit with the wrong undergarments. This chapter explains how to make your outfit look even better with only a few purchases and a few key tricks.

Hosiery

Women have a wide variety of choices when it comes to hosiery: stockings, pantyhose, tights, knee highs, or nothing at all. I don't know how we got into such a complicated state of affairs, but I personally tend to opt for nothing at all (crazy, I know). I remember my grandmother would never leave the house, let alone go to a formal affair, without the right hosiery. But what is considered appropriate and accepted has definitely changed throughout the years. Warmth, office decorum, and what flatters your body best are just a few of the issues to consider as I take you on a journey into the world of hosiery.

Different types of hosiery styles

Hosiery styles vary in color and transparency and come in various patterns. With all these varieties, be sure to select a style that fits your body type:

- ✔ If you want to appear taller or leaner, wear a darker color or one with a simple seam up the back of the leg.

- ✔ Lighter colors, especially ones with patterns, draw more attention to your legs and can make them look wider.

The right hose or some great tights can really make an outfit. But hosiery isn't just a fashion statement; some women wear it to cover up parts of their legs they aren't fans of, like veins, blemishes — you name it. (I have a friend, in fact, who doesn't like her knees.) In addition, covering your legs is appropriate or required in certain situations, like at many offices or events. The following sections take a look at pantyhose and stockings (shown in Figure 14-1).

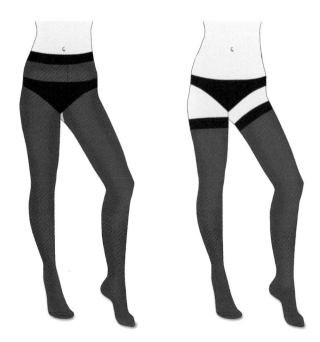

Figure 14-1: Pantyhose (left) and stockings (right).

Stockings

Stockings cover the foot and lower part of the leg and end mid-thigh. Formerly made of woven cloth, they can now be found in knitted wool, cotton, nylon, or silk.

Many women prefer stockings to pantyhose (covered in the next section) for these reasons:

- ✔ **They're not as restrictive.** Stockings can be more comfortable than pantyhose or tights, especially in warm weather.

- ✔ **They're sexier.** Stockings allow for some bare skin on the upper thigh that could inadvertently (or not) be exposed.

Use one of these methods to keep your stockings up:

- ✔ **A garter belt:** A garter belt is a piece of lingerie that goes around the waist that has "suspenders" that clip to the top of the stockings (see Figure 14-2).

- ✔ **An elastic garter:** Have you ever been to a wedding and watched as the groom pulls a garter off his new wife's leg and everyone laughs? Of course you have! Well, garters aren't just wedding souvenirs. You can use them to actually hold stockings up.

- ✔ **"Stay Ups":** Here, the inside of the top of the stocking has an elastic band added to it that allows it to, well, stay up. (Duh, hence the name!)

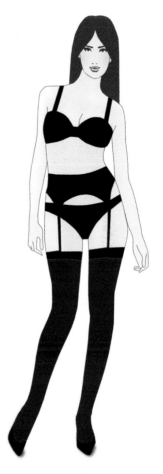

Figure 14-2: Stockings held up by a garter belt can be sexy.

Pantyhose

When women began to wear miniskirts in the 1960s, stockings, which up until then had been kept up with garters, proved to be too short. So one-piece pantyhose came to the fore (interestingly, dancers were the first to come up with the idea of sewing stockings to the leg bands of their briefs). Shortly thereafter, the majority of hosiery sales were in the form of pantyhose (see Figure 14-3). What do so many women like about pantyhose?

✔ They don't have to worry whether their stockings are sagging or attached.

✔ Pantyhose provide welcome extra warmth when it's cold outside.

✔ Because pantyhose use a stretch material, they provide extra support, which has a slimming effect on the legs (and, if the pantyhose are control top, to the tummy as well).

Figure 14-3: Regular (left) and control top (right) pantyhose.

Hosiery rules

Manufacturers have come up with a wide variety of hosiery textures and designs, including fishnet, fencenet (which has a wider webbing), stripes, checks, and other woven designs. You can also find them with bows, lace panels, and in a rainbow of colors. They can be opaque, medium sheer, or completely sheer. Other advances include a seamless toe or sandal-foot that you can wear with sandals and other open-toe shoes.

The following list offers a bit of guidance to help you decide what style looks best on you and some pointers on how to wear them:

- ✔ **Creating a slimming effect:** To get a slimming effect, wear dark hose. An alternative is to wear medium sheer, which is more slimming than very sheer or opaque because it allows for some shading on the leg. Also, wear hose that echo the color of your outfit — a navy skirt or dress with navy hose and navy shoes, for example — to elongate the appearance of your body.

- ✔ **Using hosiery as an accessory:** Wearing a simple black dress with a patterned pair of tights or stockings make your legs the centerpiece of your outfit.

- ✔ **Getting a dressier look:** Hosiery with a sheen is considered dressier and makes your outfit fancier.

  Stocking thickness is measured in *denier*. The lower the denier number, the sheerer the garment. (Stockings knitted with a higher denier are less sheer but more durable.)

For comfort and style, be sure to keep these tips in mind:

- ✔ **If you wear flesh-colored hosiery, make sure it matches the color of *your* flesh.** Having legs a different color than your arms (either because they're too dark or too light) looks funny.

- ✔ **Knee highs, a variety of hosiery to be worn under pants, leave marks on your legs that show for some time.** If you wear them during the day and intend to go barelegged at night, take them off well ahead of time.

- ✔ **If you wear a garter belt to hold up your stockings, make sure the belt matches the color of the stockings.** Also, adjust the straps so that the front straps are two inches shorter than the back ones. That way, they don't show if your skirt gets hiked up, such as when you sit.

- ✔ **You put the garter belt and stockings on first and your panties on last.** Otherwise, you have to remove everything when you go to the bathroom.

- ✔ **Never wear hosiery with open-toe shoes or sandals (see Figure 14-4).** *Never.* No exceptions. In fact, I'm getting anxious just thinking of that outfit!

Figure 14-4: Don't wear hose with open-toe shoes!

How much should you spend on hosiery? You can get a good pair of brand-name hose or stockings for $12 to $25, and they'll last a while if cared for properly. Get the right size (hosiery that's too tight wears out more quickly), and wash them before you put them on to help the material stretch a little (this also helps them fit better). Hand-washing is preferable, but if you must wash hosiery in a washing machine with other clothes, put them in a lingerie bag to protect them.

Bras

The bra has a history that stretches back several thousands of years. But it wasn't until the early 20th century, when Warner, a huge bra manufacturing company, began selling bras in various cup sizes that the "modern" bra was born. Since then, bra manufacturers have been using their creativity to design bras for almost every purpose and occasion.

Types of bras

Women wear bras to prevent sagging, to provide shape for a particular look, and to add a layer of opacity to a sheer top. Today, more than 20 different types of bras are available — not to mention all the varieties of designs available for each type. Here is a brief description of the most common categories:

- **Full-support bras:** This type of bra fully envelops the breast (see Figure 14-5). The objective is to give the breast as much support and concealment as possible. Full support bras include *minimizers* (for large-breasted women who want to appear smaller) and *underwire bras* (which have wire built into the cup to help support, lift, and shape the breasts).

Figure 14-5: The bigger your cup size, the more support you need.

✔ **Seamless bras:** Designed more for sheer or fitted clothing (see Figure 14-6), seamless bras are perfect under a T-shirt because no lines show. These come with underwire and padding if you're looking for a little boost, too!

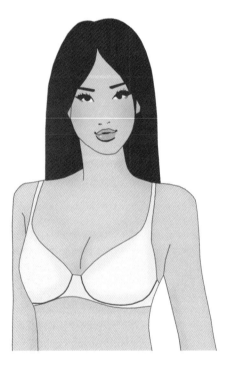

Figure 14-6: Seamless bras minimize the visual effect a bra has on your clothes.

✔ **Strapless bras:** Strapless bras, or *bandeau bras,* are designed to be worn with strapless tops or dresses, and tops that don't fully cover the shoulders.

✔ **Convertible bras:** These bras have removable straps that you can wear in a variety of ways (see Figure 14-7): over the shoulder, crisscrossed in the back, as a halter, as a T-back, or without the straps. The crisscross style is great for underneath a racerback tank or a sleeveless top.

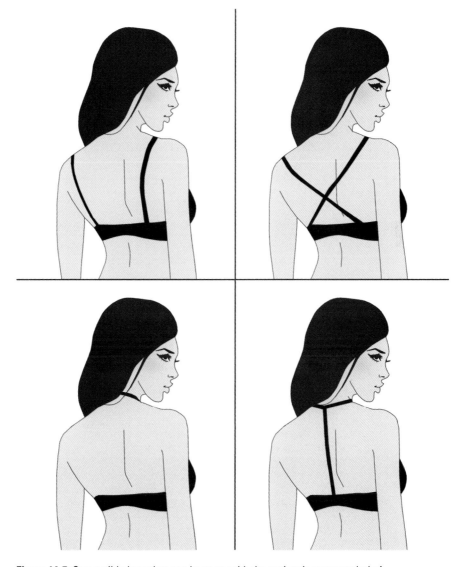

Figure 14-7: Convertible bras that can keep up with the variety in your wardrobe!

If you don't have a convertible bra, try the Hollywood Hook-Up (www.Hollywoodfashiontape.com), shown in Figure 14-8. This device converts your bra into a racerback, saving you from having to buy a new bra.

✔ **Plunge bras:** These are ideal when you wear low-cut garments but still have enough coverage to feel comfortable.

©Jeremy Winter, Hollywood Fashion Tape, Inc.

Figure 14-8: A hook-up turns a regular bra into a racerback.

✔ **Shelf bras:** These bras support the breast but don't cover it, giving the appearance that you're not wearing a bra.

✔ **Demi bras:** These bras leave the top half of the breast exposed and are good when you wear a top with a deep neckline.

✔ **Padded bras:** Padded bras are designed to increase the appearance of the volume of the breast.

✔ **Push-up bras:** These bras create more cleavage by using padding or gel to push up the breast. One of the most well-known push-up bras is the Wonderbra.

✔ **Adhesive bras:** These are latex-free adhesives that you place on your nipples to hide them. They give no support at all. Wear them with backless dresses or when you want the braless look but want to maintain a hint of modesty.

Many brands sell nipple concealers. Most are discarded after use (don't worry; it doesn't kill when you take them off!). I love Low Beams; they're $10 at www.barenecessities.com.

✔ **Specialty bras:** This category includes a variety of bras such as

• **Nursing bras:** These open up to allow a nursing mother to feed her child without removing the bra.

• **Longline bras:** The base of these stretch down to your waist to hold in your tummy.

Each style of bra comes in an assortment of fabrics, colors, and designs. As long as the bra fits you properly (see the next section) and is flattering on you, feel free to play with different options.

Have a variety of designs so that you have something appropriate to wear underneath any top you put on. If you wear a light-colored or sheer top, for example, wear a nude or flesh-toned bra that won't show through the fabric. If you wear a lot of black or heavier materials on top, you can play with darker-colored bras or bras with designs or lace, because you won't see those things through the shirt.

How many different types of bras you need depends on your lifestyle. If you have one type of bra that you like and wear every day, having a supply of those suffices. But if you attend events where you're likely to wear a strapless gown or one with a plunging neckline, even if these events occur only once or twice a year, then you want to have some of those types of bras in your drawer. If you're active and engage in various sports, you need some sports bras. Whether you ever stock up on sexy bras is a personal decision, but it's a good idea, because even if you don't dress overtly sexy, just knowing you're wearing a sexy bra underneath can do wonders to your mood and your psyche, and give you that extra boost of confidence!

Getting fitted by a pro

Experts say that something like 8 out of 10 women aren't wearing the right bra size. Let this section help you avoid being one of those unfortunate women.

Why is it so important for a bra to fit perfectly, you ask? Walk down the street and see all the women whose flesh bulges out of their bras in one place or another, and that's one answer. Then ask your women friends how many find their bras comfortable, and that gives you another. A bra that fits properly leaves you looking and feeling your best. A bra that's too tight is uncomfortable, and one that's too loose doesn't give you the necessary support. Finally, a well-fitting bra makes you look slimmer. Here's why: Your rib cage is your thinnest point. If you're like most women, the lower you go below your rib cage, toward your belly, the wider you are. So you want to show off that rib cage, but you can't do that if your breasts are sagging and covering most of it up. If your bra fits you correctly, however, your breasts look perky and stand out from your rib cage, making it visible.

Your correct bra size is very difficult to figure out on your own. To get fitted properly for a bra, go to the lingerie department of a department store or to a lingerie shop. The staff at either of these places can provide the expertise you need. Fittings are free at most department stores, and you don't generally need an appointment. Ask for the lead specialist (she's had the most experience). And keep in mind that you can't get a proper measurement with your bra on. So you're going to have to take it off and allow the expert to measure you. Don't allow modesty to prevent you from getting fitted for the perfect bra; these experts have seen everything and are very professional.

Get yourself professionally fitted at least once a year, and more often if you've undergone any dramatic weight loss or gain.

Shopping for bras

Almost all department stores have a lingerie department stocked with a wide variety of merchandise and the salespeople necessary to help with size and style. You can also go to any of the many lingerie shops and boutiques. Victoria's Secret is always a good choice, too, because it has many locations and a large variety of styles at reasonable prices. You can also find specialty bra stores, where the personnel not only fit you for a bra but also alter the bra for you right at the store. These are often more expensive, but you're sure to get the perfect fit and finest quality.

Wherever you shop, follow these steps to find a bra that fits properly (Figure 14-9 shows the different parts of a bra):

1. **Put it on the loosest fitting.**

   A bra stretches over time, and you'll have to tighten it eventually, so you want to start out with room to tighten it.

   Over time, the elastic in a bra stretches, and you'll notice that the bra rides up your back and doesn't support your breasts. When that happens, go to the next set of hooks. When you've exhausted the hooks, it's time to get a new bra.

2. **See whether you can run one finger comfortably around the inside edge of the band.**

   If you can't, it's too tight. If you can fit two fingers, then it's too loose.

3. **Take a look at yourself in the mirror.**

   Do your breasts bulge out the sides or the top? Unless it's a push-up bra that you want to boost your figure, bulging breasts means it's too tight.

4. **Check out the *gore,* or middle of the bra in the front.**

   It should be flat against your chest. If it's being pushed away from you, either the cups are too big or the band is too big.

5. **Move around and see how it feels:**

   • Bend over to make sure that your breasts don't flop out. If they do, that's a sure sign that the bra is too big.

   • Put your arms over your head. If the band slips, it's too big, but if it cuts, it's too small.

   • Twist your torso left and right. The bra should move with you, staying firmly in place.

6. **Pay attention to how the straps feel and how the cups look.**

   Are the straps weighing down your shoulders? If they need to be that tight for the bra to feel supportive, then the band size is not right. If the bra has wrinkles in the cup, the cup is too big.

When buying a bra, consider two key aspects: look and comfort. If you find a bra that you like that has both qualities, then where you buy it doesn't matter. But if you're dissatisfied with most of the bras you wear, I suggest you go to either a quality department store or a lingerie shop and spend whatever it takes to get a perfect bra.

Each manufacturer turns out slightly different bras in the same size, and that's true season to season. So if you find a bra that fits perfectly, you may want to buy several.

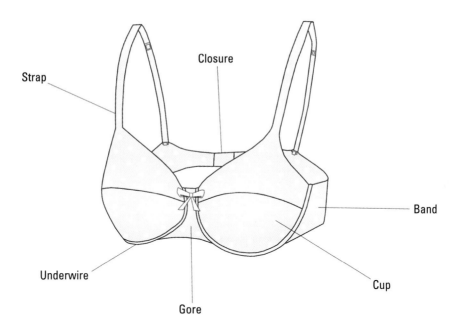

Figure 14-9: The parts of a bra.

Bra care

Bras have elastic in them and can be delicate, especially those with underwire and padding. By taking proper care of your bras, you can extend their life. Some tips:

✔ **Don't wear the same bra two days in a row.** By rotating bras day to day, you allow the elastic to recover.

✔ **Wash them correctly.** Hand-washing your bras is best. If you must put them in a machine, place them in a lingerie pop-up bag. And use a detergent that doesn't contain lanolin, which breaks down elastic. Brands made for lingerie or that are ecologically friendly don't contain lanolin. (Unfortunately, the laundry detergents you commonly find at the grocery store do contain lanolin.)

Panties

Shopping for panties is a lot less complicated than shopping for bras. Most of your decisions have to do with personal preference. What style is most comfortable for you (full brief, bikini, or thong)? Which cut is going to give you the coverage you need for the outfit you plan to wear? Do you prefer, silk, nylon, or cotton? Do you have a preference about color and design? And, most importantly, which cut is the most flattering on your body? Following are the different types of panties (many of which you can see in Figure 14-10):

✔ **Briefs:** The traditional standby, briefs today come in low cut (perfect if you're wearing low-cut jeans) and high cut (which give you the illusion of a longer leg).

✔ **Bikini:** These offer less coverage than briefs but still cover your behind. Low-rise bikinis are good when you wear low-rise pants. Some are called *string bikinis* because the sides are thin, like strings.

✔ **Thongs:** In the early 1990s, women began wearing thong underwear so they would no longer have visible panty lines (VPL). Thong underwear has only a thin strip of fabric connecting the front of the panty to the back. This style doesn't cover your butt, and it definitely feels different from traditional briefs and bikinis. Women who wear thongs swear by their comfort, so before you definitely decide they don't belong in your underwear drawer, you may want to at least try one. You may be pleasantly surprised by their comfort and by the way your clothes look and feel over them. (There's something to be said about the way you feel psychologically when you're wearing one, too!)

Don't be afraid to wear a thong, even if you don't think it'll be flattering on you. Because a thong provides so little coverage, your body actually looks better and you have no panty lines to worry about. Without elastic to dig into your skin, it gives you an overall smooth look.

✔ **G-strings:** G-strings are similar to thongs, except that the connector is only a string rather than a strip of fabric.

✔ **Boy shorts:** This style of panty, which offers complete rear coverage (more like an actual short, hence the name), also eliminates VPL by extending further down the leg. The only drawback is that it's another layer under your clothing. If you're trying to appear thinner, go with a thong or G-string to avoid that extra layer between you and your pants, skirt, or dress.

✔ **Seamless panties:** These use spandex in the material to hold the panty in place and eliminate the seam around the thigh.

As for materials, cotton panties are the easiest to care for, but silk is the most luxurious. And undies made from microfiber wick away moisture, making them good for those who exercise. Why limit yourself to one style? It makes sense to have a variety for different occasions. What you pick to wear each day will be a function of your outfit, your activities, and — mostly — your mood.

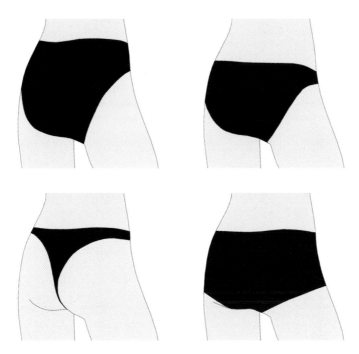

Figure 14-10: Clockwise from top left: Briefs, bikini, boy shorts, and thong.

Shapers

Body shapers are amazing inventions that help improve your appearance by holding you in and smoothing you out. They use compression to make you appear smaller. Shapers come in a variety of styles from full-body shapers to ones that cover your stomach and upper legs. Which type you choose depends on where you think you need the most help. The original shapers were called *girdles* and were designed to keep a woman's belly in. Panty girdles added hips and thighs. Today you can find control briefs, control capris, control camisoles, and control slips. You can wear a shaper under everything from jeans to an evening gown.

When I do "Ambush Makeover" on NBC's *Today* show, I put everyone — whether a size 2 or a size 20 — in Spanx (see Figure 14-11). An alternative to Spanx is Assets, a less expensive line sold at Target.

Some tips on wearing and caring for shapers:

- ✔ You can wear a shaper with or without panties. Your choice.

- ✔ If you wear a shaper on your lower half, don't forget to wear a bra that fits properly and enhances your upper half. You want the whole look to be flattering and seamless — the perfect foundation underneath your outfit.

- ✔ Make sure you follow the washing instructions for the particular garment. Because you're investing in a piece like this, take care of it properly.

You want to be comfortable in your clothing in order to be productive and enjoy your day. So dress to flatter your body type, and if you get a little help from a shaper where you need it, you'll be ready for anything.

©SPANX

Figure 14-11: Spanx.

15

Accessories

Less is more!

Lisa Rinna, Actress

I have this fabulous pair of gold earrings (see the back cover picture). Without fail, every time I wear them, somebody stops me. The earrings cost under a hundred dollars, and I definitely got my money's worth. I wear them with jeans and a T-shirt or a simple black dress. But no matter what I wear them with, they're always a showstopper. Everyone needs a few accessories like that — pieces that can take an outfit from good to great.

This chapter shows you how to use accessories to take your wardrobe from simple to sizzling in a flash.

Scarves and Shawls

Unless you're a big celebrity or have an unlimited bank account, it's unlikely that you have a big enough wardrobe to wear a new outfit everyday (would be nice, right?). You can make your outfits look different every time you wear them, though. It's all about one word — accessories.

Here's an item you probably have in the back of your closet: a printed scarf. Scarves have the power to expand your wardrobe by making each outfit look different, especially if you tend to wear monochromatic tops. Because the focus of the outfit is the scarf, no one will notice that you're wearing the same white top you wore last week. Solid scarves can also make an outfit pop. If you wear a multi-colored top, you can add a solid-colored scarf for a little extra flair.

Scarves, particularly ones made of silk, take up very little room and don't require much care. (Unless you get them dirty, you rarely need to dry clean them.) What's also great is that they're available in all price ranges. You can get a great one for $20 or splurge on a designer scarf and spend hundreds. With a scarf, you can get away with spending a little less because the price doesn't affect how the scarf fits you.

Winter scarves

Winter scarves are those you wear when you cozy up in front of the fire! Even though many of us are all bundled up in the winter, you can still look chic. Use your winter scarf to make a statement (see Figure 15-1). Here are some tips:

- ✔ **Have a couple different scarves to match your winter coats.** Because you may wear your winter scarves almost every day in cold weather, go with solids or classic weaves like plaid, houndstooth, or herringbone.

- ✔ **Feel your winter scarves before buying.** Some wool can be scratchy. (If you're buying online or through a catalogue, make sure to check the return policy.)

- ✔ **If you can, choose natural fibers.** Cashmere is a great option if you can afford to splurge on your scarf. *Pashmina* (a type of cashmere woven in Kashmir from goats that live high in the Himalayas) scarves are also very popular. Scarves made from man-made fibers generally aren't as cozy and luxurious as those made from natural fibers.

Figure 15-1: Stay bundled up and still look chic.

Summer scarves

Ah, summertime! Now I know the last thing you want to do when it gets really nice out is bundle up, but you can wear scarves even when it's warm to make an outfit complete. How? Use your scarf as an accessory to bring an outfit together. In the summer, I like to wear a white T-shirt with white jeans and tie a bright scarf around my neck. I also like to use my scarf as a belt, as in Figure 15-2. You probably didn't realize your scarf had so many uses!

Figure 15-2: A new way to wear your favorite scarf.

Using a brooch to keep your scarf closed is another option. (I love using my grandmother's old pins to make a statement.)

Tying a scarf: A quick how-to

Did you know your scarf can go from being a shirt to a purse in seconds? Turning a scarf into unexpected items is so much fun to do — always a show-stopper. Figure 15-3 shows the different ways to tie a scarf.

Figure 15-3: Different ways to use a scarf.

Around the neck

Tying a scarf around your neck is certainly the classic way to wear it, and it keeps you looking chic without making you too warm. Wearing a scarf like this can make an otherwise plain suit pop. If you wear one in the summer with a T-shirt, your outfit is more complete. Remember, when you wear a scarf this way, it's part of your outfit and you'll want to keep it on, even when you're indoors.

To tie a scarf around your neck, as shown in Figure 15-3, follow these steps:

1. **Fold the scarf into a triangle.**

2. **Starting with the point, fold inward until the scarf is one long line.**

3. **Tie it around your neck in either of the following ways:**

    - **If the scarf is long:** Start with it in the front of the neck and wrap it around the back and then back to the front. Tie a knot in the front.

    - **If the scarf is short:** Place it around your neck and tie a knot in the front.

    You can wear the knot either on the side or in the middle.

Around the waist

I love this look. Instead of using a conventional belt, try looping your scarf and threading it through the loops of your pants. This makes any outfit more fun (and is especially great with jeans). To turn a scarf into a belt (refer to Figure 15-2), follow these steps:

1. **Fold the scarf into a triangle.**

2. **Starting with the point, fold inward until the scarf is one long line.**

3. **Put it through the loops of jeans or slacks and tie a knot in the front.**

Or you can just tie it like a sarong over your jeans, as in Figure 15-3. Here's how:

1. **Fold scarf into a triangle.**

2. **Wrap around your waist and tie the two ends at one hip.**

As a halter top

To tie a scarf like a halter top (see Figure 15-3), use a large square scarf (one that's at least 36 inches square) and then follow these steps:

1. **Place the scarf on a flat surface with the dull side facing up.**

2. **In the middle of the scarf, tie a tight small knot.**

3. **Take the two points directly across from each other and tie them around your neck.**

4. **Tie the remaining two corners around your waist and tie a knot around your back.**

As a pocketbook

Yes! Another one of my favorites. Your scarf can be transformed into a pocketbook (refer to Figure 15-3). Use a 36-inch square scarf and follow these steps:

1. **Place your scarf on a flat surface with the dull side facing up.**

2. **Take the two points diagonal from each other and tie a tight knot in the middle of the scarf.**

3. **Take the remaining two points and tie another knot (only 4 inches from the top).**

   This becomes the handle of your new, fabulous pocketbook.

Jewelry

Your jewelry collection comprises the most personal and special pieces you own. You collect it over a lifetime, and you generally don't replace those items every season or even every few years. Often you get jewelry as a gift for special occasions or you inherit pieces from your mother or grandmother. Whether they're pieces you were given or bought yourself, real or fake, fine or costume, all can have sentimental value and make you feel special when you wear them. Knowing how to incorporate these pieces into your wardrobe is important because they can really express your personality and style.

Fine jewelry

Knowing what to splurge on and what to save on is really important. You shouldn't spend a lot on some things (like trendy tops). Other items, though, are worth investing in. Two pieces are a must in every jewelry chest: diamond stud earrings and a pearl necklace.

If you don't have the money right now to buy *major* jewelry pieces for your wardrobe, don't feel that these pieces are a *must* right now. I just want you to know what pieces to concentrate on when and if the occasion arises when you can spend money on jewelry.

You don't need to splurge on certain items. I wear faux jewelry all the time. I bought the necklace in Figure 15-4 at my favorite store, Jennifer Miller (www. jennifermillerjewelry.com). The one on the left is real and costs thousands of dollars. The one on the right (which is mine) costs under $100. Crazy, right? (No way can you tell the difference!) Getting the same look as expensive jewelry without breaking the bank *is* possible.

©Jennifer Miller

Figure 15-4: Real diamonds (left) versus fake diamonds (right).

Birthstones

Although the idea of certain stones being associated with certain months dates back to the Old Testament, it wasn't until the 18th century in Poland that the concept really took hold. Twelve birthstones exist, one for each month, and the list goes like this:

January — Garnet (deep red)

February — Amethyst (purple)

March — Aquamarine (pale blue)

April — Diamond (clear)

May — Emerald (green)

June — Pearl (white)

July — Ruby (red)

August — Peridot (pale green)

September — Sapphire (deep blue)

October — Opal (muilti-color)

November — Yellow Topaz (yellow)

December — Topaz (blue)

Some people become very attached to their birthstone and it becomes their signature stone. (Mine is diamond, so I am very attached!) If that's the case with you, then incorporate your birthstone into your style and your wardrobe choices. If you were born in May, for example, emerald earrings or a necklace can make a black dress or suit pop instantly.

Diamond studs earrings

If you can afford to buy a set of diamond studs in platinum or white or yellow gold, go for it. They'll last forever and will go with everything. I wear mine with everything from cocktail dresses to jeans and a T-shirt. Everyone, from surfer chicks to those who prefer classic attire, should have diamond studs. (They also come in clip-on.)

If you're laughing because buying expensive jewels isn't even an option right now, cubic zirconia studs are a great alternative. As long as you don't go too big, it's very hard (unless you're a jeweler) to tell that they're not real. Again, smaller studs — under 2 karats — look more believable yet significant. I wear faux diamonds when I'm on vacation and no one can tell.

A pearl necklace

Another staple that goes with many different outfits and takes you to many different occasions is a pearl necklace. Even if you prefer very casual dress, a strand of pearls will be useful for those times when you need to get dressed up. I wear pearls that my mother gave me, but if you don't have a pearl neck-lace, you can purchase your own without emptying your wallet. Pearls come in many levels of quality — the more perfect they are, the more expensive. You don't need perfect pearls. You can find necklaces made of pearls that have slight imperfections or that aren't all exactly the same size (another reason for the higher price).

Again, as with diamond studs and cubic zirconia, you can also buy a faux pearl necklace that no one will know is faux when paired with your fabulous outfit. And, if your look is a little more bohemian than classic, you can go with freshwater pearls. These are less expensive and have a different, more unusual look.

Costume or fashion jewelry

I love costume jewelry. I have people in my life (my dear friend Sandi and my mother) who have so much of it that they have a system of organization. Both use plastic bags (so they can see each piece) and organize the pieces by their general look. Every woman should explore the world of costume jewelry; you can make it work no matter what your style. A statement neck-lace, earrings, or ring can really make an otherwise simple outfit fabulous. My pearl necklace (on the front cover) is an example of how a piece of great jewelry can dress up jeans instantly.

Costume or fashion jewelry is made with materials that are much less expen-sive than fine jewelry. What looks like gold may be *gold-plated* (a thin layer of gold over another metal, most often copper or silver) or *gold-filled* (a thicker layer of gold laid over another metal, often brass). The designation *gold-filled* requires that the weight of the gold equal one-twentieth the weight of the entire piece. Eventually, the outer layer of gold is going to wear away, but how long that takes depends on the manufacturing process and how careful you are in protecting the piece.

Costume and fashion jewelry can vary in price depending on whether or not the piece has a designer name attached to it or whether the materials are rhinestones, cubic zirconia, or the more expensive semi-precious stones. Because it's more affordable, costume jewelry also enables you to buy dif-ferent pieces to go with certain outfits. When you're looking for the perfect accessory for a specific outfit, costume jewelry is a great option. You can build an outfit around a great piece.

Making your bangles and beads work

Playing around with different ways to wear jewelry is fun. Stacking several bracelets or necklaces can work, especially if you're wearing a very simple outfit. Just remember: Wear only one statement piece at a time. If you opt for a ton of bangles on your arm, go with a more subtle necklace or earrings (studs always work).

Mixing real and faux jewelry is also a good idea because the real items make your costume jewels look that much richer.

Again, be careful of how much jewelry you wear at any given moment. One piece that pops is often the way to go. A great trick to guard against over-accessorizing is to put on everything you think you want to wear while your back is to the mirror, and then quickly turn around. The first thing you see in the mirror is the one thing that may be putting your outfit over the top. If you remove that item, you're good to go. Figure 15-5 shows how too many accessories can overwhelm an outfit, but just the right number can make a great outfit even better.

Vintage jewelry

Although people don't like the idea of wearing clothes that other people have worn, many women have a different feeling about vintage jewelry. Especially with formalwear, vintage is very popular and can give you a beautifully classic look.

Vintage jewelry can be anything from a brooch you pick up at a flea market to an engagement ring you buy at an expensive antique jewelry shop. Because it's really about the look you're going for, hunting for inexpensive and unusual pieces to spruce up your wardrobe is a great idea (and can be a fun project). As with costume jewelry, or any jewelry for that matter, you want certain pieces to pop, so don't overdo it when you wear vintage jewelry. Try wearing one piece at a time and make that the focal point of your outfit. No one will be able to tell if it's real or not, and you will get a chance to show your personal flair.

Figure 15-5: How not to accessorize (left) and how to accessorize (right).

Hats

I have hair that needs to be blown out or I look like I stuck my head in a socket. Hats are often my best friends on the days I just can't bring myself to blow out my hair for an hour.

That said, before you add a bunch of hats to your wardrobe, you definitely have to be comfortable with wearing them. Hats worn for warmth in winter are definitely easier to get away with than ones that are pure fashion statements. Hats certainly aren't for everyone (some people just don't look good in them), but if you learn what works for you, hats are another way to achieve a different look, not to mention save you from a bad hair day!

The following is a list of the basic hat types:

- **Baseball cap:** Baseball caps are sporty and look best with workout clothes or jeans and a T-shirt. They are most commonly worn when outside watching a sporting event or concert or when running around doing errands on a bad hair day. They are not especially fashionable, but they can be cute on the weekend.

- **Beret:** The French beret is made of soft wool in a multitude of colors. You can personalize it by pushing the crown to one side or the other, wearing it at many different angles, or even adding a brooch or pin to it. Berets are great for keeping warm *and* making a fashion statement. They're a perfect addition to your fall wardrobe when the temperatures start dropping. Use a beret to top off a cute sweater, jeans, boots, and a wrap; or wear one with your new fall coat. Because you can mold them however you like and wear them in a number of ways, decide where it looks best (tilted right or left, or pushed more forward or back) and is most comfortable for you.

- **Cowboy hat:** The traditional ones are great if you live in the West but hard to match with anything other than jeans. However, straw versions of these are very popular in the summertime. The straw ones look great with a sun dress or a bathing suit on the beach.

- **Fedora:** Fedoras were originally made of soft felt. Like cowboy hats, nowadays fedoras can even be found in straw. This is a very stylish-looking hat and is generally worn to add flair to an otherwise simple outfit (see Figure 15-6).

Figure 15-6: A hat can serve as the statement piece of an outfit.

✔ **Sun hat:** These are usually made of straw or light canvas and have a wide brim to protect your face and neck from the harmful effects of the sun. Sun hats are great for the beach or just being out on a sunny summer day and work with almost any summertime outfit.

The only thing you have to be careful of when you wear hats is looking too gimmicky. You don't want to appear as if you're in a costume. Choose a hat that's in style and make sure your personality is one that can carry it off before you incorporate that look into your wardrobe. Hats can land you in the hands of the fashion police when not worn correctly. If you have thoughts that the hat you chose may look silly, it likely does. I often ask my co-writer Dana if a hat looks good on me or if it's too much. This is a time when a friend's opinion helps a great deal.

If you're looking for a hat that's hard to find, try a vintage shop. As with jewelry, they're great places to find that one-of-a-kind piece.

Bags

You'd be surprised how big a fashion statement a bag can make. Just as hemlines go up and down according to the latest trend, bags get bigger and smaller accordingly.

Types of bags

A great bag can actually make an entire outfit. You could be wearing jeans and a plain white top, but if you carry a fabulous statement bag you can change your whole look. Handbags come in a variety of categories, including:

✔ **Baguette:** A long, thin bag named after the French bread. Fashionistas set the trend with these when Fendi came out with these "it" bags.

✔ **Clutch:** This size bag works with everything from jeans to formal wear. The more dressed up you are, the less you're supposed to carry. When you're at your most elegant, the only bag to carry is a small clutch (in most cases without a handle). These small bags force you to be very selective about what you take with you. However, a clutch is also appropriate if you don't have much to carry and are just running to meet a friend for lunch or a casual dinner.

✔ **Duffle:** A take-off on the bags carried by sailors, a duffle bag is a large, roundish bag with a zipper on the top that holds your entire life and then some. Often more useful and durable than fashionable, this bag is perfect to hold everything you may need for day-to-day running around with the kids!

✔ **Evening bag:** Evening bags are usually clutches and often small enough to fit in your hand or under one arm. The level of detailing further declares how dressy a bag is. Fancier evening bags have a lot of detailing — like beads, sequins, and metallic fabric — that make them stand out. Some evening bags have a thin strap, handy when you need your hands to carry a drink during the cocktail hour, and the strap can usually be tucked inside if you want it to be simply a clutch. Judith Leiber is known for her beautiful evening bags that are uniquely shaped to match a woman's interests and personality. (I was once given an evening bag shaped like a bird.)

✔ **Hobo:** These soft, crescent-shaped bags with a long handle are meant to be worn over the shoulder. Hobo bags are very stylish and also practical because they can hold a ton of stuff. They're unstructured and go with clothing that is more casual or flowing.

✔ **Kelly bag:** This rectangular bag with a metal clasp is the epitome of luxury (see Figure 15-7). In addition to the traditional look, some are made from exotic leathers like alligator or ostrich. The prices can go as high as $27,000; and that goes for vintage bags as well as new ones.

Figure 15-7: The Kelly bag.

Grace Kelly made these bags famous in 1956 when she used one to hide her pregnancy from prying photographers.

✔ **Messenger:** Originally created to carry mail or messages, this type of bag is large and, when the strap is placed across the back and chest, leaves both hands free. Today, you see it carried by both men and women in most large urban areas.

✔ **Satchel:** The traditional satchel bag is very much like a messenger bag, but the name has also been attached to other smaller bags with shorter handles that can be carried in your hand.

✔ **Shoulder:** Any bag that has a strap long enough to go over your shoulder is a shoulder bag.

✔ **Tote:** A tote bag is a large bag with an open top that's good for carrying everything from groceries to a weekend's worth of bikinis (see Figure 15-8).

This list should also include the simple handbag, because most bags that are sold don't actually fit into a particular category. The simple handbag is available in a wide variety of shapes and sizes, with an amazing assortment of pockets and flaps on the inside to help you to organize your life. Those of you who juggle a million things every day are going to need a bag that's functional and practical as well as cute!

Figure 15-8: A tote bag is perfect for a day at the beach.

Luxury bags

High-end designer bags are definitely a luxury item. They are beautiful and well made (it can take up to 20 hours to make a hand-crafted bag). However, most of them cost upward of $1,000, so having even one can be a stretch for most people.

If you want that designer bag for a special event but don't want to spend designer prices, try www.bagborroworsteal.com. This site allows you to rent luxury bags by the week or the month at prices that start from $50 and go to $200 (depending on whether or not you're a member and how long you keep it).

Picking a handbag

Just as you wouldn't choose a pair of pants or any other item of clothing simply by the way it looks on the shelf, you shouldn't choose a handbag that way, either. Here are things to consider when buying your next handbag:

- ✔ **Consider what color and style you need.** Handbags get paired with so many different outfits, so consider carefully what color and style you need. My advice:

  - **Cover the basics first.** Get a neutral bag that goes with everything. If you already have that great black bag and you want to invest in a new bag, go for a different color. If you tend to wear mostly neutrals, a bag in a fun color can be a great accent piece.

  - **If you're buying a bag to go with a specific outfit, wear something similar to that outfit when you go shopping.** This way you'll know that you're making a smart purchase that matches the outfit you plan to wear it with.

- ✔ **Check to see that the bag balances your size.** A bag shouldn't overwhelm you if you're on the smaller side. Just like your clothing, you want your bag to look right proportionately and enhance your overall look.

- ✔ **Determine whether it complements your basic body shape.** If you're more round-shaped, you want to offset that with a square-ish, structured bag. But if you're very angular, a round-shaped bag (like a crescent-shaped Hobo) may be better for you.

- ✔ **Compare the bag color to your shoe color.** It always looks polished to have shoes and a bag that complement each other. Having said that, the days when bags and shoes have to match exactly are gone. Putting together an outfit in which all your accessories work together without being too matchy-matchy lets you express your personal style *and* look current at the same time.

For Eyes: Spectacles

Of course glasses are used for their obvious purpose — to correct your vision — but they can also work as a great accessory. It comes as no surprise that many designers have come out with their very own line of frames. As with clothing, trends come and go in the optical world. Investing in frames that best suit your face before splurging on ones that may be hot only this season is definitely the way to go.

Matching frames to face

Faces, just like bodies, come in general shapes. Your face can be oval, oblong, round, square, or triangular. Recognizing the shape of your face assists you in determining what type of frame suits you best.

- ✔ **Oval:** An oval face looks good in just about any type of frame (see Figure 15-9).

- ✔ **Oblong:** Oblong faces are much longer than they are wide. Frames that sit in the middle of your face break up that long line.

- ✔ **Round:** To deemphasize the roundness of your face, choose frames with more straight lines.

- ✔ **Square:** To deemphasize a square face, choose frames that are more rounded (see Figure 15-10). Glasses that are heavier on the top also give a lengthening effect.

- ✔ **Triangular:** Avoid large frames that make the upper portion of your face look bigger. Also stay away from bright colors, because these also draw attention to the top half of your face.

Figure 15-9: Aviator glasses go well with an oval-shaped face.

Skin tone and hair color also play a role in deciding which frame colors are right for you. Your glasses are meant to flatter and enhance your face, not overwhelm it. If your skin is very pale and you wear very dark glasses, for example, the glasses will stand out so much that people won't appreciate the rest of your face.

The length of your nose is another factor to consider. If you have a short nose, wear lighter glasses that sit high on your face to maximize the visible length; if you have a long nose, glasses with a *double bridge* (two bars) can make it seem a bit shorter. Large frames can balance a large nose, but small frames only accentuate the size.

Figure 15-10: A round frame pairs well with a square-shaped face.

Putting Your Best Foot Forward: Shoes

High heels or ballet flats go with everything.

Liz Lange, Fashion Designer

*Y*our obsession with shoes may have begun when you were 2 years old and you stepped into a pair of your mother's high heels. Eventually you grew up enough to shop for your own. How much fun! Carrie Bradshaw from *Sex and the City* took shoe shopping to a whole new level. Whether you live in a big city, in the suburbs, or on a farm, every woman should strut in style!

The great thing about new shoes is that they can reinvent any outfit in your closet. That little black dress you already own, for example, will look so much better with a fabulous new pair of strappy sandals. Buying a new pair of shoes also gives you that extra boost of confidence and makes you feel sexier with every step. This chapter shows you how to shop for comfortable, stylish shoes without breaking the bank.

Crash Course in Shoe Shopping

When you're heading out the door to go shoe shopping (lucky you!), first make sure you know what you're looking for. If warmer weather is coming and you don't have any sandals to go with your dresses, for example, then plan to buy a great pair of strappy shoes. Or if you have a garment you'd love to wear but don't have the right shoes to go with it, keep an eye out for just the right shoe. I once had a fabulous dress in fuchsia, but didn't have the right shoes to wear with it until I found the perfect pair of gold high-heel sandals.

My point? Have a goal when heading into a shoe store. Taking this approach makes your shopping excursion both practical *and* fun. Without a plan, shoe shopping is going to hurt your wallet, not your feet.

First steps: Getting ready

Just as with clothing, do your research and prepare before you go shoe shopping:

✔ **Look through some fashion magazines to see what's in style.** Are chunkier heels or stilettos in style? Are toes pointy or more rounded? What height are the boots? Are flats in? With an idea of what you're looking for, you're better prepared to hit the stores without all the choices overwhelming you.

Some of the trendier designs probably won't be in style for very long. If you decide to go with something very trendy, try to find an inexpensive version. That way, when the trends change in the coming season, you haven't wasted a ton of money on shoes you don't want to wear anymore.

✔ **Make sure you have the right hose or socks when you go to try on shoes.** If you're looking for sneakers, you need the kinds of socks you'd wear with the sneakers. If you're buying pumps or boots, you need a thin sock or stocking — whatever you plan to wear underneath. (Most shoe stores provide stocking-like disposable peds you can use when you try on shoes.) Because sandals are worn with bare feet, you'll be fine when trying those on.

If you know you'll be shopping for shoes, make sure the footwear you have on comes off easily, especially if you're visiting more than one store. Who wants to waste time tying laces when you could be looking for more potential buys!

Paying attention to fit

I love the look of high heels. I think many outfits look better and sexier when heels are worn. With that said, I am a huge fan of flats, too. Regardless of whether you're wearing heels or flats, neither will be comfortable if it doesn't fit properly. That's why in this section I begin with the basics: how to find the right shoe size for you.

Measuring your feet — both of them

Taking an accurate foot measurement requires more than just slipping your foot into one of those foot measurement devices. To get the right measurement, follow these suggestions:

- ✔ **Make sure to get *both* feet measured at a shoe store.** Your feet may not be the same size. It's not uncommon for one foot to be bigger than the other. A slight difference between one foot and the other may not matter, but if the difference is as much as half a size, it does. If one foot is bigger than the other, buy footwear that fits the bigger foot.

- ✔ **Stand on the foot measurement device, rather than put your foot on it while sitting.** Your foot gets wider when you stand.

- ✔ **Get your feet measured toward the end of the day.** Feet tend to swell as the day goes along. At the end of the day, they're at their fullest.

- ✔ **Get your feet re-measured every so often.** As you age, your foot size may change.

Taking shoe shape into consideration

Just because you know the size of your feet doesn't necessarily mean that every shoe of that size fits you comfortably. The basic shape of the shoe is called the *last* (see Figure 16-1). Variations in the last can mean that, while one size 8 shoe fits you like a glove, another size 8 shoe could be too big or too small.

When you try on shoes, pay attention to how they feel. While the level of comfort a shoe provides should be apparent, here are a few specific things to look for:

- ✔ **The toe box:** This is the part of the shoe where your toes go. You want the toe box to be big enough to accommodate all five of your toes comfortably. If it's too big, your foot will slide around and you'll end up with blisters. And if it's too small (your toes will be a little cramped when you try them on), you'll wish you never bought them after only a few hours wearing them.

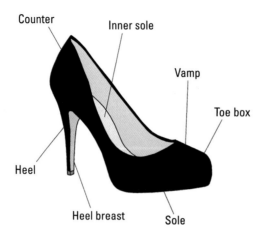

Figure 16-1: The parts of a shoe.

- ✔ **The vamp:** This part of the shoe covers the top of the foot. Depending on how high the arch of your foot is, a shoe vamp may or may not fit comfortably. Different brands cut differently, so find one that fits you correctly.

- ✔ **Sole:** One part that you're probably very familiar with, the sole is the bottom of the shoe. The soles of sneakers have ridges and are made of rubber to provide traction, while leather soles are thinner and more fashionable. Dancing, anyone? The thicker the sole, the more comfortable walking is, because the thickness protects your feet from the hard ground below.

- ✔ **Counter:** The counter is the back part of the shoe. If there's too much space between the back of your foot and the counter, your foot moves too much, and all that rubbing will cause a blister. As long as the shoe fits your foot properly in every other way, try the next shoe size down for a better fit — or if you're between sizes, try a shoe pad.

- ✔ **Heel:** The heel supports the back of your foot, determines the height of the shoe, and contributes to the shoe's style. The heel height can vary from half an inch to 5 inches.

Just as with clothing, each shoe manufacturer produces a slightly different fit, even if the sizes are all 8s. Some lines are narrower, some wider, and so on. When you find a shoe you like and that fits, check out the entire collection from that designer, which more than likely will fit you correctly and comfortably. Knowing which lines of shoes fit comfortably and which don't gives you a head start when you're shoe shopping in person or online.

If at all possible, try on shoes *before* you buy. If you purchase your shoes online, you may have to send the shoes back if they don't fit. Although returning merchandise can be a pain, it's a lot less painful than wearing shoes that don't fit!

Some people are under the impression that all shoes have to be broken in — *not* true! An uncomfortable pair of shoes may become a little more comfortable over time, and the use of a shoe stretcher can help. Still, don't count on this when buying new shoes. Your best bet is to find shoes that fit you comfortably in the store; more than likely, they'll be comfortable the first time you wear them, too.

Don't assume the shoes inside a box are new just because a salesman brings them from the storeroom. Take a good look at the shoes before you try them on. Especially look at the bottom: If the shoes have been returned, you can easily see signs of wear and tear on the sole. A returned shoe isn't necessarily one you shouldn't buy; just make sure the shoes are comfortable and have nothing wrong with them. Sometimes you can ask for a discount if the wear is noticeable.

It's a shoe-in! Shoe care tips

To maintain your shoes so they last and look great for as long as possible, follow these suggestions:

- ✔ **Shine them.** Shining shoes not only improves their appearance but protects them as well. It doesn't have to be an onerous chore: Just keep some polish and a few rags near where you watch TV. Waxes and liquid polish add gloss to a shoe but don't offer as much protection as creams and paste, which penetrate and moisturize the leather. So if you're out in bad weather, you scuff your shoe, or you just notice that they're looking dull, break out the polish.

- ✔ **Have them resoled and repaired when necessary.** The soles and heels get more wear and tear than the uppers. Having your shoes resoled when they're worn down is great way to extend the life of your shoes, as long as the uppers are in good shape. And even if the uppers need a little fixing too, a reputable shoe repair place should be able to make them as good as new.

Have your favorite shoes (the ones you wear all the time because you love them) professionally cleaned and maintained at the end of the season, before you store them away for next year. (Don't bother doing this with trendy shoes that you aren't going to wear again next year.)

Shoe psych 101

Most women have a strong attraction to shoes. Some of the cutest pictures my mother has of me show me strutting around the house in her high heels. Wearing high heels signifies coming of age. Another attraction to shoes is that, in any shopping expedition, you can almost always find a pair of shoes that fits. Many women get frustrated when shopping for clothing because finding something that looks perfect is often difficult. But because body type doesn't necessarily determine what type of shoe looks good on you, two very differently shaped women can buy the same pair and both feel like a million bucks.

Shoe Styles

Certain styles of shoes are appropriate for certain situations. A pump, for example, is appropriate for the office. A flip-flop is appropriate for the beach. Knowing what style works where narrows your choices when shopping for that certain occasion.

Pumps

Pumps, a variety of which are shown in Figure 16-2, are shoes that cover the toe box, have anywhere from a low to high heel, and are usually slipped on without any fastening. They're accepted as the traditional business shoe for women. Pumps can range from conservative, basic, low-heel, black leather, and nondescript to high heel, pointy toe, and sexy in any range of fabrics and colors.

Figure 16-2: From left: Classic black pump, peep-toe pump, kitten heel pump.

Current pump styles change with the trends. Straps across the top of the foot turn a simple pump into a *Mary Jane pump*. Another variation is the *T-strap pump*, in which a circle of leather surrounds your ankle and a strap descends down toward the toe box of the shoe. A *peep-toe pump* has the toe area cut out to expose the tips of your toes.

Mules

Take the back off your pumps and what have you got? A mule (see Figure 16-3). You can wear mules when you go shopping, when you go to work, or when you head out for the night. The key is the shoe. Mules come in a variety of styles, from pumps to sandals. (*Any* backless shoe is considered a mule.)

Don't wear pantyhose or tights with mules. Because a mule has no ankle support, your foot will slip. Plus it looks ridiculous!

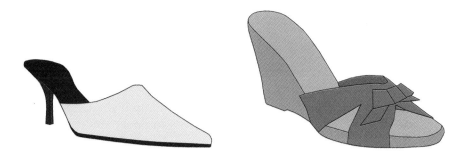

Figure 16-3: From left: A classic mule and a wedge mule.

Flats and sandals

Don't let anyone tell you that flats aren't sexy! They're not only very sensible shoes, but they can be very stylish, too. They're super comfortable (as long as the fit is right) and can take you from day to night. In fact, most women welcome the current trend of wearing flats (I'm in flats of some sort 75 percent of the time) because comfort is key. In addition, designers are making both beautiful dressy and casual flats, giving women more choices when putting an outfit together. Everything from ballet flats (see Figure 16-4) to dressy sandal flats are available.

Because soles of flats are just that — flat — you may be more comfortable if you get a pair that have a cushioned insole. When shopping for flats, bring an insole with you if you think you may want to add it. That way, you can make sure the fit is correct when trying them on.

By definition, sandals replace the top of the shoe with different combinations of straps so that most of the foot is left bare. Here's a look at the two types of sandals:

✔ **Casual sandals:** These are a great way to change up your wardrobe for the summer months. Casual sandals can range from flip-flops to strappy flats to ribbon-tie wedges. While rubber flip-flops are most appropriate for the beach, you can find plenty of open-toe sandals for summer that are suitable for the office or a casual dinner. Casual sandals look great with everything from jeans to sundresses.

✔ **Dressier sandals:** These are considered appropriate for formal occasions. Strappy sandals with high heels can be very dressy. Some are made of leather and others satin, and some have embellishments. Metallic sandals, such as gold or silver (see Figure 16-4), are very popular with evening wear because they're neutral but give you a little more flair than basic black. Don't be afraid to dress up your jeans with high-heel strappy sandals for a night on the town!

Figure 16-4: Ballet slippers (left) and dressier gold sandals (right).

I feel compelled to say this, even though I'm sure you already know it: Don't wear sandals if your feet aren't ready for them. If you don't have time to get a pedicure, just take off your polish and make sure your toes look neat. Nothing is worse than a fab pair of sandals with a not-so-fabulous pair of feet!

Sneakers and sport shoes

Sneakers come in a wide variety of styles (see Figure 16-5) and you'll definitely be able to find a pair that suits your needs both in comfort and style. Just remember that while sneakers can be a style statement, especially if your style is on the sporty side, they don't complement every outfit. There are definitely times when sneakers (like Converse) can make an outfit really adorable. But for the most part, sneakers are for the gym and days when you're just lounging or running the kids around.

Figure 16-5: Different styles of sneakers.

Boots

I'm a big fan of boots. I love everything from casual UGGs (sheepskin boots) to high, black leather boots. I just love whipping mine out when fall comes around. As much as I love boots, though, I believe they have a time and a place. Wear boots during the cooler months and store them away during warmer ones. Why? First, it makes old things seem new again: If you store your boots for the summer, you can look forward to wearing them again in the fall and they'll feel like new. Second, boots are too warm to wear during the summer and much of the spring. Some people do it, but I think it's fun to vary up your look and give everything in your wardrobe a shot!

You can choose from a variety of boot styles, depending on your look and your body type. Your choices include ankle boots, knee-high boots, and above-the-knee boots. Boots also come in a variety of heel heights (flat to low-heel to high-heel) and heel styles (chunky, wedge, or stiletto). The boot itself can be pull up, zipper, or lace-up. And did I mention the toe shape? The toe can be pointy, square, or round. Figure 16-6 shows a few boot styles. As you can see, you have a lot of options!

Any type of boot can look sexy. My ex-boyfriend loved when I wore a fitted hoodie sweatshirt with leggings and UGG Boots. As long as you pair your favorite boots with the right outfit, you can turn your look from drab to fab instantly!

Figure 16-6: From left: Knee-high stiletto boots, low-heel riding boots, and high-heel ankle boots.

Because boots are more noticeable than shoes (after all, they can come halfway up your leg), you want them to have the appearance of high quality and style, which means you have to spend a little more. I bought a pair of Jimmy Choo boots four seasons ago, and although they were very expensive, they are still standing strong. Classic boots are worth spending on. A great pair of leather knee-high boots (with a heel or flat) is a great investment. When searching for that great pair of boots, take into account the clothing in your closet, the occasions you plan to wear them, and how much you can spend on them.

Boots are great with jeans. Try these looks; either option gives you the fashionable look of wearing boots and the confidence that comes with that:

✔ **Tuck a pair of skinny jeans into knee-high boots.** This is a great look if you want to show off your legs.

✔ **Pair ankle boots with boot-cut or flared jeans.** Wear the jeans over the boots.

Cowboy boots are in a category unto themselves. They come in and out of style as a fashion statement. If the occasion or location fits, or if you are a true cowgirl, these boots are great. Otherwise, better to invest in a pair of fashion boots that better suit the needs of your wardrobe.

Finally, many women have taken to wearing high rubber boots in an assortment of wild colors and designs (see Figure 16-7). These boots are perfect for a rainy or snowy season. They protect your clothing, keep your feet dry, and make a fashion statement at the same time. They come in basic neutral colors and in a variety of brights. Just make sure that if you decide to go for a fun pair in a bright color, the rest of your outfit is neutral. Rain boots are meant to be fun and brighten up a dreary day. If you know how to make them work into your wardrobe, go for it. If not, stick with the neutrals.

Figure 16-7: There's a way to make rain boots look fashionable.

Honing In on Heel Heights

Nothing says sexy like a high heel. Your legs look better when wearing high heels because your calf muscles are flexed, shortened, and more defined. High heels also elongate the appearance of your legs, making you look longer and leaner (see Figure 16-8).

Figure 16-8: Nothing says sexy like a high heel.

Two things affect heel height:

- ✔ **The size of the shoe:** The larger the shoe, the higher the heel. If you get a size 6 shoe with a 1-inch heel, you get a 1-inch heel height. But order that same shoe in a size 11 and the heel height is 1½ inches. The heel height has to be in proportion to the size of the shoe. Because a size 11 shoe is obviously bigger than a size 6 shoe, the heel height is greater, too. Sometimes women with size 11 shoes don't want that added height, so they adjust the heel height downward.

- ✔ **Where the heel height is measured from:** The heel height can be measured from the center of the heel or from the back. Measuring from the back results in a higher measurement. This consideration may be important when you want everyone wearing the same heel height, like in a bridal party. (By the way, the wedding industry measures shoes from the inside of the heel.) If you're only choosing for yourself, be aware that different shoes with the same heel height printed on the box may have noticeable differences in the actual height. The likely culprit for this discrepancy is the location of the measurement; center, back, or front of the heel.

Part VI
The Part of Tens

The 5th Wave — By Rich Tennant

©RICHTENNANT

"Okay, let's try it again without the keychain. While we're at it, let's lose the sweat-pants-under-the-summer-skirt look."

In this part . . .

Have you ever walked down the street and noticed a woman with her underwear sticking out of her pants? Yikes! Well, at one point or another, we've all been fashion victims — but never again! In this section, I offer tips on how you can avoid the all-too-common fashion mistakes. And because I often leave my house in the morning and am gone for the the entire day, whatever I'm wearing at 7:30 a.m. has to work at 7:30 p.m., too. In this part, I give you tricks for going from day to night in a flash! You can also find a list of my favorite fashion Web sites here.

17

Ten Fashion Faux Pas and How to Avoid Them

- -

In This Chapter

▷ Knowing what to show and what not to show

▷ Avoiding other mistakes

- -

*F*aux pas is a French expression that in English means something you're not supposed to do. In this chapter, I list ten fashion mistakes you want to avoid at all costs.

Over-Accessorizing

You've heard the old saying "less is more," right? Like many old sayings, it's lasted for a reason. Wearing big statement pieces to express your personal style is definitely fun and fashionable, but you don't want to wear too many statement pieces at one time. Pick one piece that you want people to notice. Wear a chunky necklace, chandelier earrings, or a cute hair accessory. Wearing all of them at once overwhelms your overall look, distracts anyone from looking at your face, and makes you look like you tried too hard to be matchy-matchy. (For more information on how to accessorize, see Chapter 15.)

Problematic Panties

Doesn't the title say it all? Panties should always be worn under, not out of, your clothing. Obviously, panties sticking out of your jeans or slacks is a giant no-no. Make sure (and you can even test this) that no matter what your pose — sitting, standing, or bending to pick up a pen — your undergarments don't expose themselves (see Figure 17-1).

Your jeans or pants are there to cover your rear and flatter it. If your underwear is sticking out, chances are good that your outfit is doing nothing for your entire midsection and backside. Don't draw unwanted attention there by letting your panties, or worse, your rear, stick out of them. Yikes!

Figure 17-1: Keep your panties covered.

Wearing White to a Wedding

As is tradition, the bride will (most likely) be in white, so you shouldn't be. In addition to white, avoid ivory, cream, ecru, eggshell, linen, or any other nearly white color. People often question whether black is okay to wear to a wedding. If it's a nighttime affair, then yes, black is totally chic. However, if it's a daytime affair, stay away from black. For more on dressing for special occasions, head to Chapter 11.

Baring Your Stomach

Baring your stomach — unless you're wearing a bathing suit — is another giant no (see Figure 17-2). Just as showing your rear isn't the height of fashion sophistication, neither is showing your stomach. Even if you can get beyond the lack of sophistication, it's not a flattering look for most women. A cropped top cuts you right in the middle and draws all the attention to your waist. Believe me, you can look sexy in many ways; showing your stomach is not one of them.

Figure 17-2: Avoid showing your stomach.

Wearing Hose with Open-Toe Shoes

Gasp! Seeing the seam of pantyhose across someone's toes in an open-toe shoe gives me hives! If you're wearing sandals, it's probably warm out, and you don't need hose. If you're wearing pantyhose, it's probably cold enough out to warrant closed-toe shoes. Even if you came up with what seemed like a logical reason to pair hose and open-toe shoes, the look is an absolute no. No exceptions! Head to Chapter 14 for more hosiery rules.

Part of being fashionable is dressing appropriately for the season and the weather. If it's hot, wear sexy sandals and go with bare legs. If it's cold, pair the hose or tights with great boots or pumps. Of course, you can also wear open-toe sandals (sans hose) in the winter with an evening dress, as long as you're not outdoors for an extended period.

Wearing High Waters

Wearing capri pants is one thing; wearing pants that are meant to be full length but that fall too high on your leg is quite another (see Figure 17-3). Make sure your pants hit the top of your shoe (or foot, if you're wearing a sandal). You don't want to look like you're ready for a flood.

Wearing pants that are too short not only takes away from the long, clean line that is supposed to make you appear taller and thinner, but it also looks like you bought the wrong size, got them hemmed improperly, or shrank them in the wash — none of which is good.

Too much

The most common fashion faux pas is to overdo it. That could mean wearing too much jewelry, too much perfume, too much makeup; showing too much skin; or wearing too tight a dress or too high a heel. You may think that, because so many of the outfits seen on the fashion runways are over the top, exaggeration has a part to play in everyday fashion, but that's not so. Remember, all fashion is an accessory to the person wearing the clothes, you. If you overdo it, then *you* will get overwhelmed. So while you always want to make a style statement, you never want to be a fashion victim. If you abide by the golden rule — less is more — you'll always be able to avoid becoming a fashion faux pas.

Figure 17-3: Pants aren't supposed to look like they shrank in the wash.

Wearing White Underwear under Anything Sheer

If you're wearing a sheer top, choose flesh-toned undergarments. These come in a variety of shades, so you can find one that matches your skin tone. The flesh-toned color of your bra, camisole, or slip gives the illusion that you don't have anything on underneath, while everything really remains covered and hidden. This way, you get the full effect of the beauty of the sheer top or dress without the distraction of the wrong undergarment. When you wear white underneath something sheer, the white is all you see (see Figure 17-4). This is especially true if you're somewhere where you may be photographed — such as a wedding. The flash of the camera will pick up the white undergarment, making it even more noticeable in the picture than it is in real life.

Figure 17-4: White undergarments under sheer tops can be distracting.

Wearing All Denim

I love denim. Jeans are a great staple in most everyone's wardrobe. A jean jacket is the perfect complement to white pants, khakis, or a cute dress. Still, don't wear jeans and a denim jacket together as an outfit. The look is straight out of the 1980s and is too matchy-matchy. With so many mix and match options for jeans and jean jackets, pair denim with pretty much anything other than more denim. (For more on how to wear denim, see Chapter 5.)

Showing Your Bra Straps

Your bra straps should never be showing. If you're wearing a spaghetti strap dress, opt for a strapless bra. If you're wearing a racerback tank top, go for a racerback bra. Letting your straps show takes away from your outfit, and your bra straps are often the first thing people notice (see Figure 17-5). You can find convertible bras in all different sizes and with all different levels of support. (Head to Chapter 14 for more on undergarments.)

Many bra companies have begun to make fashionable bra straps that are meant to be shown. This look is very casual and therefore inappropriate for work and many other occasions. Exercise caution with fashionable straps, and remember, a cleaner look is always safe and stylish.

Figure 17-5: Keep your bra straps hidden.

Wearing Clothing That's Too Tight

Clothing is unflattering when it's too tight. I know, I know — you love that top and you must have it. Unfortunately, the only size you can find is a size smaller than you wear. What do you do? You put the garment down and walk away! We've all bought the top we *had* to have knowing it was too small. But no matter how fab the top, if you have to squeeze yourself into it, it's a total no. Walking around in clothing that's too tight is not only uncomfortable; it's also unfashionable (see Figure 17-6). You don't want to be the woman in a fabulous outfit that's too small.

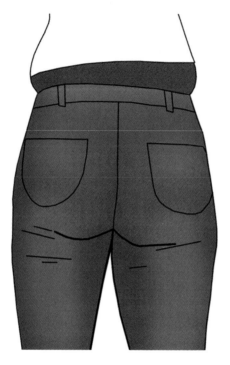

Figure 17-6: Avoid clothes that are too tight.

18

Ten Ways to Go From Day to Night in a Flash

*W*hether you're heading to a planned event or a last-minute soiree, you want to look your best, even when you don't have the time you'd like to primp and polish. No worries. In this chapter, I give you ten ways to transform your look from day to night. With these tips, you'll look like you spent hours digging through your closet to find the perfect outfit!

From Simple to Sizzling

If you know you're going out after work, slip on a simple black dress in the morning with whatever shoes are office-appropriate. Take along some jewelry, a clutch, and a pair of dressy sandals. When your work day is done, all you need to do to totally transform your look is put on the jewelry (the right amount of bling can spice up that little black dress), trade in your day bag for the clutch, and don your dressy sandals (see Figure 18-1). In no time flat, you have a whole new look!

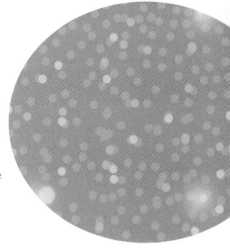

Figure 18-1: The little black dress takes you from day to night in a flash.

A Silky Transformation

Simply by changing the way you wear a silk scarf, you can change your whole look. All it takes is a little creativity, a few seconds, and the right scarf (a 36-inch square works, or if you want more coverage, go bigger). During the day, tie the scarf around your neck and pair it with a suit and tank. At night, take the scarf off your neck, remove the tank and suit jacket, and tie the scarf as a halter top (see Figure 18-2). Chapter 15 explains how to turn a scarf into a halter. Who knew a simple scarf could take you so far?

Figure 18-2: A little creativity with a scarf gives you a new look almost instantly.

Cubicle to Cocktails

If you're going out after work, there's no need to pack an extra outfit. Simply wear a suit. Underneath, put on a sexy tank that barely shows when the jacket is closed (see Figure 18-3). When you're ready to go meet your friends for cocktails, take off your jacket and you'll be ready for that cosmo!

Figure 18-3: Less can be more when dressing up for an evening out.

A Shirt to Take You Anywhere

A white button-down shirt is suitable for almost any occasion. During the day, pair it with jeans. At night, put it with a dressier skirt or slacks. Add a bold necklace or chandelier earrings for a little pop (see Figure 18-4). The look is not only sophisticated, but understated and sexy as well!

Figure 18-4: Trade in your slacks for a dressy skirt when going out on the town!

Tote to Clutch

If you're heading to a party after work, don't let your bag be the sign that you didn't have time to run home and change. An overflowing tote is never stylish. To avoid this dilemma, throw a clutch in your purse (pack some mini-makeup in your evening bag, too). That way when you're running out of the office for your fabulous plans, you'll look chic from head to toe!

Accessorize, Accessorize!

Never underestimate the power of accessories. If you're in a simple dress during the day and want to dress it up for dinner, you don't need to change your outfit;

you can simply change your accessories. Pick two pieces to make your outfit pop (shoes don't count!). Choose a bracelet and earrings, a necklace and statement ring, or a pair of earrings and a belt (as pictured in Figure 18-5). Any such combo will do the trick. Have fun with your choices, and don't be afraid to mix metals. The only caveat? Don't overdo it. (See Chapter 15 for details on how to avoid over-accessorizing.)

Figure 18-5: The right accessories can dress up any outfit.

Shoulder Bag to Clutch

Invest in a bag that has a chain or strap you can take off or tuck inside. If you're shopping during the day and want to be "hands-free," you can use the strap. At night, when you just want to wear a clutch, you can tuck the strap inside the bag and *voila!* Most major department stores carry these types of bags. With most chain-strap bags you can tuck in the strap. Look around and find one you can wear with many different outfits; it's a great staple for any wardrobe.

Day Casual to Dinner Chic

A simple sweater set is a great staple. Paired with a pair of slacks, it's always classic and clean — a great look for the office. Dress it up for night by taking the cardigan off, tying it around your neck, and pairing it with a fun skirt, sandals, a clutch, and accessories (see Figure 18-6). Now you're ready to dance the night away in style!

Figure 18-6: Maybe you never thought you could use a sweater as an accessory, but you can.

It's a Wrap!

You can wrap many dresses in different ways to get different looks. American Apparel makes a great and inexpensive one that's very easy to figure out and experiment with. Don't be afraid to come up with your own way to wrap a versatile dress…whatever works best on your body works! Here's an example: For daytime, wrap the two straps of the dress around your waist and tie a knot in the back (I wear this look all the time). Pair with a T-shirt and cardigan and you're ready to shop the day away! For nighttime, tie the two straps around your neck to make a halter dress (see Figure 18-7). Get out those fab new earrings you've wanted to wear and a pair of high heels, and you're ready to dance into the night!

Figure 18-7: Tie the garment as a skirt or a dress depending on where you're heading!

Best Foot Forward

Higher heels are sexy and great for nighttime, but few women can walk around in them comfortably all day. You could bring another pair of shoes with you, but there's another solution: Camileon Heels, shoes that, with a simple move, have a heel that goes from low to high in a flash (see Figure 18-8). And they look nice, too! To buy a pair, go to www.camileonheels.com.

©Richard Quindry, Camileon Heels

Figure 18-8: With these shoes, you switch from low to high heels in no time.

19
Ten Great Fashion Web Sites

In This Chapter

▷ Tapping into fashion knowledge

▷ Finding sample sales and other great bargains

▷ Accessing world-class stylists

*T*he World Wide Web is just that when it comes to fashion: a world wide resource that lets you explore the entire world of fashion without having to leave your house. Through the Web, you can learn about the hottest designers, buy clothes and accessories for the best prices, and find the help you need to become as fashionable as possible. This chapter lists ten of my favorite sites to check out, but remember: The Web is ever-changing, so be sure to explore all the possibilities it has to offer.

www.style.com

Vogue has long been the leader of the pack as far as what's hot in the fashion world, and this is the magazine's Web site. It's one of the top resources when you want to find out about upcoming trends and up-and-coming designers. Not only can you find the latest info from the magazine here, but you can see all the fashion runway shows from the American and European collections. If you're curious what your favorite designer is showing for the upcoming season, or you just want to browse around to see what's current, log on to www.style.com.

www.usmagazine.com

If you want to check out the latest trends and see what celebrities are wearing, *Us Weekly* has you covered. You can check out what stars are wearing when they're shopping and on the red carpet. You can see how your favorite celeb takes the looks of her favorite designers and makes them her own. *Us* not only has pictures of all the celebs in the most current fashions, but it also tells you where the celebs shop so that you can check out their favorite stores, too. In addition to celeb photos, *Us* has a few fashion pages with the latest pieces and Web site links telling you where to find them.

www.hautelook.com

Hautelook.com has great *sample sales*. When designers (including high-end designers!) produce too much merchandise and have leftover stock at the end of the season, they have sample sales. These sales unload merchandise at a discount because they won't be able to sell it again next season. A variety of sizes and styles are usually available, but it's first-come, first-served — so you have to be quick when you hear about a sale.

After you register (don't worry — registration is free), you receive e-mails about upcoming sales. The sales last for 24 to 48 hours and feature great designers for bargain prices. So for all you fashionistas who think you can't afford that piece you're coveting, keep an eye out for sample sales: You never know what will end up here! For more information on sample sales and how they work, go to Chapter 7.

www.gilt.com

Another great site for sample sales (refer to the preceding section), gilt. com is the place to go if you want access to designer creations for less. Because both Web sites have access to different designers' merchandise, it's worth registering at both so you don't miss out on anything. Again, registration is free. What great bargains!

www.priorities.com

This Web site lets you access the hottest looks for less. I love this line because it specializes in winter coats and stylish jackets, which can often be hard to find (especially at reasonable prices). You can order and have your items shipped. The site offers a full refund policy, so don't worry about sizing problems. You *can* return!

www.jennifermillerjewelry.com

I've mentioned this site numerous times throughout the book. It's my go-to Web site when looking to make an outfit complete with accessories. You can find great pieces for under $100; every time I wear something from them, I'm the talk of the party. This site really allows you to look like a million bucks without spending it. The gold big hoop earrings I'm wearing on the back cover of the book are from `jennifermillerjewelry.com`, and they're always my go-to party earrings.

www.michellejonas.com

Michelle Jonas Designs has everything from dresses to shorts, and each item is perfect for travel. Every piece goes from day to night and folds up easily to fit in your suitcase. All the items are very reasonably priced, and believe me, not only will you live in these pieces when you're traveling, but you won't want to take them off when you're back home, either! If you prefer to try things on, check out the Web site for the address of a store near you.

www.25park.com

The mission of 25Park is to provide designer merchandise that consumers can't find easily in stores. 25Park offers a "quick-guide," designed to give customers suggestions on what to wear to special occasions. It also donates a portion of each sale to a different charity each month and ships items in recycled packaging.

www.dailycandy.com

DailyCandy is a guilty pleasure — without the guilt! This site runs the gamut from fashion to beauty to food and culture. Just log on to access all the site's areas. Click on "Fashion" to see the newest and latest in the fashion world. You'll find highlights of the newest designers, Web sites, boutiques, and anything else to do with fashion. You can also browse the site by city, to see what's new in your area. Because almost everything listed links to its own Web site, you don't have to live in one of the major U.S. cities to take advantage of all `dailycandy.com` has to offer.

www.fordmodels.com/fordartists

If you're looking to hire a professional stylist, this Web site is a great place to start. These experienced, professional stylists work on photo shoots, commercials, and TV. They have online portfolios you can browse, and the agency has offices throughout the country. So if you live near one of the major cities, you can hire a stylist locally. If you don't live near a major U.S. city, the stylists travel as well (expect higher fees if travel is involved).

Index

● *E* ●

● *F* ●

Business/Accounting & Bookkeeping

Bookkeeping For Dummies
978-0-7645-9848-7

eBay Business
All-in-One For Dummies,
2nd Edition
978-0-470-38536-4

Job Interviews
For Dummies,
3rd Edition
978-0-470-17748-8

Resumes For Dummies,
5th Edition
978-0-470-08037-5

Stock Investing
For Dummies,
3rd Edition
978-0-470-40114-9

Successful Time
Management
For Dummies
978-0-470-29034-7

Computer Hardware

BlackBerry For Dummies,
3rd Edition
978-0-470-45762-7

Computers For Seniors
For Dummies
978-0-470-24055-7

iPhone For Dummies,
2nd Edition
978-0-470-42342-4

Laptops For Dummies,
3rd Edition
978-0-470-27759-1

Macs For Dummies,
10th Edition
978-0-470-27817-8

Cooking & Entertaining

Cooking Basics
For Dummies,
3rd Edition
978-0-7645-7206-7

Wine For Dummies,
4th Edition
978-0-470-04579-4

Diet & Nutrition

Dieting For Dummies,
2nd Edition
978-0-7645-4149-0

Nutrition For Dummies,
4th Edition
978-0-471-79868-2

Weight Training
For Dummies,
3rd Edition
978-0-471-76845-6

Digital Photography

Digital Photography
For Dummies,
6th Edition
978-0-470-25074-7

Photoshop Elements 7
For Dummies
978-0-470-39700-8

Gardening

Gardening Basics
For Dummies
978-0-470-03749-2

Organic Gardening
For Dummies,
2nd Edition
978-0-470-43067-5

Green/Sustainable

Green Building
& Remodeling
For Dummies
978-0-4710-17559-0

Green Cleaning
For Dummies
978-0-470-39106-8

Green IT For Dummies
978-0-470-38688-0

Health

Diabetes For Dummies,
3rd Edition
978-0-470-27086-8

Food Allergies
For Dummies
978-0-470-09584-3

Living Gluten-Free
For Dummies
978-0-471-77383-2

Hobbies/General

Chess For Dummies,
2nd Edition
978-0-7645-8404-6

Drawing For Dummies
978-0-7645-5476-6

Knitting For Dummies,
2nd Edition
978-0-470-28747-7

Organizing For Dummies
978-0-7645-5300-4

SuDoku For Dummies
978-0-470-01892-7

Home Improvement

Energy Efficient Homes
For Dummies
978-0-470-37602-7

Home Theater
For Dummies,
3rd Edition
978-0-470-41189-6

Living the Country Lifestyle
All-in-One For Dummies
978-0-470-43061-3

Solar Power Your Home
For Dummies
978-0-470-17569-9

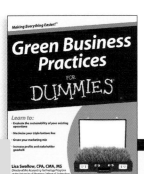

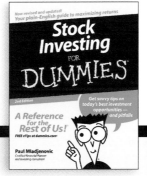

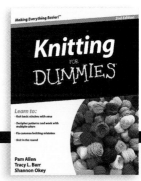

Internet
Blogging For Dummies,
2nd Edition
978-0-470-23017-6

eBay For Dummies,
6th Edition
978-0-470-49741-8

Facebook For Dummies
978-0-470-26273-3

Google Blogger
For Dummies
978-0-470-40742-4

Web Marketing
For Dummies,
2nd Edition
978-0-470-37181-7

WordPress For Dummies,
2nd Edition
978-0-470-40296-2

Language & Foreign Language
French For Dummies
978-0-7645-5193-2

Italian Phrases
For Dummies
978-0-7645-7203-6

Spanish For Dummies
978-0-7645-5194-9

Spanish For Dummies,
Audio Set
978-0-470-09585-0

Macintosh
Mac OS X Snow Leopard
For Dummies
978-0-470-43543-4

Math & Science
Algebra I For Dummies
978-0-7645-5325-7

Biology For Dummies
978-0-7645-5326-4

Calculus For Dummies
978-0-7645-2498-1

Chemistry For Dummies
978-0-7645-5430-8

Microsoft Office
Excel 2007 For Dummies
978-0-470-03737-9

Office 2007 All-in-One
Desk Reference
For Dummies
978-0-471-78279-7

Music
Guitar For Dummies,
2nd Edition
978-0-7645-9904-0

iPod & iTunes
For Dummies,
6th Edition
978-0-470-39062-7

Piano Exercises
For Dummies
978-0-470-38765-8

Parenting & Education
Parenting For Dummies,
2nd Edition
978-0-7645-5418-6

Type 1 Diabetes
For Dummies
978-0-470-17811-9

Pets
Cats For Dummies,
2nd Edition
978-0-7645-5275-5

Dog Training For Dummies,
2nd Edition
978-0-7645-8418-3

Puppies For Dummies,
2nd Edition
978-0-470-03717-1

Religion & Inspiration
The Bible For Dummies
978-0-7645-5296-0

Catholicism For Dummies
978-0-7645-5391-2

Women in the Bible
For Dummies
978-0-7645-8475-6

Self-Help & Relationship
Anger Management
For Dummies
978-0-470-03715-7

Overcoming Anxiety
For Dummies
978-0-7645-5447-6

Sports
Baseball For Dummies,
3rd Edition
978-0-7645-7537-2

Basketball For Dummies,
2nd Edition
978-0-7645-5248-9

Golf For Dummies,
3rd Edition
978-0-471-76871-5

Web Development
Web Design All-in-One
For Dummies
978-0-470-41796-6

Windows Vista
Windows Vista
For Dummies
978-0-471-75421-3

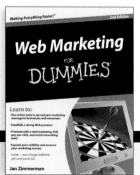
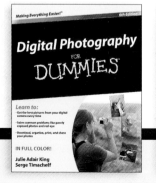